This unique, heartfelt, and visionary book penetrates to the deepest questions of the human journey, and offers touching and inspiring poetic images to guide us. Oman Ken brings the wealth of his experience and deep insights as a welcome roadmap to awakening. I recommend Journey of *The Great Circle* to anyone dedicated to fathom the mysteries of life and advance on your own healing journey.

— *Alan Cohen, bestselling author of* **A Course in Miracles Made Easy**

In his book, **Journey of *The Great Circle***, Oman brings forth "pearls" of wisdom - and has strung those pearls together in a compelling narrative and practice. Bottom line: If you find yourself going around in circles in life, go around THIS circle, and you will spiral to a higher and brighter view.

— *Steve Bhaerman, aka Swami Beyondananda "cosmic comic" and co-author with Bruce Lipton of* **Spontaneous Evolution: Our Positive Future and a Way to Get There From Here.**

Oman's book inspires us to embark on a sacred journey and exploration of what life is truly about - and what really matters. Here is a book that can be utilized every day to polish the Diamond of our Souls.

— *Rama Jyoti Vernon, co-founder of* **The Yoga Journal** *and author of* **Yoga: The Practice of Myth & Sacred Geometry**

With the poetry of a passionate artist - and the perspectives of an intuitive scientist, Oman Ken has written a visionary book. Utilizing his unique system of daily practices, he lays out the vision and pathway for a more peaceful and compassionate world.

— *Reverend Max Lafser, Unity minister and former chairman of* **The Center For International Dialogue**

I know first-hand the power and beauty of a 365 daily transformation practice. Oman's deep reflection and soul searching has devoutly created this profound and poetic work. Use this book as a daily practice to soar into the heights of your soul. You will forever be transformed.

— *José R. Fuentes, Co-Founder and Facilitator of the Sedona Integral Group*

Oman's book, Journey of *The Great Circle,* is too rich with meaningful poetic and creative thinking not to be experienced. Through his 365 contemplative exercises, he brings a great gift to the human family for our next leap in wholeness. I celebrate this new work, for I know the reader will be assisted in their spiritual unfoldment.

— *Bruce Kellogg, Unity minister*

Journey of *The Great Circle* is Oman Ken's epic masterpiece to passionately hone and master the best in us. Four seasonal volumes of brilliant creativity weaving consciousness, science, art, history, and evolutionary spirituality. Stunningly written and organized. You will be blessed.

— *Enocha Ranjita Ryan, Transformational Healing Artist*

As a minister, I would highly recommend Oman's book to inspire other ministers with meaningful themes for Sunday talks. Each of the 365 contemplative narratives is rich with powerful ideas and inspiration. Oman's book is such a meaningful gift for humanity as well as a practical pathway to a better world at this crucial moment in human development.

— *Marshall Norman, former Unity minister of Madison, Wisconsin*

JOURNEY OF
THE GREAT CIRCLE

DAILY CONTEMPLATIONS FOR CULTIVATING INNER FREEDOM
AND LIVING YOUR LIFE AS A MASTER OF FREEDOM

SUMMER VOLUME

OMAN KEN

BALBOA.PRESS
A DIVISION OF HAY HOUSE

Balboa Press books may be ordered through booksellers or by contacting:

Balboa Press
A Division of Hay House
1663 Liberty Drive
Bloomington, IN 47403
www.balboapress.com
844-682-1282

Cover art designed by Oman Ken – and created by Mark Gelotte.

Graphic art designed by Oman Ken – and created by Mark Gelotte.

Photography of Oman Ken by Charles Ruscher

ISBN: 978-1-9822-6837-4 (sc)
ISBN: 978-1-9822-6838-1 (e)

Print information available on the last page.

Balboa Press rev. date: 06/23/2021

✻ CONTENTS ✻

June 20	Gifts of Summer	Solstice Means "The Sun Stands Still"
June 21	Qualities Within the Seasons of Life	Humanity's Collective "Illusion"
June 22	The Great Story of Awakening	Natural Patterns Within the Seasons
June 23	*Journey of Awakening*	High Observation Point on the Mountain
June 24	Cultivating the Mastery of *Being* and *Becoming*	The Foundation is Only the First Phase
June 25	Inner Freedom	What Is My Life Truly About?
June 26	The Integral Stage of Consciousness	Many Different Stages of Awareness
June 27	Aligning With *the True Self*	Four Synchronized Rowers

June 28	*The Great Circle*	A Year as a Metaphor for Wholeness
June 29	*The Great Circle* of Awakening and Contribution	As the Wind Increases to a Strong Gale
June 30	*The Great Circle* of the Medicine Wheel	A Multitude of Universal Paradoxes
July 1	Alternative Ways to Describe *The Great Circle*	Using Many Words to Portray One Thing

This book is dedicated to the children of the world,
the hope for our future.

May they be inspired and supported
by those who are helping to make the world a better place,

those who are consciously transforming their lives
by learning to live and express their fullest potential,

and those who are contributing their creative gifts and talents
to the unfolding of a more enlightened global society.

Questions are the seeds of tomorrow's harvest
and when planted in the fertile soil of an open mind and heart,
their insightful fruits burst forth
from *the Infinite Ground of Being*.

✳ WHAT IS – JOURNEY OF *THE GREAT CIRCLE* ✳

JOURNEY OF *THE GREAT CIRCLE* is a collection of 365 contemplative narratives designed as a daily transformative practice for the purpose of personal transformation. The annual collection of narratives is divided into four volumes, Winter, Spring, Summer, and Autumn each beginning on either the solstice or equinox. Each of the 365 narratives has a specific spiritual theme to help you gain a more expansive understanding of what really matters - and points you to how to live a life with peace of mind and inner freedom.

The various themes of the narratives involve insights from spirituality, quantum physics, the evolutionary perspective, the study of visionary archetypes, healing, and transformative practice. **Journey of *The Great Circle*** can be thought of as "a spiritual map of an awakening life".

A life of inner freedom is when one consciously realizes the perfection that's always unfolding within - and within all of life. Living with this awareness allows the natural states of peace, happiness, joy and harmony to effortlessly arise. It is a life of one who has devotedly learned to love others and all of life unconditionally - and who has gained the joyful awareness of serving the wellbeing of others. In these writings, one who attains this level of mastery is referred to as a **Master of Freedom**.

We are all natural-born storytellers with a mandate from *Life* to generate the most fulfilling and creative story of life we can imagine. Every day is a new opportunity to make our life story a little more glorious, a little more fulfilling, a little more creative. We are the authors of this story in every moment of our lives based on the intentions we choose, either consciously or unconsciously. For most people, in order to have the most glorious, fulfilling, creative, and peaceful life requires some form of spiritual practice necessitating conscious attention each day.

Journey of *The Great Circle* utilizes a transformative system of daily practices that can help you:

1) Experience a life of peace, happiness, joy, harmony, and fulfilling creative expression.

2) Prepare for the day's activities and surprises that await you so you can meet each situation from the "sanctuary" of heart wisdom, gratitude, and centeredness.

3) Connect to the inner guidance of the heart so you may live you life with ease and grace.

4) Learn to love every expression of life unconditionally.

5) Maintain a conscious alignment with *a Greater Power*. *A Greater Power* has been called myriad names, including but not limited to, *the Source of Life, the Infinite Presence of Love, God, the Great Spirit,* and *the Infinite Intelligence of the Universe.*

When **Journey of *The Great Circle*** is used on a daily basis it will help cultivate inner freedom and assist you in fulfilling your sacred destiny of an awakened life as a **Master of Freedom**.

For many of us who have a strong yearning
to explore the spiritual facets of our nature,
the deep existential questions of life are "effective tools" our minds can use
to help shape and build the ever-unfolding contours of our destinies.

✳ PREFACE – THE GENESIS ✳

I WAS STANDING ALONE on a large wooden stage in front of a thousand people performing my original songs with my two dear companions - my acoustic guitar and my lyrical voice. I had also created a photographic slide show to visually animate the poetic images of my songs, which projected on a large screen behind me.

As the strings of my guitar rang out, I was offering the last song of a two-week concert tour where I had traveled through the lush Northwest in late spring. As the musical notes of this final composition came to an end, I felt something was very wrong. I could feel a turbulent energy within my ailing body crashing through every cell. My physical form was in some kind of crisis, and from that moment on, my life would never be the same.

The Story of How This Book Came To Be

Life seems to lead each of us on an adventurous journey in which we must ultimately make important choices based on the many possible roads and different turns that come before us along the way. When we were young, most of us conjured up some sort of future vision about how our life would unfold when we grew older. Yet usually for most of us, there was a plethora of surprises and unpredictable twists along life's journey. This book is the surprising result of one of those twists.

In 2005, after numerous years of steadily declining health, a mysterious illness had become a major challenge, and I became deeply frustrated and depressed. I lost most of my physical energy and was very fatigued and exhausted. A heat sensation would rush up into my head each day accompanied by reddish flushing of my chest, neck, and head. At times I felt an internal shaking in my body that was strange, frightening, and uncomfortable. Because of these curious symptoms, I had to adjust my entire life. My musical career came to a halt, and I had to adapt to a new expression of who I was and what I did. I was no longer able to tour around the country performing concerts and retreats with my music. I lost all motivation and energy to record music in my home studio as I did in previous years. And I was barely able to perform at short local events - such as conferences and weddings in order to pay monthly bills.

Because of these increasing physical challenges, I spent many years and lots of money seeing numerous doctors, naturopaths, nutritionists, chiropractors, hypnotherapists, spiritual counselors, health wizards, and a "host of pretty cosmic characters" to find a resolution to my situation. I did get a little help here and there, but for the most part, nothing seemed to work ongoing. My health kept declining slowly. I got very angry at life. At God. At the *Infinite Intelligence* that was supposed to be good and fair. What was happening to me did not feel fair.

I thought of myself as "a spiritual person" because I did a host of "spiritual things". I meditated every day, read spiritual books, attended self-help workshops, exercised regularly, ate a fantastic array of organic food, projected what I thought was a positive attitude toward life, served people with my uplifting music, donated money to environmental organizations - and therefore in my mind,

I did everything "right". Why would someone like me, who is "spiritual" and is doing everything "right", suffer from a physical condition that felt so "wrong"? Over time, I was getting more and more depressed, even suicidal. After a long period of feeling this way, I got very tired of living a depressed life and decided to take more responsibility for my healing.

When I made this shift in awareness, one of the ways I chose to responsibly deal with my ongoing depression was to re-dedicate my life to my spiritual practice. I did this by spending more time in Nature, so I could deeply contemplate my personal situation. I wanted to find out what, if anything, I was supposed to learn about myself from this challenging opportunity I was dealing with.

At that time I had been living in Sedona, Arizona for eighteen years. I received the inner guidance to spend one day a week out in Nature alongside a beautiful wooded creek called Oak Creek and use this time to explore my inner spiritual quest. Each week at the water's edge I would spend five to seven hours in contemplation and inquiry, and then wrote down any insights or realizations. I wanted to use this time in Nature to gain insights about what I could discover about myself from my increasing health challenges and how they might relate to my life-long quest of spiritual awakening, however I understood it.

Thus this weekly ritual of sitting beside the creek, quieting my mind, and waiting began. And then insights started to come. And they continued to emerge each week with different spiritual themes and different life perspectives for me to consider. The thought came to me that it would be easier to remember these insights at a later time if I could find a simpler form to record them, rather than writing long paragraphs of prose as in a spiritual journal. Previously, I had done a lot of journal writing, but I noticed I had a tendency to not go back and read my journals very often. Therefore, I wanted to devise another way to record my thoughts.

I decided to use the basic circular form of the Native American medicine wheel with its four cardinal points and a center point. I picked four primary concepts of each theme or idea I was exploring during my contemplations and wrote them down in four short phrases or sentences in the location of the four cardinal directions (west, south, east and north).

I named these thematic circles Contemplation Circles. Each Contemplation Circle was focused around a spiritual theme that would help point me to *a Transcendent Reality* and to an expanded vision of living my life with inner freedom. I perceived these circles as spirtual maps of consciousness - or theme targets - or wheels of distinction that empowered and supported my spiritual journey and the restoration of my health. Through these ongoing contemplations, I have received beneficial insights that have served the wellbeing of my body, heart, and mind, and have helped me to expand the way I love and accept myself.

Over many years of working with these Contemplation Circles on a daily basis, I began to see applications for them in various aspects of my spiritual practice. They started to organically have a life of their own. I was inwardly guided regarding how to use them in contemplation practices, affirmative prayer, foundational transformative practices, and to gain ever-larger perspective of my life, including my physical challenges.

In 2007, I experienced a transformational workshop called the Big Mind Process facilitated by Genpo Roshi, a Buddhist teacher and author. I was deeply moved by the ability of this process to bring a person to a direct experience of profound states of transcendence so quickly and effectively. The next morning, I began to create my own Contemplation Circles around my experience of the Big Mind Process. It felt natural to use a set of specific circles in a sequential form in my daily meditations. The result was very powerful. The depth of my meditations took on a new level of sublime communion, and I began to notice a much greater experience of self-love and acceptance of my life.

I used this system of meditation for a year, continuing to receive fulfilling results - and was then guided to put this meditation process into a form that could be shared with others. The first book I wrote is called, **Master of Freedom**. This book was written as a universal creation story that portrays "The Great Story" of the creation of the Universe, the 13.8 billion year process of infinitely intelligent evolution. **Master of Freedom** is the archetypal story of life awakening throughout the Universe - in relation to our current human journey of transformation, the spirituality of humanity. It offers a poetic glimpse of our sacred destiny, which is to live an awakened life of inner freedom - and to learn to love all of life unconditionally.

Then in November of 2008, I was given the inner guidance to take 365 of my 400-plus Contemplation Circles and organize them in such a way as to write a thematic narrative for every day of the year. I started writing these narratives on December 21, 2008, the Winter Solstice. That year, I wrote a 350-word narrative for 365 consecutive days. This daily set of contemplative narratives, accompanied by its adjacent Contemplation Circle, I called **Journey of The Great Circle**.

I do not call myself a spiritual teacher, nor am I some kind of healer, psychological counselor, or expert of esoteric spiritual studies. I am simply a conscious person who is passionate about living life fully and discovering what really matters, but also a person, like many, who has suffered a great deal during my life adventure. Yet by some form of *grace*, I have embraced the conscious awareness to take responsibility for my healing, and through inner transformative work have gained a greater experience of inner freedom.

Initially, I did not begin this time of deep contemplation in Nature with a pre-conceived idea to write a book. The creative process of these contemplations grew over time on its own, and I feel this book was written through me rather than by me. I was benefiting tremendously from these contemplations and insights, living with greater peace, happiness, joy, and harmony, and my guidance informed me to put them into a book for the benefit of others.

The Daily Practice of Being an *Artist of Life*

JOURNEY OF *THE GREAT CIRCLE* is a daily transformative program to assist people interested in developing larger perspectives of what life is truly about in order to cultivate an ongoing experience of inner freedom and an awareness of loving oneself and others unconditionally. It uses *the evolutionary perspective* to help create an understanding of the "Bigger Picture" of our human reality.

This system of contemplative practices focuses on the daily practice of being an *artist of life* in which a person lives in a state of inner freedom, maintains an ongoing alignment with *Life*, and learns to effectively contribute his or her creative gifts and talents in service to others - and to all of life. In this series of narratives, living in inner freedom is described as an awakened individual (referred to as a **Master of Freedom**) who has discovered how to live life masterfully and who has learned to respond to every experience with gratitude, surrender, and complete acceptance of what is.

The insights from **Journey of *The Great Circle*** assist in understanding that this universal awakening is a part of the intrinsic evolution that's taking place everywhere in the Cosmos. Thus it's taking place on our little blue planet - and is also taking place within you and me. Every person has the potential to be a conscious self-reflective human being becoming aware of the natural unfolding of evolutionary principles within the Universe and throughout the Earth. When we become aware of, and deeply study, *the evolutionary perspective* (the unfolding perspective of the Universe that has been naturally evolving for 13.8 billion years) and we perceive how we are all an integral part of this constant and ever-expanding evolution, we then begin to understand that this *journey of spiritual awakening* is one of the most natural processes unfolding within every human being. It is just one step in the never-ending unfolding journey within a vast Universe of Infinite Awakenings.

The Intention for Journey of *The Great Circle*

This book is designed to assist individuals to respond to life's challenges with harmony and grace, as well as to understand the blessing and obligation it is to contribute one's unique gifts and talents to the creation of a more glorious world. In other words, these narratives are designed to inspire people to cultivate inner freedom and to joyously offer their creative gifts to others as an *artist of life*.

My intention in sharing this book
is that it be helpful
in discovering the magnificence
of who you really are.

My hope
is that the contemplative practices in this work
may aid you
to more easily navigate your life
to a place of peace and inner freedom.

✳ INTRODUCTION – POLISHING THE DIAMOND ✳

Bringing Light to *the Art of Life*

IMAGINE WALKING THROUGH AN ART MUSEUM that displays many exquisite masterpieces of paintings and sculpture. Now visualize that it's late at night when all of the lights are turned off - and every room is completely dark. In this moment you would not be able to see anything in the museum. All of the magnificent works of art would be right in front of you, but without any light to illuminate them, you couldn't enjoy them.

Now imagine that you light a match. The sudden light from the match would allow you to get a glimpse of some of the artistic majesty around you. Yet if you turned on a strong flashlight, it would provide even more illumination for you to enjoy a bigger spectrum of the art collection. And, of course, if the main lights in the museum were suddenly turned on, you would be able to appreciate the total experience of beauty and grace from all the masterpieces around you.

Certainly before the overhead lights were turned on, the art and sculpture were right there close to you the entire time, but were veiled and hidden in the dark. But with the aid of the light, you were able to observe what was always present.

Similar to the lit match, the flashlight, or the main lights in the museum, ever-greater spiritual awareness (ever-larger perspectives of what our life is truly about and what really matters) is like a powerful light that comes into "the mansion of our heart and mind" to illuminate the reality we perceive. More expansive perspectives of reality transform "the darkness of our mind", so we can easily see the truth, goodness, and beauty that is always there. What is always present within us, and what *the Essence of Life* yearns for us to fully experience, is the radiant magnificence of who we really are. We are constantly being invited by *Life* to rediscover our ever-present magnificence - by turning on the light of our conscious awareness.

There is a constant stream of *Transcendent Energy*, a *Field of Unlimited Creativity*, which surrounds us and permeates within us in every moment. This *Boundless and Transcendent Creativity* is who we really are. Yet sometimes "the darkness" of our habitual belief in separation, fear, and other loveless thoughts can inhibit us from seeing our own beauty, our own "magnificent work of art". Every one of us is a living masterpiece that is ever-evolving, a creative work in progress. Our life is the outer creative expression of our inner development. We are continually learning to unveil the exquisite beauty and majesty of who we truly are. Each day we fashion the blank canvas of our life to create the next version of our masterpiece. Every day we're embarked on a journey of learning to artfully live our lives in a way that expresses the natural states of peace, happiness, joy, and harmony. These are the natural states of our *True Eternal Nature*.

Greater spiritual awareness is what naturally nurtures the creative artist within us - or what we can call *the artist of life*. There are many time-tested ways to cultivate *the artist* within us - and to turn on "the light of our spiritual awareness", including meditation, self-inquiry, deep contemplation, and devotional prayer - to name a few. Yet another important way is to fully recognize that in the present moment, our life is always unfolding perfectly just as it is - for life simply is the way it is. This sublime recognition is a radical acceptance of our life.

The Daily Practice of *the Art of Life*

Like being helplessly and powerfully drawn toward some mysterious invisible magnet, we seem to be constantly pulled by unseen forces that attempt to compel us to seek for something other than what we already are. Our modern society, as well as the unconscious people around us, sometimes tell us that we are not OK the way we are, that we are somehow flawed and need to be fixed, that something within us is not right, and that what is wrong in us must be changed into what others believe is right.

The unconscious result of our society's dysfunctional conditioning is that it keeps pulling us away from the creative power of the present moment. This kind of social conditioning persists in attempting to catapult us to some future reality where, at some illusory time, our lives will hopefully be fixed, changed, holy, or enlightened. It falsely promises that we will finally be transformed into what we've been taught by others to believe life should actually look like.

If we habitually succumb to "the mysterious pull of this magnet", this collective illusion propagated within our society, then we typically begin our personal quest to be fixed, or to rid ourselves of our flaws, by first trying to eliminate our suffering. And sometimes from a religious point of view, this illusory quest compels us to attempt the pursuit of spiritual enlightenment - or some kind of spiritual transformation, so we may someday be like the elevated saints and gurus we have learned to venerate.

Of course there is nothing wrong with gaining inspiration from the wealth of great spiritual wayshowers that have come before us, especially if they're pointing us to our own innate power and invincible *True Nature*. Yet seeking to be fixed, as if we were broken, can become the kind of illusory spiritual quest in which we join millions of other people across the globe in seeking something to magically transform our lives, but which in actuality, we already have and already are. *We already are, and have always been, the perfect expression of truth, goodness, and beauty that the Infinite Intelligence of the Universe perfectly unfolds within us through a natural process of universal and personal evolution.* We are all living in a boundless *Field of Unlimited Creativity* which is always present to further our inner development and spiritual evolution.

As we intentionally open our heart so we may explore an even deeper and more meaningful spiritual quest, we begin to feel the inner attraction of an authentic "spiritual magnet", our true *journey of awakening*. This *journey of discovery* is primarily about the full realization of who we really are. This "attraction" is the natural tug of *the Transcendent Impulse* within us. It is the natural impulse to learn that, in the present moment, our life is unfolding perfectly just as it is.

Over time we begin to recognize the perfection unfolding within the creative expressions in every form of life. We are part of that perfection which includes each living creature on our planet and every phenomenal structure within the Universe. This awareness allows us to be truly grateful for everything, to humbly surrender our attachments and resistance, to fully accept ourselves just as we are, and to celebrate the essential Oneness of which we are a part.

This is *Life's* universal invitation to love and accept ourselves completely and unconditionally with all of our individual flaws and personality traits. It's a heightened recognition that the challenging parts of our life are not problems, but rather sacred gifts we can use to "polish the diamond" within us. We use these gifts so we may transform into a more radiant expression of our highest self. We attain this awareness - not by being habitually attached to getting rid of our suffering or our challenges - but by embracing each challenge as "a gift in disguise" offered for our personal and collective transformation. These are life's exquisite opportunities to let our pain or suffering point us to what our life is truly about - and what really matters.

As we arrive at this level of spiritual awareness, we become immune to the societal influences and programming of "the magnet of dysfunctional conditioning". We then experience a transformative shift from living under the unconscious urge of constantly seeking for what we do not have - to celebrating the magnificence of who we already are and joyously living *the art of life*.

Being and *Becoming*

Living our lives in the present moment is where true creativity exists, as well as the genuine experience of unconditional love. Authentically living in present moment awareness, or Presence, allows us to be consciously aware of two fundamental and paradoxical streams of life that are constantly expressing within us: *Being* and *Becoming*.

Being is the absolute reality where everything in our life is unfolding perfectly just as it is. A life that is unfolding perfectly is one that lives in the sacred sanctuary of present moment awareness. With this awareness there's a knowing that because of the perfection in our life, there is nothing to do and nowhere to go, and that nothing needs to be changed, altered or fixed. *Being* is also an awareness of the Oneness within all of life, and in that Perfect Oneness rests the experience of true happiness and peace of mind.

At the same time, living in Presence allows us to experience the paradoxical and complimentary stream of life called *Becoming*. The journey of *Becoming* is the constant natural yearning within us to develop our highest potential, to strive for ever-higher levels of awareness, to expand into new horizons and uncharted territory of unlimited possibilities, and to poetically "reach for the stars". This ongoing personal growth and inner development comes from an intrinsic longing to contribute to the creation of a more glorious world within an awareness of joy and creativity, rather than from an awareness of needing to fix something that is wrong with us - or the unconscious attachment to relieve our suffering.

Cultivating Inner Freedom

There are many beautifully written self-help books, which certainly play an important role in elevating a person's conscious awareness and alleviating suffering. As it has been already stated, **Journey of *The Great Circle*** is not about helping you change the outer circumstances of your lives, fix your emotional or psychological flaws, or get rid of your problems. These writings aim to inspire you to live a life of devoted practice so as to cultivate inner freedom, self-love, and an unconditional love for all of life. Yet with this wealth of self-cultivation, the areas of one's life are constructively affected. This book is also designed to point you to the conscious awareness of your *True Eternal Nature*, the supreme holiness and magnificence of who you really are.

It's pretty obvious that everyone has their own set of difficult opportunities to deal with, and there doesn't appear to be any way to bypass life's many challenges. Some challenges can be very hard to cope with, yet challenge is one of the most natural parts of evolving life. For without the dynamic challenges, chaos, and turbulence within the Universe there would be no galaxies, nor stars, nor planets. Thus there would be no intelligent life on Earth, and there would be no conscious awakening within you and me.

Therefore, with intention, we can choose to use our challenges as sacred gifts in order to become ever more free. We can make use of these opportunities to consciously develop a more awakened awareness, for true healing is learning to maintain a perfect balance within us that supports the evolution of all of life. No matter how much money we have, how great our health may be, how wonderful our marriage or significant relationship is, or how successful our career may be unfolding, we will always be presented with challenging situations that will invite us to expand our ability to experience true inner freedom.

Inner freedom does not come from changing the external conditions of our lives, but is fostered from how we're able to respond to the events and challenges of our life from inside the chamber of our heart. The heart is the integral part of us we must keep open and aligned with *the Source of Life*, so the sublime energy of *Limitless Love* can continuously flow through us unimpeded.

Embodying Inner Freedom

Inner freedom is the unconditional love and acceptance of ourselves and others in which we fully realize that our life is unfolding perfectly just as it is. Since the nature of life is to move through continuous cycles of order and chaos, balance and imbalance, challenges will always be an intrinsic and important part of our ever-evolving life. A masterful ability to love and accept life just the way it is, simply witnessing these experiences without judgment, allows for inner freedom to be embodied within the everyday unfolding of life's constant stream of challenges and treasures.

Just as turning on the main lights in a darkened museum allows us to see all the artistic masterpieces present, as we illuminate the light of our own awareness to the supreme majesty and magnificence of who we are, we re-establish our ability to live in self-mastery. In these writings, a person who realizes and lives with this elevated awareness is referred to as a **Master of Freedom**.

Transformative Practice

This innate yearning to embody inner freedom and joyously express our unique creativity is enhanced by developing a system of personal practice that helps us consciously live our visionary intentions. Through the use of daily transformative practices, we "polish the diamond of our inner being" and use the personal expressions of our creativity to help manifest a more peaceful and compassionate world. Transformative practice is what establishes new belief systems, new world views, new perspectives of life, and new behavior. Practice is what also slowly eliminates destructive habits and dysfunctional patterns in our life.

As we develop a more expanded awareness, "life becomes practice" and "practice becomes life". And both our life and our practice are informed and guided by consciously living in a state of Presence, a state of present moment awareness. From this state, we practice *the art of life*, like a musician practices his or her instrument, or a painter practices his or her craft, to co-create with life in sculpting a more beautiful world. Whether we practice the piano or tennis, compose a symphony, develop a life-enhancing personality trait, or help to relieve hunger on our planet, transformative practice is all about living in the joy of being an *artist of life*. It's about jumping into the natural stream of evolving life that inwardly directs us towards truth, goodness, and beauty - and towards expressions of unconditional love and service to others.

The essence of this book is intended to inspire and provide the mechanisms for the power of daily practice. Each day presents a unique awareness perspective to contemplate regarding the nature of your life. Each day provides an opportunity to expand your awareness of what your life is truly about - and what really matters. It is of great benefit to bring these contemplations out into the glory of Nature - to sit next to a creek - or lie upon the earth at the top of a hill - or lean against a tall tree. As you exercise the "muscles" of your *body, heart, mind, and Spirit* each day with steady determination and commitment, you are assisting *Life* in creatively sculpting its next expression of awakening within you.

Remember that you already are, and have always been, a supremely gifted *artist of life*. There is no one else who can create the exquisite masterpieces which only you can create. So while you enjoy your daily practice as you read and contemplate each day's theme within this book of narratives, you are practicing *the art of life*. And remember that your daily practice is not only for your personal benefit. We are all intimately connected as one global family as we ascend the infinite ladder of awareness. Our daily practice benefits all the men, women, children, and myriad creatures of the world. Practice well.

✳ <u>You Are A Diamond</u> ✳

You are a perfect diamond
    Longing to become more perfect
        A luminescent jewel
            Shimmering upon the necklace of this ephemeral world
           Forged from the supreme fire
               Within the heart of the Universe

You are a multifaceted gem of sublime majesty and grace
    Through which *Life* focuses its celestial starlight
        So it may glisten endlessly within you

You are a beloved *artist of life*
    Fashioning unparalleled hues upon the blank canvas of each new day
        To create the next rendering of your magnificent masterpiece

You are an invincible prism of the *Soul*
    Chiseled into form so *the Fullness* of the Cosmos can savor
        More of the luminous spectrum of its sensual wonders and hallowed glories

You are an ascending aeronaut spiraling heavenwards
    Climbing the infinite ladder of possibility
        Navigating tumultuous storms and immaculate skies
            Terrestrial chaos and galactic order
               The sacred gifts you use to share the omniscient nature of your truest self

You are a sovereign sculptor of untethered intentions
    Each one polishing the ever-effulgent diamond of your life
        So you may launch new portals of pristine freedom
            For the invisible lines of destiny to dance through you

Your mission - to dance with the *Light*
    Your purpose - to polish the perfection
        Your meaning of it all - to give for the good of all

It's just what diamonds
    Who spend their life *Being*
        In the course of *Becoming*
            Do

There is an innate spark of *Infinite Creativity*
radiating at the very core of everything
which has animated the entire Universe for 13.8 billion years,
and it is this *Essential Impulse* that directs and governs
the perpetual unfolding of the entire Cosmos.

❋ HOW TO BENEFIT FROM THIS BOOK ❋

The Daily Narratives and Contemplation Circles

JOURNEY OF *THE GREAT CIRCLE* has been designed to provide a set of contemplative narratives of various spiritual themes to be used as a daily transformative practice for cultivating peace of mind and inner freedom. Engaging daily in this form of inner development, especially for an entire year, you will be inwardly pointed to the most natural ways to experience greater peace, happiness, joy, and harmony.

Each of the 365 contemplative themes has a narrative displayed on the left page and a corresponding Contemplation Circle on the right. The Contemplation Circle illustrates a short summary of the daily narrative in four concise statements or words. Each Contemplation Circle can be used to quickly reconnect and summarize the primary ideas that have been described in the narrative.

The Contemplation Circles are typically read in the clockwise direction starting with the north node (top quadrant) yet there are often variations of how the Circles can be read. Many have arrows pointing in a specific direction for further contemplation. Generally, the counter-clockwise direction of the Circles represents the evolution of consciousness, and the clockwise direction represents the evolution of creation.

The Four Seasonal Volumes

The complete set of 365 contemplative narratives has been divided into four seasonal volumes. Each has a specific theme for its series of daily practices. The Winter Volume is oriented toward practices for the **cultivation of spiritual wellbeing**; the Spring Volume for **wellbeing of the mind**; the Summer Volume for **wellbeing of the heart**; and the Autumn Volume for **wellbeing of the body**.

Each of the four volumes contains sixteen primary Contemplation Circles that are repeated in all four volumes. The specific Contemplation Circle is the same within each volume, but the narrative is different, allowing you to explore and gain a deeper understanding of the main theme.

How to Use the First Two Seasonal Narratives – June 20th and June 21st

The first two narratives of this volume, June 20th and June 21st, explore the spiritual meaning and transcendent qualities of the summer season. Both of these narratives have two dates printed at the top of the page. This is because the summer solstice, the first day of summer, will usually occur on one of those two dates depending on the relationship of the Earth's orbit with the Sun for any given year. The title of the first narrative is written as "Gifts of Summer - June 20 or 21" and the second is written as "Qualities Within the Seasons of Life - June 20 or 21".

When the summer solstice takes place on June 20th, read the first two narratives as they are sequentially laid out. When the summer solstice occurs on June 21st, read the narrative entitled

"Qualities Within the Seasons of Life"" first, and then read "Gifts of Summer" on June 21st, the actual day of the summer solstice for that year.

Transformative Practices

A primary intention of this book is to encourage the use of daily transformative practice as a means to discover effective ways to embody and anchor the ideas and concepts into the heart as a direct experience. Consistent self-cultivation is the center of spiritual development. Throughout each of the four volumes there are a series of transformative practices that may be incorporated into one's daily life. The prominent focus is based upon four foundational transformative practices. These are:

1) meditation, 2) contemplation, 3) appreciation, and 4) prayer.

It is suggested for the spiritual development of the reader that some form of each of these four practices be experienced frequently. Change usually happens slowly and incrementally through constant repetition on a daily basis. In order to master a sport, an art, a science, or a business, one must practice ardently. It takes this same effort to develop our spiritual nature.

You may be interested in exploring the suggested meditative practices in the narrative from January 14th called "Meditation Practices" in the Winter Volume or explore various meditation practices that you discover elsewhere. You can also explore a specific form of the practice of contemplation in the narrative from April 5th called "A Contemplation Practice" in the Spring Volume. Daily appreciation is seemingly straightforward, yet you may get additional inspiration from the July 6th narrative called "Spheres of Appreciation" in the Summer Volume. And you may deepen your exploration of the power of prayer in the October 8th narrative called "The Practice of Prayer" in the Autumn Volume.

Daily Affirmation Statements

At the top of each contemplative narrative is a short affirmation printed in italics. This affirmation expresses one of the key themes within the daily narrative. For best results, the affirmation can be repeated at various times throughout the day. In the back of the book, all affirmation statements are printed for each day within a given volume. They are designed to be copied onto a piece of 8.5" x 11" paper. You can cut along the dotted lines and then take the individual affirmation with you as a reminder of the theme you are embracing for that specific day.

Visionary Archetypes as Transformative Practice

A visionary archetype is similar to the image of a distant horizon, for it represents qualities and virtues of ever-higher levels of human consciousness that we can envision on our personal horizon, yet desire to embody right now in our life. It is a poetic image of our greater potential or possibility, which we have yet to realize, until we have bravely traveled past boundaries of our current beliefs about who we think we are.

Visionary archetypes are symbolic templates that point us to higher stages of inner development and to the qualities and realms of creative expression we strive to achieve. They can be thought of as pictorial representations of superior moral qualities which can empower and motivate us to reach for something greater in ourselves, a promise of a more positive future for our life.

We can use these archetypes as a spiritual tool and blueprint of potential to assist us in imagining a more perfect expression of ourselves, and to hold within us an expansive vision of what is possible. It is suggested that each person seek their own inner guidance regarding how to use these visionary archetypes as a means to envision and embody the highest possibilities of who they really are.

Throughout each volume there are four sets of visionary archetypes that can be used as a transformative practice to envision and embody one's creative potential and spiritual sovereignty. The four sets are: 1) The Archetypes of Spiritual Awakening, 2) The Archetypes of Life Mastery, 3) The Archetypes of Higher Knowledge, and 4) The Archetypes of Conscious Contribution.

The Archetypes of Life Mastery, the Archetypes of Higher Knowledge, and the Archetypes of Conscious Contribution are all visionary archetypes. The Archetypes of Spiritual Awakening are four archetypes that represent our *spiritual journey*, or *journey of awakening*. The ultimate culmination of our *journey of awakening* is consciously living a life of inner freedom represented by the archetype of the **Master of Freedom**. All of the other visionary archetypes are facets of our unlimited potential, pointing to our sacred destiny as a **Master of Freedom**.

A Tool of Inner Guidance

There are additional ways to benefit from this book other than consecutively reading the daily narratives. You can also utilize this book to find guidance and inspiration by opening any volume to any place within the seasonal narratives, reading that specific narrative, and discovering how the narrative applies to your life at that moment. In this way, **Journey of The Great Circle** becomes "a tool of inner guidance" and can be used when you need a form of spiritual guidance or when you are seeking a moment of inspiration for your day.

The Great Circle as "a Spiritual Map of an Awakening Life"

The Great Circle is a map of consciousness and creation. It is a way to clearly understand the dynamics at play in our world and in our life. **The Great Circle** illustrates how our <u>inner development</u> determines and gives creative shape to how our <u>external reality</u> is expressed in our life. It portrays the universal dynamics relating to <u>our inward expansion of awareness</u> mirrored as <u>our outward creative expression</u>.

The primary function of **The Great Circle** as a transformative tool is to simply portray a useful collection of thoughts and ideas for the purpose of deeply comprehending the nature of existence. With this awareness we develop a greater understanding of what our life is truly about and thus cultivate an unconditional love for each expression of life.

There are many examples of traditional iconic images that represent **The Great Circle**, such as the Yin Yang symbol, the Star of David, the Medicine Wheel, and the Sacred Cross. In this book, the following symbolic image, *"The Great Circle Portal - a Window Into Being and Becoming"*, is also used to visually illustrate **The Great Circle** as "A Spiritual Map of an Awakening Life".

This image has been placed at each chapter of the contemplative practices to subconsciously assist you in deepening your understanding of the universal dynamics that are at play in the world and in your life. It can also be used to cultivate a comprehension of your purpose in life, your life mission, the meaning of life, and an awareness of your *True Nature*. Here is the significance of the Circle:

First, there is both a vertical line and a horizontal line within the larger circle of the image. The vertical line represents *Being* - or *Infinite Intelligence* - or God (*the Divine Transcendent* aspect of life). The horizontal line represents *Becoming,* our *journey of inner development,* our *spiritual journey.*

Over the vertical line within the large circle there is a Vertical Infinity Sign (a figure eight) that perpetually descends to the bottom of the circle and then ascends to the top repeating continuously. This Vertical Infinity Sign represents the constant yearning of our current physical lifetime (bottom circle) to merge with *the Transcendent, the Source of Life* (top circle) and *the Transcendent* (top circle) that constantly yearns to manifest ever-new expressions of creativity in our current physical lifetime (bottom circle). This natural and constant yearning (which is both the longing for spiritual awakening and spiritual embodiment) exists within us and within all forms of life. It is called *the Transcendent Impulse.*

The Vertical Infinity Sign represents *the Transcendent Impulse* as the top circle merging with the bottom circle - Consciousness merging with Creation - God merging with the Universe - *Divinity* merging with humanity - *Spirit* merging with the body - *Infinite Intelligence* merging with the myriad forms of Nature - *The One* merging with the Many.

The top circle within the Vertical Infinity Sign is a cosmic tunnel, like an inter-dimensional portal or quantum vortex, constantly moving towards the center. The center of this circle represents God, *the Source of All That Is, Universal Consciousness.*

The bottom circle has a Black Centerpoint or Singularity which represents material form, the physical body, or a focused point of creative manifestation.

The thick black line from the center of the top circle to the center of the bottom circle represents the perpetual alignment and Oneness of our current physical incarnation with *the Divine Transcendent (God, Infinite Intelligence, the Source of Life).*

Master of Freedom Logo

This image represents our *Fully Awakened Self,* one's *True Eternal Nature* completely experienced and lived within one's physical body. It is the embodied realization of a person who lives a life of inner freedom, loves all of life unconditionally, and serves the good of all with their creative gifts and talents. It is every person's sacred destiny to embody the *Awakened Self* and fully experience life as a **Master of Freedom.**

Infinite Awakenings Logo

This image represents the perpetual evolution - or the constant "awakenings" - that naturally take place in every aspect of Nature symbolized by the diamond, the flower, the bird, and the human being.

At one time, millions of years ago, there was only a plethora of green vegetation on the planet. The beautiful manifestation of flowers had not yet arrived on the evolutionary scene. But over time and with gradual development, evolving life eventually found a way to empower a brand new emergent form to arise; the very first flower.

For the first flower to take shape on Earth, a radical shift in consciousness was required within the plant kingdom. This new expression of vegetative form could poetically be thought of as an "enlightenment" or "awakening" of the plant kingdom. A similar kind of radical shift in consciousness also occurred in the mineral kingdom with the first diamond - and millions of years later, in the animal kingdom with the first flight of a bird.

The same expansive evolutionary impulses in consciousness are happening right now throughout the world as they continuously have from the beginning of the Universe. Each person on the planet is now, consciously or unconsciously, evolving and developing into his or her destiny as an awakened human.

The Story of Awakening Within the First Narratives

In the conceptual design of **Journey of The Great Circle**, there is a poetic interweaving of themes within the first four contemplative narratives of each volume. Together these four narratives reveal "a hidden archetypal story" regarding every person's *spiritual journey of discovery*.

The first four narratives in the Summer Volume are:
1) Gifts of Summer
2) Qualities Within the Seasons of Life
3) The Great Story of Awakening
4) *Journey of Awakening*

The daily practice of contemplative narratives can easily be accomplished without the understanding of this conceptual design. Yet for those who are interested, the concept of how these four narratives are woven together is described at the end of the book in the section called "The Story of Awakening Within the First Narratives".

Life as Practice

One of the foundational themes within the contemplative narratives of **Journey of The Great Circle** is to experience the spiritual power of daily transformative practice. In order to embody something that we desire in our life, it usually requires dedicated practice and committed perseverance.

When we intend to align our awareness with *the Source of Life*, it also takes practice to embody this alignment as an ongoing experience in every moment. When we intend to be grateful for all that we're learning from every experience of our life, it takes practice. When we intend to live a life of inner freedom, it takes practice. When we intend to love all of life unconditionally, it takes practice.

If a person is committed to the practice of learning to play the piano, in the beginning it requires a lot of focused attention on every detail of how to move the fingers across the keyboard. Yet over time as one implements daily exercises and perseverance, eventually playing the piano becomes natural and effortless. It is as if some invisible *Field of Energy* is playing through the person - as the piano becomes a natural creative extension of his or her body.

The same thing occurs with spiritual practice. For with the daily dedication of placing our attention on the spiritual desires of our heart, we naturally and effortlessly learn how to respond to life's glories and challenges with ease, grace, and conscious responsibility. This is what these 365 daily contemplative narratives are designed to help you manifest in your life. There comes a sacred moment on our journey of discovery when we deeply recognize the authentic joy of practicing each day to be the best version of ourselves. And in that sublime moment, daily transformative practice becomes one of the most fulfilling and meaningful facets of our life.

Therefore practice with all the vibrant joy in your heart so you may walk through this life, gracefully and naturally, as a **Master of Freedom**.

The Essence of Life is at this time
asking us to learn to be a better version of ourselves.
We are all being invited to evolve
to a whole new evolutionary expression
of what it means to be human.

DAILY CONTEMPLATION PRACTICES FOR SUMMER

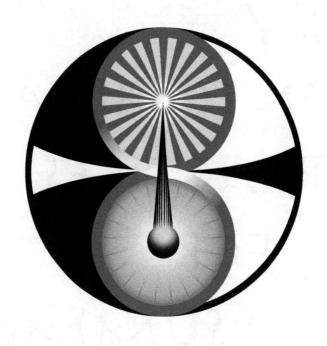

1

THE DANCE
OF THE INFINITE
SEASONS

GIFTS OF SUMMER

Today I consciously deepen my understanding of the meaning of my life.

Once again in the northern hemisphere of our planet, it's the first day of the summer season,
  The beginning of a new quadrant of time within the endless seasonal cycles,
    The one moment during the year when the apparent path of the Sun overhead
      Travels across the sky at its most northern arc along its annual journey.

Today is referred to as *the summer solstice (solstice means "the Sun appears to stand still")*
  And the Sun's most northern journey across the sky makes it the year's longest day -
    For from this day on, the Sun's overhead path will once again return southward.

In relation to our personal journey, the season of summer points us to **the service of others**,
  For it's a time that reminds us to deepen our generosity of spirit to the people around us
    Using the creativity that's been inspired and seeded during "the spring of our life".

Summer is a time when the outer fruits of the trees, as well as "the inner fruits of our lives"
  Are yearning for ample nourishment - so that life's garden is better able to flourish.

It also symbolizes "the ripening of the fruits of our *Soul*" in relation to the quality of **surrender**,
  For it's a time of renewing our commitment to let go of everything in our life
    To *the Infinite Intelligence* that's constantly animating us each day.

Similar to our vegetable and flower gardens that have been planted during spring,
  In life we must learn to be patient and know "our harvest will appear at the proper time".

Just as gardens need plenty of nourishment, this time is for nourishing the power of our **love**
  Concerning all sentient beings - and expanding our care and compassion for all of life.

Furthermore during this season, we can learn "to increase the bounty of our kindness"
  By intentionally cultivating, in every moment, the heart-centered ways
    We consciously choose to respond to life regarding each situation we encounter.

The better choices we make (based on the more inclusive perspectives we're aware of)
  The more peace of mind and harmony we're able to experience.

Conscious heart-centered choices help us use our unique gifts to serve and bless others
  And give us greater clarity about the larger purpose and meaning of our life.

The season of summer is, typically, a natural time when more people are active outdoors
  Enjoying the warmer days, the radiant sunshine, and one another,
    When more people genuinely feel an instinctive urge to experience community.

In a symbolic way, this season is a time that helps us expand our awareness
  Of how we can better **contribute our creative gifts and talents to the collective,**
    To the larger community of our friends, co-workers, and fellow citizens.

We can use the longest day of the year - *the summer solstice*, with its radiance of solar light,
  As a time to look within so we may deepen our understanding of the meaning of our life.

Circle of the Gifts of Summer
(Transcendent Qualities Within the Seasons of Life)

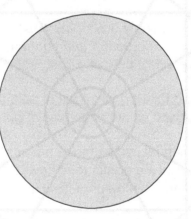

SERVE
"THE MANY"
**A TIME OF USING
THE CREATIVITY THAT
I'VE CULTIVATED DURING
"THE SPRING OF MY LIFE"
AS A WAY TO DEEPEN
MY SERVICE TO OTHERS**

**CONTRIBUTION
TO COMMUNITY**
**A TIME OF EXPANDING
MY AWARENESS OF HOW
TO BETTER CONTRIBUTE
MY CREATIVE GIFTS AND
TALENTS TO MY FRIENDS
AND COMMUNITY**

SURRENDER
**A TIME OF RIPENING
"THE FRUITS OF MY *SOUL*"
BY SURRENDERING
EVERYTHING TO *INFINITE
INTELLIGENCE* - WHILE
PATIENTLY LETTING
"MY HARVEST" UNFOLD**

**UNCONDITIONAL
LOVE FOR LIFE**
**A TIME OF INCREASING
THE BOUNTY OF MY
LOVE, MY GENEROSITY,
MY KINDNESS, AND MY
CARE AND COMPASSION
FOR ALL OF LIFE**

QUALITIES WITHIN THE SEASONS OF LIFE

My life is interconnected with the lives of all people through a vast Field of Universal Energy.

Everything in the world is interconnected with every other material expression in the Universe
For all phenomenal forms in the Cosmos are inwardly directed to evolve and develop
By the same *Infinite Intelligence* that animates all of creation.

However there is one *illusion* that a majority of humanity has unconsciously agreed to live with
Which is: the world is seen as many isolated objects that are separate from one another
Rather than perceiving reality as "one infinite sea of radiant energy in motion"
That is all interconnected as "one universal dance of life".

Of course, this long-standing collective illusion also includes the common accepted belief
That all people are separate from one another - and are not connected as a Unity.

Quantum physics has revealed that everything is one continuous flow of universal energy
Emerging into countless unique forms from the formless dimensionless *Unified Field*,
"The One" Source of All That Is.

Yet our human sense perceptions seemingly determine separate individual forms in the world
In order to consciously participate in creation and contribute our gifts to its progression,
Whereas, in actuality, there exists only one vast *Field of Universal Energy.*

Our life becomes ever more rich and fulfilling when we're able to see our everyday reality
With both *the eyes of <u>unity</u>* - as well as with *the eyes of <u>duality</u>*.

Typically, most people think of the annual cycle of the seasons as four distinct periods of time,
But from the perspective of unity, it's a continuous flow of one moment to the next,
One ceaseless and unbroken movement of the eternal now.

Obviously, it has been helpful for us humans to define and categorize the individual seasons
So we may better communicate certain conceptual ideas about them to one another.

There can be benefit in learning to distinguish the individual components of the annual cycle
(Known to us separately as winter, spring, summer, and autumn),
And yet, at the same time, to maintain a conscious awareness of its wholeness,
In other words, learn to embrace its duality and its unity - simultaneously.

As we contemplate the meaning of our life (**serve *"The Many"***) which we intuit in **summer**,
We can also be mindful to renew ourselves (**align with *"The One"***) sensed in **winter**,
To express our personal creativity (**outward expression**) realized in **spring**,
And to develop our potential (**inward expansion**) recognized in **autumn**,
Yet we can still sustain a conscious awareness of the totality,
Of the interconnected flow of the complete seasonal cycle.

So in order to deepen our awareness of the transcendent qualities of the summer season
(Serve *"The Many"*, surrender, unconditional love for life, contribution to community),
We can learn to see them in a much wider context, as part of a larger whole,
One infinite sea of radiant energy in constant motion.

Circle of Qualities Within the Seasons of Life

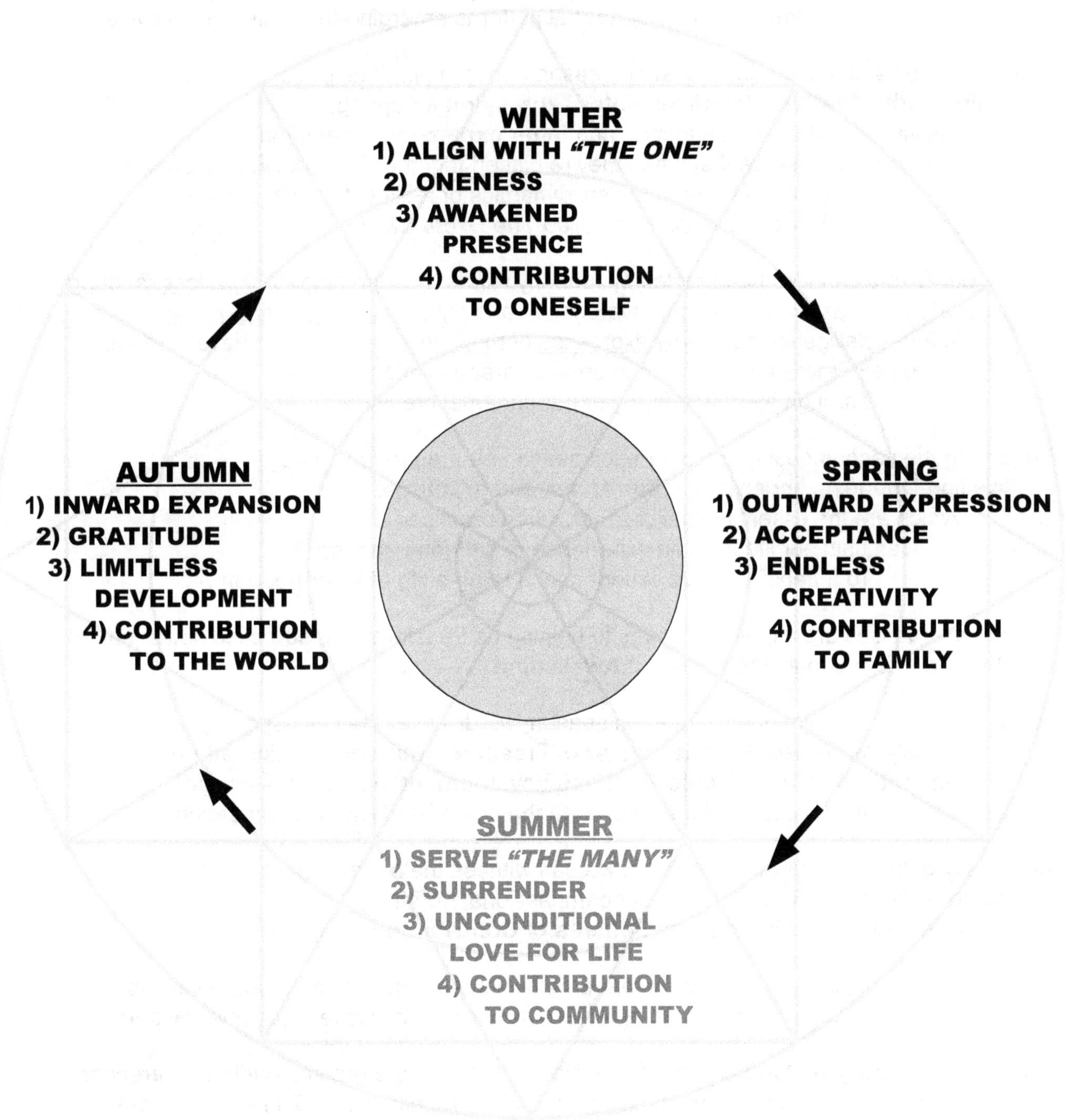

WINTER
1) ALIGN WITH *"THE ONE"*
2) ONENESS
3) AWAKENED
 PRESENCE
4) CONTRIBUTION
 TO ONESELF

SPRING
1) OUTWARD EXPRESSION
2) ACCEPTANCE
3) ENDLESS
 CREATIVITY
4) CONTRIBUTION
 TO FAMILY

AUTUMN
1) INWARD EXPANSION
2) GRATITUDE
3) LIMITLESS
 DEVELOPMENT
4) CONTRIBUTION
 TO THE WORLD

SUMMER
1) SERVE *"THE MANY"*
2) SURRENDER
3) UNCONDITIONAL
 LOVE FOR LIFE
4) CONTRIBUTION
 TO COMMUNITY

THE GREAT STORY OF AWAKENING

Every day has meaningful opportunities to learn to serve the wellbeing of others.

If you were to observe the various characteristic qualities within each of the four seasons
And then began to notice the way they thematically interconnect with one another,
You might distinguish some key natural patterns emerging from this annual cycle.

When you look at the first quality of each season from the previous page
(**Align with *"The One"*** for winter, **outer expression** for spring,
Serve *"The Many"* for summer, and **inner expansion** for autumn),
You can observe that when they're placed together in a specific pattern,
They express four universal dynamics of reality at play in our life
Which collectively is called *The Great Circle*. (see June 28th)

The Great Circle can also be depicted by four key words: <u>interior</u>, <u>exterior</u>, <u>formless</u>, and <u>form</u>
Illustrating that as we expand our awareness - and <u>align with *the Source of Life*</u>,
Infinite Intelligence <u>outwardly expresses</u> our <u>inward expansion</u> and development,
By externally mirroring our internal awareness into the world
Through <u>the many forms</u> of our personal creativity.

Regarding the second quality listed for each season on the preceding page,
We find **Oneness**, **acceptance**, **surrender**, and **gratitude**,
Which are the essential qualities that, when practiced daily,
Can shift our life from an experience of suffering and fear
To a transformative experience of living a life of inner freedom.

These four qualities are important means to helping us transform our, so-called, lower nature
And are referred to as the **Pillars of Awakening**. (see July 10th)

When we look at the third quality for each season, we discover the key aspects (see Aug. 17th)
Of our Fully Awakened Self, **the Master of Freedom**, which are **awakened presence**,
Unconditional love for life, **limitless development**, and **endless creativity** -
And these vital qualities point us to the potential of who we can become.

And finally of the last four qualities listed, we can witness the natural impulse within us
To **contribute to others** through our compassionate offerings
And through the four primary **Spheres of Contribution**. (see Aug. 27th)

For each one of us, these basic natural patterns (which emerge within the four seasons)
Portray an unfolding *spiritual journey*, or Great Story, which we're all an integral part of.

It's **The Great Story of Awakening**, of consciously cultivating a greater spiritual awareness
Gained from a growing understanding of life via our reflections on *The Great Circle*,
Which leads us to the expansive possibilities for inner and outer transformation
As we learn to embody the attributes of the **Pillars of Awakening**,
Through which we are offered the *grace* of inner freedom
Expressed within every person as a **Master of Freedom**,
And this awakened awareness longs to be shared
By way of the four **Spheres of Contribution**.

Circle of The Great Story of Awakening
(My *Spiritual Journey* In Relation to the Infinite Seasons of Life)

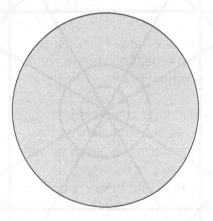

THE GREAT CIRCLE
MY *JOURNEY OF AWAKENING*
IS TO MINDFULLY EXPAND MY
AWARENESS OF WHAT IS TRUE
AND SERVE THE GOOD OF ALL
+ + +
WIN - ALIGN WITH *"THE ONE"*
SPR - OUTWARD EXPRESSION
SUM - SERVE *"THE MANY"*
AUT - INWARD EXPANSION

SPHERES
OF CONTRIBUTION
I RESPONSIBLY SUSTAIN
BALANCE REGARDING
MY CONTRIBUTIONS TO:
+ + +
WIN - MYSELF
SPR - FAMILY
SUM - COMMUNITY
AUT - THE WORLD

PILLARS
OF AWAKENING
WITH DAILY PRACTICE I
TRANSFORM SUFFERING
INTO INNER FREEDOM
+ + +
WIN - ONENESS
SPR - ACCEPTANCE
SUM - SURRENDER
AUT - GRATITUDE

MASTER
OF FREEDOM
ULTIMATELY I DISCOVER
HOW TO MASTER THE KEYS
TO LIVING AN AWAKENED LIFE
+ + +
WIN - AWAKENED PRESENCE
SPR - ENDLESS CREATIVITY
SUM - UNCONDITIONAL LOVE
AUT - INNER DEVELOPMENT

JOURNEY OF AWAKENING

My life is a perpetual journey of discovery - a quest to live an awakened life of inner freedom.

Every morning as the new day emerges from the darkness of night,
    The fiery Sun blankets the Earth with its comforting warmth
        And the dawning light beckons us to begin another adventure of life.

Yet why are we actually here, where is our life really headed,
    And what is this human adventure truly about which we embark on each morning?

In order to fully embrace the answers to these foundational questions of life,
    We must courageously "climb the mountain", and stand once again "at the summit",
        Where we can more easily ascertain a wider perspective of our entire journey.

This is the hallowed place of self-inquiry where we can gain a much larger vantage of our life
    And where it may be easier to perceive that our lives have purpose and mission,
        Creative momentum and meaning.

From this grand perspective of the "Big Picture of our life",
    We can, so to speak, "learn to take off the habitual blinders over our eyes"
        By expanding our awareness of what our life is truly about,
            Gaining a greater understanding of what really matters,
                And cultivating our **inner development** and creative potential.

From this expanded vantage of reality, it becomes obvious
    That our life can be much more fulfilling and meaningful
        When we discover how to transform our personal suffering into inner freedom
            Through a dedicated process of releasing
                Our dysfunctional habits and loveless beliefs
                    That do not further, or support, the advancement
                        Of our *spiritual journey* - **our transformative quest**.

Through the intentional shedding of our old habits,
    We can embody a more compassionate and caring way
        To express the moment-to-moment choices and actions of our life
            By opening our heart to these more heightened stages of awareness.

And then with the discipline of transformative practices - such as meditation and mindfulness,
    We, in time, can learn to **embody the mastery of living a life of inner freedom.**

Our journey naturally leads us to the discovery that to live our life with ever-fulfilling meaning
    We must use our creative gifts and talents to **contribute to the good of all**.

One of the most effective ways in which we maintain the over-arching vision of this adventure
    Is to, each day, "ascend to the summit where we feel our union with *the Infinite*",
        In other words, align our awareness with *the Source of Life* in the core of silence
            So as to reconnect with what really matters - and with who we really are
                While preserving a strong commitment within our heart
                    To continue the cultivation of our ***journey of awakening***.

Circle of the *Journey of Awakening*
(Key Stages of the Transformative Quest For Inner Freedom)

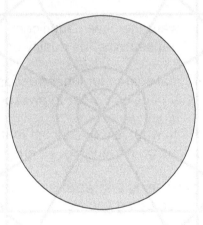

DEVELOPMENT
FIRST STAGE:
I EXPAND MY AWARENESS
OF WHAT MY LIFE
IS TRULY ABOUT AND
WHAT REALLY MATTERS,
FOSTER MORE INCLUSION
OF OTHERS, AND DEVELOP
MY UNLIMITED POTENTIAL

TRANSFORMATION
SECOND STAGE:
I ENGAGE IN PRACTICES
THAT HELP ME TRANS-
FORM MY BELIEFS WHICH
NO LONGER SERVE *LIFE*
INTO MORE CARING,
COMPASSIONATE, AND
LOVE-CENTERED BELIEFS

MASTERY
THIRD STAGE:
I EMBODY THE MASTERY
OF LIVING A LIFE OF INNER
FREEDOM THROUGH MY
DAILY ALIGNMENT WITH
THE SOURCE OF LIFE AND
COMMITMENT TO TRANS-
FORMATIVE PRACTICE

CONTRIBUTION
FOURTH STAGE:
AS I LIVE A LIFE OF INNER
FREEDOM, I CONTRIBUTE
MY CREATIVE GIFTS
AND TALENTS
TO THE GOOD OF ALL
- AND HELP CO-CREATE
A BETTER WORLD

CULTIVATING THE MASTERY OF *BEING* AND *BECOMING*

Each day I cultivate a life of inner freedom using the gifts of daily transformative practice.

When structural engineers build a tall skyscraper in some city business district,
  They first construct a sturdy foundation that supports the weight of the lofty tower.

At one point in this process, when the first stage of construction is complete,
  They must shift their focus away from the foundation
    In order to start working on the next stage of the structure's design.

In a similar fashion, each of us is involved in a continuous process of "building our future life",
  And we must at some point, mindfully shift our focus away from our *egoic foundation*,
    Which, through ignorance, has erroneously placed belief in the illusion of fear
      And instead, become conscious of what is true (what our life is truly about)
        By expanding our awareness and transforming our loveless beliefs.

The egoic self has been a crucial step in the survival of our species and prior cultural evolution,
  Yet the *ego* is just the basic foundation for the possibilities of what we truly can become.

So in order to consciously blossom toward the new magnificent expression of our future self,
  We must embark on a journey of transforming the quality of our inner experience.

This is a *journey of discovery*, a personal search for inner freedom,
  A path of mastering key aspects of our life in order to awaken to who we really are.

Life is constantly inviting us to relax into what is (i.e. - accept that our life is unfolding perfectly)
  And discover how to be a conscious co-creator (i.e. - learn to create our heart's visions).

This *journey of life - the journey of awakening* that we're all embarked on - is a spiritual quest,
  A quest for mastery of what is called *Being* and *Becoming* ("what is" and "what can be").

Being is an awareness inviting us to cultivate gratitude, surrender, acceptance, and Oneness,
  So we may focus our daily attention on **learning to deepen our love for all of life**.

Cultivating the mastery of *Being* also requires letting go of our negative emotional energy
  That unconsciously affects our choices and actions, by purifying and healing our heart
    Using **the transformative practices of forgiveness and release work**.

Our natural innate impulse of *Becoming* invites us to learn to master **the power of intention**
  So as to manifest our visions and build new neural pathways of our *Fully Awakened Self*
    Using our intention, imagination, and prayer while aligned with *the Source of Life*.

Becoming can also be fostered by focusing **healing energy** in the form of high frequency *Light*
  Through our body using sound, ecstatic dance, sacred geometry, and healing facilitators
    In order to experience and embody new levels of health and creativity.

As we align our heart and mind each day with *the Natural Intelligence* that abides within us
  And "build higher stages of awakened awareness" upon the foundation of our life,
    We are guided to inner freedom - and more able to help co-create a better world.

Circle of Cultivating the Mastery of *Being* and *Becoming*

(Key Practices to "Accept What Is" and "Create What Can Be")

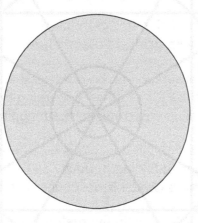

**THE PILLARS
OF AWAKENING**
EACH DAY I MINDFULLY
CULTIVATE THE FOUR
AWAKENING ATTRIBUTES:
GRATITUDE, SURRENDER,
ACCEPTANCE & ONENESS
- AND LEARN TO DEEPEN
MY LOVE FOR ALL OF LIFE
(BEING)

**THE MIRACLE
OF CONSCIOUS
CO-CREATION**
I CO-CREATE VISIONS
OF POSSIBILTY USING MY
INTENTION, IMAGINATION
MEDITATIONS & PRAYERS
AS I STAY ALIGNED WITH
THE SOURCE OF LIFE
(BECOMING)

**THE ALCHEMY
OF *LIMITLESS LOVE***
I FOCUS HIGH FREQUENCY
LIGHT THROUGH MY BODY
TO EXPERIENCE HEALTH
AND CREATIVITY - USING
SOUND, ECSTATIC DANCE,
SACRED GEOMETRY, AND
HEALING FACILITATORS
(BECOMING)

**THE SONG
OF FORGIVENESS**
I ACCEPT THAT MY LIFE
IS UNFOLDING PERFECTLY
JUST AS IT IS - AND THUS
I RELEASE ANY NEGATIVE
EMOTIONAL ENERGY
USING THE PRINCIPLES
OF FORGIVENESS
(BEING)

INNER FREEDOM

I accept what is, embrace that my life is unfolding perfectly, and love myself just as I am.

Just for the fun of it, take a moment and ask yourself the following questions:
  "What is the purpose or reason I wake up every morning?" -
    "Why do I experience certain situations such as relationships, various careers,
      Doing creative projects, recreational adventures, or attending school?" -
        "What is my life truly about?" - *"Why am I here?"* - *"Who am I?"*

Many religious scholars and philosophers have postulated that what life is actually about
  Is learning *the spiritual lessons of life* - so we can eventually experience true freedom.

Some suggest that life is about deeply investigating the interior world of our heart and mind
  So we can ultimately discover how to live an awakened life of inner freedom,
    But then that brings up yet another question - *"What actually is **inner freedom**?"*

Surely we all have our different concepts regarding what *inner freedom* means to us,
  So listed below are a few fundamental ideas of possible meanings we might investigate.

Inner freedom can be thought of in relation to **the Pillars of Awakening**, (see July 10th)
  For it requires we learn to live with **gratitude, surrender, acceptance,** and **Oneness**.

Therefore from this vantage, *inner freedom* can be described as living our life in such a way
  That we are in constant **gratitude** for what we're learning from every experience of life
    And authentically appreciating ourselves for the magnificent gift of who we are.

Inner freedom can also be described as the conscious awareness
  Of fully embracing that our life in unfolding perfectly just as it is
    And, thus, **accepting what is** (which is accepting all things the way they are).

Furthermore, it can be thought of as living with the maturity and heart wisdom
  To let go of our attachments, **surrender everything in our life to *a Greater Power***,
    And relinquish searching for what we already have,
      Which is the majesty and splendor of this eternal moment.

And to put it another way, *inner freedom* can be expressed as the awareness we embody
  In which we sustain an **alignment with *Life*, maintain awareness of our Oneness,**
    And compassionately love others - and all of life unconditionally.

So from "the Big Perspective", the reason we wake up every morning and why we are here
  Is to learn to fully love and accept ourselves, to fully love every expression of life,
    And to share our love with others through our compassionate acts of service.

Inner freedom is consciously realizing the perfection that's always unfolding within all of life,
  For as we learn to <u>be grateful</u> for, <u>surrender</u> to, accept, and be <u>one</u> with, life just as it is,
    The natural states of peace, happiness, joy and harmony arise in our awareness.

Therefore, when we are aligned with *Life* - and gratefully celebrate every experience we have
  While fully loving and accepting ourselves, as well as every part of life - we are free.

Circle of Inner Freedom
(In Relation to the Pillars of Awakening)

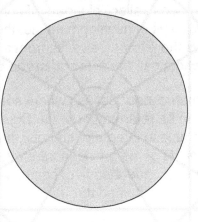

ONENESS
INNER FREEDOM –
A SUSTAINED ALIGNMENT
OF MY AWARENESS WITH
THE SOURCE OF LIFE
AND AWARENESS OF MY
ONENESS WITH ALL OF LIFE
- WHILE LOVING OTHERS
UNCONDITIONALLY

GRATITUDE
INNER FREEDOM –
LIVING MY LIFE IN SUCH
A WAY THAT I AM IN
CONSTANT GRATITUDE
FOR WHAT I'M LEARNING
FROM EVERY EXPERIENCE
- AND APPRECIATING
MYSELF FOR WHO I AM

ACCEPTANCE
INNER FREEDOM – MY
CONSCIOUS AWARENESS
OF FULLY EMBRACING
THAT MY LIFE IS
UNFOLDING PERFECTLY
JUST AS IT IS - AND THUS
ACCEPTING ALL THINGS
THE WAY THEY ARE

SURRENDER
INNER FREEDOM –
LIVING WITH THE HEART
WISDOM TO LET GO
OF MY ATTACHMENTS
TO MY DESIRES
- AND TO SURRENDER
EVERYTHING IN MY LIFE
TO *A GREATER POWER*

THE INTEGRAL STAGE OF CONSCIOUSNESS

In the quiet of my heart, I integrate the many aspects of my life into an expression of harmony.

Modern psychologists have discovered (through the science of precise observations)
    That every person naturally grows through a series of specific stages of development -
        While historians have observed that societies, cultures, religions, and nations
            Progress, over time, along similar stages of unfolding development.

But of course, not all people, societies, cultures, religions, or nations
    Grow at the same pace of development simultaneously (at identical rates of learning),
        Which makes it possible for different levels or stages of human awareness
            To all take place on Earth within humanity at the same time.

We can think of these various stages of awareness as analogous to a modern family
    That's made up of many unique individuals with different ages and life experiences
        Who each have diverse levels of personal development and maturity,
            Yet are all living together as one family within the same home.

Spiritually exceptional people have been called "pioneers of consciousness", or "wayshowers",
    Or those who live at very high levels of development (i.e. the leading edge of evolution),
        For their awareness allows them to perceive life from a wide vantage of inclusion,
            Which some philosophers call **the integral stage of consciousness**.

The integral stage is a level of human consciousness where some highly developed individuals
    Live with an awareness that can be referred to as "the Big Picture perspective of reality"
        In which these people are able to integrate, embody, and harmoniously include
            All of the different aspects of the previous lower stages of consciousness,
                The various stages of understanding, compassion, and cooperation
                    That humans have attained through time - up to the present.

The *integral stage of consciousness* (that **embraces and includes** all other preceding stages)
    Means a person is able to integrate, and unify, key aspects of awareness in one's life
        By learning to live with, and accept, the mystery and paradox of life that states:
            "Each of us is a unique individual expression of *the Source of All That Is*,
                Yet simultaneously in some incomprehensible way,
                    Our *True Eternal Nature* is also - the same as *the Source*".

Thus, those who are spiritually liberated have learned to **merge** their "heart of compassion"
    With *"the Mind of the Universe"* while living their life in service to the good of all.

Some scholars propose that the endless expansion of awareness unfolding within humanity
    Suggests there's a natural impulse deep within each one of us
        That perpetually invites us to discover who we really are
            So we may truly experience an awareness of our Oneness with all of life.

Could it be that our actual "human job description", or what we can call our "purpose in life",
    Is to learn to integrate and unify all aspects of our life into one expression of **harmony**,
        And then to help integrate and unify every form of life, person, society, and nation
            Into "an embodied collective expression" of a harmonious world?

Circle of the Integral Stage of Consciousness

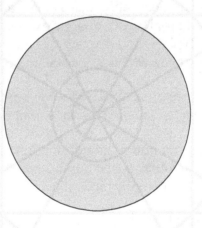

INCLUSION
THE INTEGRAL STAGE –
**EMBRACING
AND INCLUDING ALL
OF THE DIFFERENT STAGES
OF CONSCIOUSNESS
THAT EXIST IN THE WORLD
INTO ONE UNIFIED WHOLE**

PERSPECTIVE
THE INTEGRAL STAGE –
**PERCEIVING "A BIG
PICTURE PERSPECTIVE
OF REALITY" IN WHICH
I INTEGRATE ALL LOWER
LEVELS OF AWARENESS
INTO A TOTALITY**

HARMONY
THE INTEGRAL STAGE –
**MY EXPERIENCE
OF INTEGRATING AND
UNIFYING ALL ASPECTS
OF MY LIFE
INTO ONE EXPRESSION
OF HARMONY**

MERGE
THE INTEGRAL STAGE –
**THE MERGING OF MY
"HEART OF COMPASSION"
WITH *"THE MIND OF
THE UNIVERSE"* - AS I LIVE
A LIFE IN SERVICE
TO THE GOOD OF ALL**

ALIGNING WITH *THE TRUE SELF*

Today I align my awareness with who I really am, my True Self, the Essence in me that is eternal.

The large majestic rivers that snake their way through the hills and valleys of the world
  Seem to maintain a steady current as they advance toward some distant ocean.

If someone were to place an empty four-person racing rowboat on one of these waterways,
  It would effortlessly float down the river, "captured" by the constantly moving current.

Even without the racing team on board to row the boat downstream,
  It would, in time, make it on its own - swept along by the pull of the ever-flowing water.

But if four synchronized rowers of a racing team were in the boat rowing down the river,
  This added energy would certainly quicken the boat towards its ultimate goal.

There is a natural impulse within each of us yearning to discover higher stages of awareness,
  In other words - an inborn intuition inviting us to expand our consciousness.

If we feel this natural longing tugging at us - and desire to live a life of greater love and service,
  We can take intentional action to realize our goal by examining who we believe we are,
    Letting go of any loveless beliefs, and aligning our awareness with our *True Self*,
      The *Limitless Essence* in us which is eternal and unbounded.

As a metaphor, our life can be thought of as similar to a rowboat traveling down a flowing river
  Swept by a current that's moving us toward *"the Ocean of our True Nature"*.

As we gain more inclusive perspectives and a greater understanding of what life is truly about,
  We also recognize we can consciously assist our journey down *"the River of Life"*
    By "picking up the oars" (i.e. the many tools of awareness available to us).

One of "the oars", or transformative awareness practices, for **aligning with our *True Self***
  Is using daily **meditation** (or some form of quieting the mind)
    In order to directly experience our *Eternal Nature*.

The practice of **contemplation** and inquiring into *life's existential questions*
  Helps us align with our *True Self* by gaining awareness of what really matters
    And more clearly understanding our life from "a Big Picture perspective".

Another valuable exercise we can incorporate is to sustain a practice of **mindfulness**
  Which is simply witnessing our passing thoughts and emotions without judgment.

And it certainly is beneficial to maintain a healthy body, enjoy meaningful relationships,
  And foster a nourishing environment in which to live,
    For, of course, it's so much easier to align ourselves with *the Transcendent*
      When we're experiencing states of physical and emotional **wellbeing**.

The simple fact that we're alive means we are, right now, "flowing down *the River of Life*",
  Yet *Life* is constantly inviting us "to pick up the oars", to align with our *True Self*,
    And "to actively row our boat" towards our next horizon of luminous possibility.

Circle of Aligning with *the True Self*
(Transformative Awareness Practices)

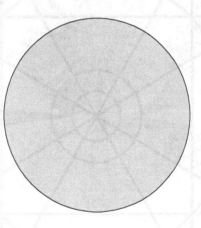

MEDITATION
**I USE DAILY
MEDITATION
OR PERIODS OF SILENCE
TO QUIET MY MIND
IN ORDER TO DIRECTLY
EXPERIENCE
MY *ETERNAL NATURE***

WELLBEING
**I MAINTAIN A HEALTHY
BODY AND
ENVIRONMENT AS WELL
AS MEANINGFUL
RELATIONSHIPS
THAT SUPPORT
MY ALIGNMENT
WITH MY *TRUE SELF***

CONTEMPLATION
**I CONTEMPLATE
LIFE'S EXISTENTIAL
QUESTIONS REGARDING
WHAT REALLY MATTERS
WHICH HELP ME ALIGN
MY AWARENESS WITH
MY *TRANSCENDENT
SELF***

MINDFULNESS
**I SUSTAIN
A PRACTICE
OF MINDFULNESS
IN WHICH I WITNESS
MY PASSING THOUGHTS
AND EMOTIONS
WITHOUT JUDGMENT**

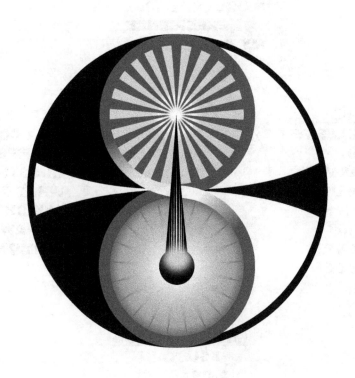

II

THE POETRY
OF
THE GREAT CIRCLE

THE GREAT CIRCLE

From the perspective of living in the present moment, my life is unfolding perfectly just as it is.

Generally, when we speak to another person about "a single year" as a specific period of time
    We are describing the temporal interval the Earth travels through space
        As it orbits one revolution around the Sun,
            And we view this interval as one complete cycle.

Yet the concept of a year as an annual cycle can be viewed in different ways,
    For example, a year can be viewed as either one complete experience of wholeness,
        Or it can also be seen as four individual seasons
            Which, collectively, make up the totality of a single year
                (Depending on which perspective we want to use at the time).

Similarly, we typically perceive *the perpetual unfolding of the evolving Universe*
    (In other words, what we define as our collective reality)
        As a wholeness, an entirety, a unity, a totality of all that is.

But in order to understand the essential dynamics of this *perpetual unfolding* more clearly
    And then to effectively communicate these dynamics with others,
        Our human mind seems to require distinctions
            Or specific ways in which to describe its characteristic individual parts.

When we attempt to communicate certain abstract ideas with one another,
    We sometimes use images or symbols in ways that can, more simply and concisely,
        Depict the complexities and diverse aspects of those concepts.

The Great Circle is "a spiritual map of an awakening life" used for thousands of years
    To illustrate the universal dynamics at play in the world - and within every human being
        As *one ever-expanding spiral of life* that's constantly and perfectly unfolding,
            But which can also be described and comprehended
                From four distinct vantage points.

To illustrate two of these primary dynamics, the transcendent (or eternal facet of life) is shown
    As **"The One"** *Source of All That Is* - from which **"The Many"** forms of life are created.

In other words - the many forms of Nature arise out of *the Infinite Intelligence of the Universe,*
    Or said this way, the rich spectrum of diversity within our Universe emerges out of *Unity*.

The natural yearning in us described as <u>*the inward expansion of our evolving consciousness*</u>
    Can also be depicted as the traditional religious desire for **spiritual awakening**,
        And it refers to our innate longing for inner development and spiritual growth.

The natural yearning in us described as <u>*the outward expression of our evolving creativity*</u>
    Can also be portrayed as our moral compass and desire for **conscious contribution**,
        And as well, it refers to our corresponding outer transformation and healing.

It might serve us to think of "a single year" as being defined in terms of either "the entire wheel"
    Or, at other times, we might think of it as "the summation of all the spokes of the wheel

The Great Circle
(A Spiritual Map of an Awakening Life)

"THE ONE"
PERFECT ONENESS,
UNITY WITHOUT FORM,
THE ONE TRANSCENDENT
SOURCE OF ALL THAT IS,
INFINITE INTELLIGENCE,
LIMITLESS LOVE,
MY *TRUE NATURE*
WHICH IS ETERNAL
(BEING)

INNER
DEVELOPMENT
INWARD EXPANSION
OF MY AWARENESS
+
INTERIOR EVOLVING
CONSCIOUSNESS
+
MY SPIRITUAL
AWAKENING
(BECOMING)

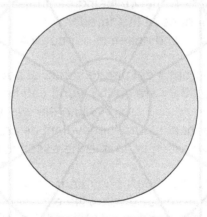

OUTER
TRANSFORMATION
OUTWARD EXPRESSION
OF MY HEALING
+
EXTERIOR EVOLVING
CREATIVITY
+
MY CONSCIOUS
CONTRIBUTION
(BECOMING)

"THE MANY"
THE PERFECTION WITHIN
EACH FORM OF LIFE,
THE MANY UNIQUE
FORMS WITHIN NATURE,
INCLUDING MY BODY,
ALL UNFOLDING
PERFECTLY
IN THE PRESENT MOMENT
(BEING)

THE GREAT CIRCLE OF AWAKENING AND CONTRIBUTION
Greater awareness of what is true leads to greater contributions of my creative gifts to others.

When a very light breeze flutters through the branches of a tree,
Its leaves are barely rustled.

But as the wind increases in intensity, the branches begin to sway
And its leaves are jostled by the wind's mounting power.

If the magnitude of the wind grows to a strong gale,
Then the entire tree will severely bend from its mighty force.

Similarly, as we consciously expand our awareness of what is true - and what really matters,
And align our awareness each day with *"The One" Source of All That Is*,
The spiritual awakening that naturally emerges in us begins "to sway and bend"
In the direction of **more personal contributions of our creative gifts**
Which are in service to others.

For as we awaken our awareness to what our life is truly about and discover who we really are,
The natural impulse to contribute to the wellbeing of others
As a spontaneous consequence of this freedom
Becomes more evident - and arises in our consciousness.

And yet, this *impulse* doesn't arise from a desperate sense of needing to change the world,
Or to make things different than they are so the world can be the way we want it to be,
Or to somehow alter the world and shape it into the way we think it should look,
But it comes from the most natural benevolent desire of sharing our love,
The Limitless Love within us that is the essence of our *True Nature*.

As "the winds of awareness" grow in our heart and mind
Through the learning achieved from our diverse life experiences
And through the inward expansion we gain from daily transformative practice,
Then our unfolding consciousness can gently lead us to a place within
Where we begin to embrace *ever-larger circles of compassion*.

Over time as we continue to develop our conscious awareness,
We are given blessed opportunities to personally experience states of Oneness,
A state of *grace* in which we know we're not separate from one another
But recognize we're all part of an interconnected global family.

Thus, we ultimately learn that through the compassionate act of serving another,
We are also giving a blessing to our self - for we're all part of one *Eternal Self.*

The exquisite scent of a rose emerges on its own as the flower naturally blooms
And keeps on giving its fragrance over the span of its lifetime.

The innate *impulse to contribute* to the wellbeing of others (which is always present within us)
Also instinctively emerges on its own as the most natural expression of our life
As we awaken to the sacred realization of who we really are.

The Great Circle of Awakening and Contribution
(The Universal Dynamics At Play In the World and In My Life)

"THE ONE"
UNITY WITHOUT FORM
+ + +
THE SOURCE OF LIFE
LIMITLESS LOVE
+ + +
MY TRUE NATURE
WHICH IS ETERNAL

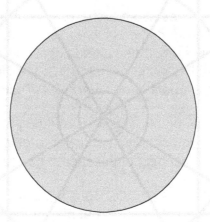

INWARD IMPULSE
OF AWAKENING
I EXPAND MY AWARE-
NESS OF WHAT
IS TRUE AND WHAT
REALLY MATTERS
+ + +
MY SPIRITUAL
AWAKENING

OUTWARD IMPULSE
OF CONTRIBUTION
I EXPRESS MY NEW
AWARENESS BY GIVING
MY CREATIVE GIFTS TO
OTHERS
+ + +
MY CONSCIOUS
CONTRIBUTION

"THE MANY"
THE MANY FORMS
OF NATURE'S
DIVERSE CREATIVITY
+ + +
IN THE PRESENT MOMENT
MY LIFE IS
UNFOLDING PERFECTLY

THE GREAT CIRCLE OF THE MEDICINE WHEEL

Today I embrace the existential paradox that I live in an ephemeral body - yet I am also eternal.

When you take the time to deeply contemplate the wonders of your *inner and outer worlds*,
    You may possibly observe that your life is rich with many perplexing paradoxes
        (I.e. the perception that two contradictory realities both exist at the same time).

For example, a number of common *existential paradoxes* can be stated as follows:
    1) God is *Infinite Love*,
        Yet, simultaneously, the world God created is riddled with suffering and pain,
            2) Everything in the Universe is part of a Unity,
                And yet we each experience life through individual separate bodies,
                    3) Timeless consciousness is all that exists,
                        And yet every expression of life is evolving in time,
                            4) There is a realm of life that's eternal,
                            Yet, concurrently, all forms of life
                            Come to a physical end.

The visual image of **the medicine wheel** is an archetypal symbol
    Which Native Americans and other cultures have used for thousands of years
        To portray, in an illustrative form, these paradoxical concepts of reality,
            And can also be used to remind us (through a traditional pictorial image)
                Of the spiritual alignment of our *Eternal Self* with our physical body.

The circle of *the medicine wheel* has no starting point and no point of finality,
    And so it expresses a unique representation of never-ending continuity
        That directs us to an understanding of the sacred nature of existence.

The image of **The Great Circle** also has paradoxical symbolism within it
    Which depicts four distinct universal dynamics at play in the world and in our life,
        And yet, at the same time, it portrays one continuous flow of reality
            That's unfolding perfectly in every moment. (see June 28th)

We can **join the symbolic aspects of *The Great Circle* with *the medicine wheel***
    To display the inward expansion of consciousness (our natural yearning to develop*)*
        Intentionally reaching toward *"The One", the Limitless Source of All That Is*,
            Which is then mirrored through the outward expressions of our <u>creativity</u>
                Manifesting as *"The Many"* <u>facets of our life</u> (including our body).

Yet all four of these essential aspects; <u>consciousness</u>, <u>creativity</u>, *<u>Source</u>*, and <u>the many forms</u>,
    Are merged as one in a perpetual spiral of existence
        That's constantly evolving and unfolding
            As the majesty of the entire Universe, as all of life on Earth,
                And as the phenomenal expressions of our mind, heart, and body.

The medicine wheel can be used to help us contemplate and embrace the existential paradox
    That our lives have individual and separate time-bound forms,
        Yet, simultaneously, they have no beginning and no end,
            Which is another way of stating that we are also limitless and eternal.

The Great Circle of the Medicine Wheel

THE NORTHERN POINT
AT THE TOP
OF THE MEDICINE WHEEL
REPRESENTS
+ + +
"THE ONE"
THE LIMITLESS SOURCE
OF ALL THAT IS

THE WESTERN POINT
AT THE LEFT
REPRESENTS
+ + +
THE INWARD
EXPANSION OF MY
CONSCIOUSNESS

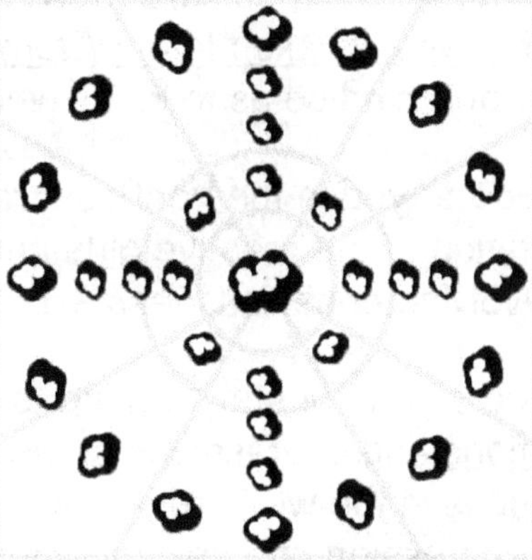

THE EASTERN POINT
AT THE RIGHT
REPRESENTS
+ + +
THE OUTWARD
EXPRESSION OF MY
CREATIVITY

THE SOUTHERN POINT
AT THE BOTTOM
OF THE MEDICINE WHEEL
REPRESENTS
+ + +
"THE MANY"
THE MANY FACETS
OF MY LIFE
UNFOLDING PERFECTLY

ALTERNATIVE WAYS TO DESCRIBE *THE GREAT CIRCLE*

Today I develop a greater awareness of what my life is truly about - and what really matters.

In some literature and poetry "the ocean" is referred to using many vivid phrases
Such as "the mighty deep", "the great waters", "the high seas", "the main",
And "the infinite depths".

Sometimes our language utilizes a wide variety of words or phrases to describe one thing
In order to gain a more enhanced understanding, or more nuances of insight,
And, at times, just to characterize life a bit more colorfully.

Similarly, if we want to deepen our understanding
Of what the various fundamental phrases of *The Great Circle* are pointing to,
The four quadrants of this circle can each be described in multiple ways.

As depicted in the left quadrant of the circle on the following page,
The inward expansive impulse of life, also referred to as <u>evolving consciousness</u>,
Is the masculine impulse within us yearning to <u>develop</u> our unlimited potential,
<u>Expand</u> our awareness as we reach toward "new horizons",
<u>Learn what really matters</u>, <u>awaken to our *Eternal Nature*</u>,
And <u>transcend</u> our mind so as to know who we really are.

The outward expressive impulse portrayed in the right quadrant of *The Great Circle*
(Which represents the manifestation of our creative gifts and contributions to others)
Is the out-picturing of our evolving consciousness expressed in the world of form.

The feminine impulse can be grasped as our innate yearning to express our evolving creativity,
In other words, it's our <u>contributions</u> and expressions of the many forms of our creativity,
It is our outward <u>manifestations</u> in the world mirroring our inner development,
And it's our continual progression of <u>outer transformation and healing</u>.

Over eons of time, humanity has given numerous poetic names to a **formless** *Greater Power*:
God, Love, Source of All That Is, The Unified Field, the Absolute, Tao, "The One", etc.

The myriad forms of the natural world can also be described in numerous ways,
Such as the Universe, Nature, all of creation, the body, the heart, *"The Many"*, etc.

The spiritual map of *The Great Circle* can be symbolically shown as four distinct components
Each with their unique roles to play in the mystery and paradox of "the dance of life".

The primary function of *The Great Circle* as a transformative tool
Is to simply portray a useful collection of words and phrases
For the purpose of communicating to one another about the nature of existence
So we can develop a deeper understanding of what our life is truly about
And thus, cultivate an unconditional love for each expression of life.

Of course, all four quadrants of this circle are all simultaneously unfolding in the same moment,
One interconnected cosmic dance perpetually spinning in perfect harmony
As *The Great Wheel of Life*.

Circle of Alternative Ways to Describe
The Great Circle

**THE FORMLESSNESS
OF PERFECTION**
+ *SOURCE OF ALL THAT IS*
+ *THE UNIFIED FIELD*
+ *INFINITE INTELLIGENCE*
+ *LIMITLESS LOVE*
+ *INFINITE PRESENCE*
+ *"THE ONE"*
+ *GOD*

INWARD IMPULSE
+ INWARD EXPANSION
+ CONSCIOUSNESS
+ TRANSCENDENCE
+ LEARNING AND INNER
   DEVELOPMENT
+ MASCULINE YANG
+ SPIRITUAL
   AWAKENING

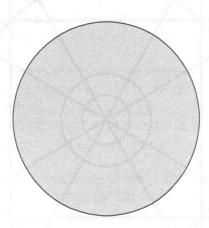

OUTWARD IMPULSE
+ OUTWARD EXPRESSION
+ CREATIVITY
+ MANIFESTATION
+ HEALING AND OUTER
   TRANSFORMATION
+ FEMININE YIN
+ CONSCIOUS
   CONTRIBUTION

**THE PERFECTION
OF FORM**
+ THE WORLD OF FORM
+ ALL OF CREATION
+ NATURE
+ THE BODY
+ COMPASSIONATE HEART
+ *"THE MANY"*
+ THE UNIVERSE

BEING AND BECOMING

My life is unfolding perfectly, at the same time, I'm here to help the world become more perfect.

The entire Universe, from the most massive distant galaxy to the tiniest sub-atomic particle,
  Is in constant motion - and yet everything within the Cosmos "arises out of *Stillness*".

For many millennia various Eastern religions, in certain places like India, Nepal, and Tibet,
  Have aimed their teachings on realizing Oneness with the *Stillness,* or *Ground of **Being**,*
    Attempting to gain personal spiritual enlightenment (awakening, self-realization)
      By sublimely merging and being one with God *(the Source of All That Is).*

On the other hand, numerous Western religions originating within Europe and the Middle East
  Have focused on acting in accord with the Will of God (i.e. "following the rules of God"),
    By cultivating pious ways of **Becoming** more loving, more moral, more virtuous
      And "obeying" Holy Scriptures so as to attain rewards with God in heaven.

Some traditional religions typically pointed a spiritual seeker to either one - or the other path,
  Either to a realization of **Being** (enlightenment) - or of **Becoming** (serving others),
    Either to fully living in the present moment - or to greater promise for the future,
      Either to Oneness with *the Transcendent* - or to personal transformation.

There is also a paradigm that has emerged as a more expansive understanding of spirituality
  Which invites us to embrace the existential paradox that **Being** and **Becoming**
    Are both essential facets of an integrated whole experience of who we really are,
      Declaring the enigma that both an *Infinitely Intelligent Transcendent Power*
      And an evolving Universe of limitless diversity - are *merged as one.*

Being is accepting "what is" - a life that's perfectly unfolding, an expression of <u>*Limitless Love*</u>,
  While **Becoming** is our *journey to Love* - or "<u>all within our life that needs development</u>".

Being can also be experienced as Oneness with *the Transcendent*
  (With *Infinite Intelligence,* with *the Source of Life* that's sensed in our body and mind),
    Whereas **Becoming** can be experienced as taking action to create "what can be",
      Our <u>*journey of discovery*</u> to evolve and contribute to a more glorious world.

Furthermore we can think of **Being** and **Becoming** in terms of present and future perspectives
  In which **Being** is <u>*Awakened Presence*</u> - the feeling of living fully in the present moment,
    In other words, the complete acceptance of the way we experience life right now,
      And **Becoming** is future, our *spiritual journey* of creating a better tomorrow.

Being is like a vast Ocean - and is sensed as our *Transcendent Self,* our *Limitless Nature,*
  Our <u>*Eternal Self,*</u> *the Unbounded Consciousness* that animates our life experience.

Becoming is like a flowing river - and is about our daily *journey of discovery*
  Of transforming the quality of our life experience, cultivating our unlimited potential,
    As well as <u>awakening to a life of inner freedom</u>.

The entire Cosmos is in constant motion, yet it naturally emerges out of *Absolute Stillness* -
  In other words, it is **Being Becoming** a more fully awakened Universe.

Circle of *Being* and *Becoming*
(A Paradox of Simultaneous and Complimentary Realms of My Life)

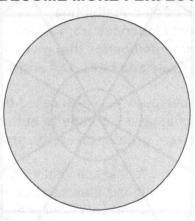

PERFECTION –
PATH OF EVOLUTION
BEING - THE REALIZATION,
IN THIS MOMENT, MY LIFE
IS UNFOLDING PERFECTLY
+SIMULTANEOUSLY+
BECOMING - MY *JOURNEY
OF DISCOVERY* TO HELP
THE WORLD EVOLVE AND
BECOME MORE PERFECT

PRESENCE –
PATH OF TIME
BEING - EXPERIENCING
MY LIFE FULLY IN THE
PRESENT MOMENT
+SIMULTANEOUSLY+
BECOMING - MY INNER
SPIRITUAL JOURNEY
IN WHICH I CREATE
A BETTER FUTURE

LIMITLESS LOVE –
PATH OF MY LIFE
BEING - EXPERIENCING
EVERY MOMENT AS
LIMITLESS LOVE
+SIMULTANEOUSLY+
BECOMING – MY *JOURNEY
TO LOVE*, WHICH IS "ALL
WITHIN MY LIFE THAT
NEEDS DEVELOPMENT"

ETERNAL SELF –
PATH OF EXPERIENCE
BEING - MY *ETERNAL SELF,
PURE CONSCIOUSNESS,*
WHICH IS UNBOUNDED
+SIMULTANEOUSLY+
BECOMING - THE *JOURNEY
OF MY LIFE EXPERIENCE*
AWAKENING ME TO A LIFE
OF INNER FREEDOM

GOD

I realize there is no place where the Omniscient Intelligence of Limitless Love is not.

It's obvious that there's an amazing diversity of fish
    Which live and swim within our planet's numerous oceans.

Just for fun, imagine that if you could ask one of these fish "to search for the ocean",
    The fish might respond by saying, *"I do not know what you're talking about"*,
        Because for fish swimming in the salty water, the ocean is everywhere
        And, thus for them, there is no place where the ocean is not.

Some religious teachers encourage their students "to search for God",
    Yet God does not need to be searched for since God is the essential core of everything,
        Is everywhere present, and thus, there is no place where God is not.

Since the time that early humans first developed conceptual language to our present day,
    The concept of God has been elegantly described in various academic terms,
        Such as **the mythic personification of *Ultimate Reality*,**
            ***The Unbounded Field* of all possibilities,**
                ***The Universal Consciousness* from which everything arises**,
            And **the *Infinite Intelligence* that gives form to,**
                And creatively animates, the entire Cosmos.

Infinite Intelligence, from a science perspective, is also called **the *Evolutionary Impulse*,**
    For it is **the organizing force of limitless creativity in the Universe**
        Which directs all form toward greater diversity, order, and cooperation.

One of the fundamental invitations from *Life* that constantly vibrates within each of us
    Is to align our awareness each day with this transcendent impulse,
        ***"The One" Source of All That Is* (the Totality of everything in creation),**
        Or what many people throughout our planet simply refer to as "God".

For thousands of years, the world's spiritual traditions have attempted to guide humanity
    By providing a wealth of religious paths, methods, and practices,
        Which can assist a person on his or her inner quest for *union with God*.

A variety of simple and esoteric techniques have served the attainment of this goal
    Such as aligning with *the Transcendent Power* through meditation,
        Creating resonance with *the Omniscient Intelligence of Love* through prayer and service,
        As well as achieving a state of *living presence* through daily mindfulness.

There is a sacred sanctuary deep within our heart, a temple of profound silence at our core,
    Where we can find a communion with this *Field of Limitless Love*.

Yet to find this hallowed place requires the commitment and willingness
    To simply pause long enough during our day so as to respond to this *inner invitation*.

The more we consciously choose to dive into this sublime sanctuary,
    The more we find that we are swimming, always and everywhere, in "an Ocean of God".

Circle of God
(Various Names for *the Transcendent Power of the Universe*)

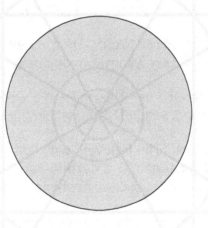

"THE ONE" SOURCE OF ALL THAT IS
GOD IS *THE SOURCE AND TOTALITY OF EVERYTHING IN CREATION, ULTIMATE REALITY,* ALL THAT EVER WAS, IS NOW, AND EVER WILL BE

THE EVOLUTIONARY IMPULSE
GOD IS THE ORGANIZING *FORCE OF LIMITLESS CREATIVITY* IN THE UNIVERSE THAT DIRECTS ALL EVOLUTION TOWARD GREATER UNFOLDING

INFINITE INTELLIGENCE
GOD IS THE *INFINITE INTELLIGENCE* THAT GIVES FORM TO, AND CREATIVELY ANIMATES, THE ENTIRE COSMOS

UNIVERSAL CONSCIOUSNESS
GOD IS *THE UNBOUNDED FIELD* OF ALL POSSIBILITIES, THE CONSCIOUSNESS FROM WHICH EVERYTHING ARISES

GOD AS "THE BELOVED"

I radiate my love to the people in my life - and honor the beauty and goodness within them.

When we use a common language to communicate our thoughts and feelings to one another,
We typically speak in one of three distinct linguistic perspectives; first, second, or third.

If we are in a conversation, the first perspective is when I am speaking to you
And this perspective uses the words "I" or "me",
While the second perspective is when you are speaking to me
And uses the word "you".

Furthermore, the third perspective is when we speak of someone else, or of something else,
That's not present with us - and thus we use the words, "he", "she", or "it".

Throughout history, humanity has referred to God in many ways and with many names,
Yet each of God's names is related to one of these three perspectives of language.

God in the first person, referring to "I" (such as God in many Eastern religions - "I Am That"),
Was thought of as *the Transcendent Source of All That Is,* or *Limitless Consciousness.*

God in the second person, using words like "You", "Thou", "Beloved", (a God we can relate to)
Was experienced as a supreme deity with whom one developed a personal relationship.

God in the third person, referring to God as "It" (signifying a God that can be spoken about),
Was seen as the animating power within Nature, within the Universe, within all Creation.

Early within humanity's evolution, God "The Beloved" was first imagined as a divine persona
That could be related to, and venerated in, **a certain sanctified form within Nature**,
Such as the Sun, the Moon, a special totem animal, a holy mountain, etc.

As civilizations began to appear - and powerful kings became the ruling authority of the people,
God "The Beloved" was then seen as a heavenly **divine king**, **a supernatural being**,
That existed somewhere outside of the Universe - and yet created everything.

In places like India and Bali, God "The Beloved" developed into **the many divine expressions
Of a multitude of personified beings** symbolizing certain virtuous qualities
Such as compassion, abundance, surrender, and courage,
And took form as diverse Gods like Shiva, Ganesh, Hanuman, or Lakshmi.

And over thousands of years, a prominent expression of God "The Beloved"
Has taken the forms of **particular enlightened avatars or spiritual masters**
Such as Jesus, Buddha, Krishna, Muhammad, and many other awakened ones.

With this distinct vantage of the second person perspective of God, the sacred place within us
Through which to merge our inner being with "The Beloved" is through the heart.

To know **God as "The Beloved"** requires we learn to connect with this aspect of the divine
Through the devotional opening of a loving and compassionate heart,
And then seeing "The Beloved" (the divine presence) in all the people in our life.

Circle of God as "The Beloved"
(Second Person Perspective of the Divine)

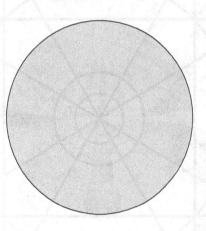

SUPERNATURAL BEING
GOD EXPERIENCED AS
A SUPERNATURAL BEING
WHO HAS CREATED
EVERYTHING THAT IS
- AND WHO I CAN
DEVELOP A PERSONAL
RELATIONSHIP WITH

SANCTIFIED FORM WITHIN NATURE
GOD EXPERIENCED AS
A FORM WITHIN NATURE
THAT IS SANCTIFIED
AND VENERATED
LIKE THE SUN, MOON,
A TOTUM ANIMAL,
A HOLY MOUNTAIN, ETC.

DIVINE PERSONIFICATION
GOD EXPERIENCED AS
A PERSONIFIED FORM -
THE DIVINE TRINITY,
THE GODDESS, SHIVA,
GANESH, LAKSHMI, ETC.
SYMBOLIZING CERTAIN
VIRTUOUS QUALITIES

AVATAR
GOD EXPERIENCED AS
A FULLY ENLIGHTENED
AVATAR OR TRUE
SPIRITUAL MASTER,
SUCH AS JESUS, BUDDHA,
KRISHNA, MUHAMMAD,
LAO TZU, AND MANY
OTHER AWAKENED ONES

III

HEART AWARENESS PRACTICES

FOUNDATIONAL TRANSFORMATIVE PRACTICES

Through my commitment to daily transformative practice, I cultivate a life of inner freedom.

In many parts of the world (during a prior period of human history)
    There was a popular social tradition in which a person who wanted to learn a trade,
        Such as a carpenter, a tailor, a baker, or a watchmaker,
            Would first become an *apprentice* to a *master tradesman*,
                An expert who demonstrated great art and skill in a particular field.

The *master* would teach the eager *apprentice* everything the student needed to learn
    In order to be proficient at their specific trade.

The *apprentice* would usually spend many years of dedicated work
    In refining his or her abilities and knowledge of the craft
        Through hours of devoted study and practice.

This *master-apprentice tradition* has declined in many parts of our modern culture
    Yet is still an important aspect of sharing wisdom and guidance
        When it comes to the pursuit of our *spiritual journey.*

Once a spiritual seeker begins on a disciplined path of conscious inward development,
    He or she usually looks for an experienced spiritual teacher, or "spiritual wayshower",
        To inspire or guide the unfoldment of their *journey of awakening.*

There is great benefit to following the ways of one who has much knowledge and insight,
    And who has already mastered certain stages of *the spiritual journey.*

Over time, through the wisdom gained from expansive perspectives and rich life experiences,
    The spiritual seeker eventually learns to follow the guidance within one's own heart,
        Or what is called "the master within" that abides within the core of every person.

Both forms of being guided by "the master", whether within or without,
    Reveal the benefits of practicing the following **transformative exercises**.

1) **The practice of silent meditation** (or whatever form of inner silence we are drawn to),
    Which stills our mind, aligns our awareness with *Life,* and points us to our *True Nature.*

2) **The practice of contemplation,** which consciously expands our awareness of what is true
    By reflecting on "the Big Questions" regarding what our life is truly about.

3) **The practice of being thankful** for the many gifts we receive each day,
    Being grateful our life is unfolding perfectly, and appreciating ourselves for who we are.

4) **The practice of prayer** in the form of asking *Life* how we are to serve, and contribute to,
    The wellbeing of others - and then courageously acting on what we receive.

In "the ever-expansive classrooms within the school of this unfolding world"
    We're all *apprentices* to the *Master* within who invites us to live an awakened life,
        As we learn, each day, to *master* a life of inner freedom and love unconditionally.

Circle of Foundational Transformative Practices
(Primary Ways to Cultivate and Maintain Inner Freedom)

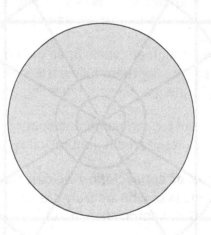

MEDITATION
THE PRACTICE
OF EXPERIENCING INNER
SILENCE SO AS TO STILL
MY MIND, ALIGN MY AWARE-
NESS WITH *THE SOURCE
OF LIFE,* AND AWAKEN
TO MY *ETERNAL NATURE*

PRAYER
THE PRACTICE
OF ASKING *LIFE*
HOW I AM TO SERVE,
AND CONTRIBUTE TO,
THE WELLBEING OF
OTHERS - AND ACTING
ON WHAT I RECEIVE

CONTEMPLATION
THE PRACTICE OF
CONSCIOUSLY EXPAND-
ING MY AWARENESS
BY REFLECTING ON
"THE BIG QUESTIONS"
REGARDING WHAT MY
LIFE IS TRULY ABOUT

APPRECIATION
THE PRACTICE OF BEING
THANKFUL FOR THE GIFTS
I RECEIVE EACH DAY,
BEING GRATEFUL MY LIFE
IS UNFOLDING PERFECTLY,
AND FULLY APPRECIATING
MYSELF FOR WHO I AM

SPHERES OF APPRECIATION

My appreciation grows each day for the many gifts and blessings I continue to receive.

A wild river naturally yearns to flow unimpeded through the countryside
    Effortlessly winding its way into valleys, past hills, through forests, or into deserts.

When a dam is built across a river to harness its potential power,
    It massively slows down the flowing current of the water
        Which then disturbs the living habitats of the creatures that live near the river
            Generating havoc to the fragile ecosystems
            And the vegetation that thrives on its banks.

At some future time, should the dam be dismantled and removed,
    And the natural flow of the river's current be restored,
        Then *life energy* along its banks could return, and the river would once again
            Nurture the native environment with its constant movement.

In a similar way, living with a lack of appreciation is like placing a dam on "the river of our life",
    Obstructing the flow of *Life Force energy* that wants to freely circulate through us.

Life Force energy longs to course through our veins in an unimpeded manner,
    Nurturing and sustaining us so we may more fully participate
        In creatively contributing to the magnificent unfolding of life.

When we appreciate, and are grateful for, the numerous spheres of experience within our life,
    We directly support the *energy* that yearns to naturally flow through our body and mind.

Of course, there are many **spheres of appreciation** we can place our attention on,
    And as we gain greater awareness of who we truly are - and what really matters,
        We can include more areas of appreciation in our life to honor.

Generally, when individuals are asked what they appreciate most,
    They primarily speak about how grateful they are for the people in their lives,
        Their spouse or partner, family members, friends, and co-workers.

Taking time to consciously appreciate the blessings of the people in our lives
    Helps keep the natural current of *Life Force energy* flowing through us.

As we continue to expand our awareness of what is true,
    Our *spheres of appreciation* grow as well, which usually includes our life mission,
        Our creative expressions, and ultimately every experience we encounter.

As we continue to consciously cultivate *a life of inner freedom*,
    We are being invited to authentically appreciate ourselves just the way we are,
        Grateful for every breath we take, and for all that is unfolding in our life.

Our life can be thought of as "a wild river that longs to flow unimpeded"
    So we can constantly experience its natural movement of radiant energy
        And ride the ceaseless current to wherever it intends to take us.

Circle of Spheres of Appreciation
(A Transformative Practice)

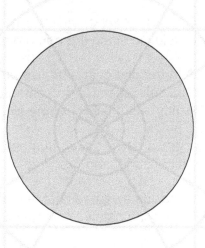

LIFE
I APPRECIATE AND GIVE
THANKS FOR:
+ *LIFE (GOD, LOVE)*
+ CONSCIOUSNESS
+ ALL OF NATURE
+ WHAT I AM LEARNING
EACH DAY

PEOPLE
I APPRECIATE AND GIVE
THANKS FOR:
+ MY SPOUSE OR
PARTNER
+ MY FAMILY
+ MY FRIENDS
+ MY CO-WORKERS

CREATIVITY
I APPRECIATE AND GIVE
THANKS FOR:
+ MY LIFE'S MISSION
+ MY ARTISTIC SELF
EXPRESSION
+ MY CAREER
+ MY CONTRIBUTIONS

PERSONAL
I APPRECIATE AND GIVE
THANKS FOR:
+ MYSELF FOR WHO I AM
+ MY HEALTH
+ MY HOME
+ MY ABUNDANCE

SERVICE

Being in service to the wellbeing of others is a natural, joyous, and fulfilling part of my life.

Every living organism within the natural world has been part of a long process of evolution
    And, thus, has added its unique contributions to the ongoing development of our planet.

Some of Nature's primal life forms have been "serving" Earth's evolution for four billion years
    Through their vital participation in the planet's constant ecological expansion.

Over eons, some species have become interconnected with other completely different species
    So as to support one another in their intrinsic drive to improve their chances of survival.

There are countless plants and animals that have developed interdependent relationships
    In which together they sustain and prosper life within one integrated ecosystem.

Around the world, novel ecosystems have emerged out of the complex interplay
    Of the mineral, plant, and animal kingdoms weaving together harmoniously.

The act of supporting one another (i.e. - of "serving" other forms of life via these connections)
    Has been a natural dynamic of evolution since the primordial beginning of biological life.

When Homo sapiens first appeared on the planet around five hundred thousand years ago,
    They developed the capacity to be self-reflective, to contemplate the "Big Questions",
        And because of this inquiry they eventually became aware of their own evolution.

Humanity's genuine evolutionary progress has required humans to become consciously aware
    Of the key role they have in contributing to, and "serving", the larger planetary system.

Service can be thought of as the conscious awareness of humanity's important part to play
    In contributing to the wellbeing of this intricately interconnected system of life on Earth.

Of course, **it's also the loving actions and choices we make that transcend our ego
    In which we use our gifts and talents to assist the needs of the greater good.**

**Furthermore, service is consciously surrendering our self-oriented agenda
    So we may support an action that benefits another, or a larger aspect of life.**

To serve is one of humanity's major ways of being aligned with *the Natural Intelligence of Life*
    That has been animating and directing all of Nature for billions of years.

**The yearning to serve is the compassionate giving of our individual time and energy
    That we contribute to the wellbeing of others.**

**Ultimately, *Life* is constantly inviting us to recognize that "serving other people"
    <u>Is the same</u> as "serving ourselves" - because in truth, we're all one global family.**

So at this dynamic and monumental time in our planet's evolution,
    Humanity is beginning to embrace a much larger vision of what it means "to serve"
        As service becomes the core of every life, business and government in the world.

Circle of Service
(A Transformative Practice)

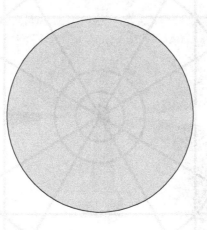

GIVING
SERVICE –
THE COMPASSIONATE
GIVING OF MY TIME
AND ENERGY
THAT I CONTRIBUTE
TO THE WELLBEING
OF OTHERS

SUPPORT
SERVICE –
SURRENDERING
MY SELF-ORIENTED
AGENDA
SO I MAY SUPPORT
AN ACTION THAT
BENEFITS ANOTHER

ASSISTANCE
SERVICE –
THE ACTIONS
AND CHOICES I MAKE
IN WHICH I USE
MY GIFTS AND TALENTS
TO ASSIST THE NEEDS
OF THE GREATER GOOD

UNITY
SERVICE –
RECOGNIZING THAT,
ULTIMATELY, SERVING
OTHERS IS THE SAME
AS SERVING MYSELF
- BECAUSE IN TRUTH, WE'RE
ALL ONE GLOBAL FAMILY

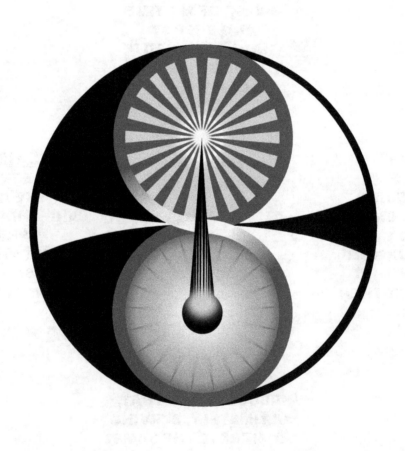

IV

THE SONG OF EMBODIED LOVE

THE NATURAL STATES THAT EMERGE FROM *BEING*

I take time throughout the day to feel the ever-present peace and harmony that's within me.

When you are sitting in a movie theater watching a feature film,
　　You typically are fully absorbed with the movie's action and story,
　　　　And can be deeply drawn into the emotions of the characters
　　　　　　Temporarily feeling your heart and mind empathetically consumed
　　　　　　　　By emotions such as fear, love, sadness, or joy.

If for some reason, such as an electrical power outage, the movie projector suddenly stopped,
　　You would then quickly become aware of the blank screen
　　　　That was present in the theater and in front of you all the time,
　　　　　　But which you weren't conscious of while fully engaged in the film.

As is usual when watching a film, we put all of our attention and focus on the moving images
　　And, for a moment, forget about the blank screen
　　　　That's always there beyond our conscious awareness.

Our everyday life is also filled with "activities and stories", so to speak,
　　In which our heart may feel the changing cycles of a plethora of moods and emotions,
　　　　Similar to what we might experience during a popular film
　　　　　　That's projected on a movie screen.

Yet when we take the time to suddenly stop for a moment to be silent,
　　We can find that behind "the activities of our life",
　　　　Beyond all of our daily thoughts, emotions, and bodily sensations,
　　　　　　Lies a host of **natural states** that are always available to us.

Thus when we're fully present to these natural states, we can experience a sublime **peace**,
　　A soaring and true **happiness**, a flow of authentic **joy**,
　　　　And a sacred **harmony** that's felt within our body.

At any time within our day - should our life get stressful or out-of-sorts,
　　We can simply stop what we're doing,
　　　　Choose a particular way to become still and inwardly quiet,
　　　　　　And connect with the natural states of *Embodied Love* that live within us.

Whenever we become aware, we can choose to stop "projecting certain old outdated images",
　　Pause the action and story of our life for a few moments,
　　　　And return to the hallowed place "behind the images"
　　　　　　That's always there and is ever-present.

Even with the conscious awareness that can come from just taking a long deep breath
　　Stopping for a brief moment to breathe,
　　　　We can instantly access this ever-present peace,
　　　　　　This field of eternal happiness,
　　　　　　　　This ocean of never-ending joy,
　　　　　　　　　　And this river of perpetual harmony,
　　　　　　　　　　　　Whenever we choose to simply "pause the movie".

Circle of the Natural States That Emerge From *Being*

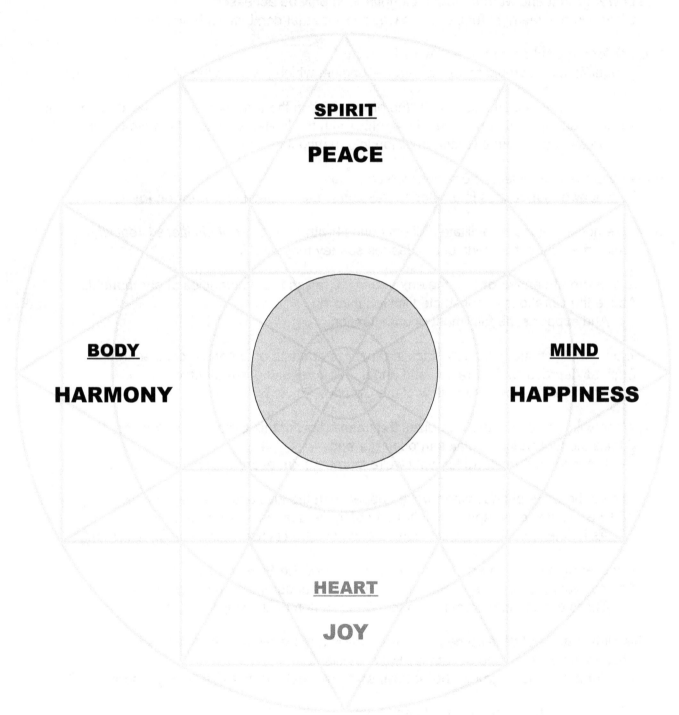

SPIRIT

PEACE

BODY

HARMONY

MIND

HAPPINESS

HEART

JOY

THE NATURAL STATE OF JOY

Joy is the natural state that arises in me when I'm fully present to each experience of my life.

The power of light and warmth from a campfire can only be accessed
> When there is the right fuel, such as wooden logs that combine with air and heat.

In order for a typical car to travel down a highway,
> It requires the appropriate fuel to turn the engine, which provides the wheels with power.

The power of our intention also needs "the proper fuel" in the form of a strong elevated emotion
> To "fuel" our desires - and then join together with the limitless power of *Infinite Creativity*
>> So as to bring our intention or vision into manifested form.

And one of the most effective emotions we can use
> To empower our desires into outer expression is the emotion of **authentic joy**.

Joyous emotion serves to facilitate a direct conduit with *the Power of Limitless Creativity*
> Which nourishes the seeds of our desires so they may take form.

As we feel **the aliveness of life**, the emotion of joy raises the frequencies of our thoughts
> Above the vibrations of constricted limited thinking
>> And supports the fulfillment of our intention.

When our emotions are habitually stuck in repetitive streams of unconstructive energy,
> Such as depression, frustration, and anger, our inner being is restricted
>> Which blocks the natural flow of the *Creative Power* within us.

Joy, along with an open heart, energizes the natural flow of this *Creative Intelligence*,
> For it's the feeling that radiates through our body
>> When we are **grateful** for what we're learning from every experience of our life.

Sometimes there are periods when we're gripped with the loveless desires of our ego
> And we recognize the apparent fulfillment of these desires is temporary,
>> As is "the fleeting joy" which comes and goes that is tied to this kind of fulfillment.

Yet as we learn to maintain **an alignment with *the Infinite Presence of Love***
> And cultivate greater awareness each day, there's another expanded level of joy
>> That's experienced from the profound realization of knowing who we really are.

At this higher stage of development, *authentic joy* is a more refined state of awareness
> That does not come and go, but is always available,
>> For at this stage, **joy is the natural state we feel when we're fully present**.

Campfires require fuel to produce light and heat,
> And cars won't travel down a highway without fuel.

The universal principle regarding the fulfillment of desires
> Requires that passionate emotion be used as a means of empowering our intentions,
>> And life is so much more fun when the frequency of joy is "fueling our vehicle".

Circle of the Natural State of Joy

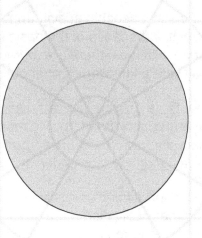

ALIGNMENT
JOY –
THE FEELING
I EXPERIENCE
WHEN I'M
CONSCIOUSLY ALIGNED
WITH *THE INFINITE
PRESENCE OF LOVE*

GRATITUDE
JOY –
THE FEELING THAT
RADIATES THROUGH
MY BODY WHEN I AM
GRATEFUL FOR WHAT I'M
LEARNING FROM EVERY
EXPERIENCE OF MY LIFE

ALIVENESS
JOY –
THE FEELING
I EXPERIENCE WHEN
I'M PASSIONATELY
ATTUNED WITH
THE EVER-FLOWING
ALIVENESS OF LIFE

PRESENCE
JOY –
THE NATURAL
STATE OF *BEING* THAT IS
ALWAYS AVAILABLE
AND THAT I BECOME
AWARE OF
WHEN I'M FULLY PRESENT

PILLARS OF AWAKENING

I let go of my attachments and surrender everything in my life to a Greater Power.

At the heart of many indigenous cultures throughout the planet
Is a traditional wisdom that states - *"every manifestation within the world*
Is comprised of four fundamental elements - **earth, water, air, and fire** *-*
Which combine together in an infinite variety of ways
To form rocks, trees, animals, people, and everything in creation".

This indigenous wisdom also states that these four basic elements relate to *the four seasons,*
Winter, spring, summer, and autumn,
And each season carries specific primary *elemental characteristics or qualities.*

Some Native American tribes speak about *four totem animals* of the medicine wheel,
Such as **white buffalo, eagle, coyote, and bear,** and each represents a certain quality
Which is connected to *the four cardinal directions,*
North, east, south, and west.

And just like the above sets of four distinct aspects arising from traditional wisdom,
We may also sense how natural it is (because of the basic nature of the human mind)
To observe, that arising from within us, there are *four foundational attributes*
Which can help us cultivate a knowing of what our life is truly about.

With awareness, we can notice that there are four key attributes or "pillars" which are essential
If we desire to live a life of authentic inner freedom (the mastery of *Being),*
And many spiritual teachers and awakened ones from around the world
Identify these "pillars" as <u>gratitude</u>, <u>surrender</u>, <u>acceptance</u>, and <u>Oneness</u>.

The pillar of *"***gratitude** *for what we're learning from every experience of our life"*
Comes from an innate knowing that we live in an abundant and empowering Universe,
And this knowing helps us respond to each life situation with heart wisdom.

"Letting go of our attachments and **surrendering** *our life to a Greater Power"*
Allows us to be courageous, yet flexible, in regards to whatever may arise,
Much like the branches of a willow tree are strong, but yielding,
As they bend to the powerful force of the wind.

*"***Accepting** *that our life is unfolding perfectly just as it is"*
Requires the unwavering faith of living with the unknown, trusting in *the Power of Love,*
And seeing our many gifts and pains from "the Big Picture Perspective of life".

And *"awareness of our* **Oneness** *with all of life"* is a pillar that's a vital key to inner freedom -
For with this recognition, we realize our interconnectedness with creation's wonders
That is experienced within every blade of grass - and within every human heart.

These four foundational **Pillars of Awakening** are like "invisible transformative vehicles"
That we must consciously cultivate in our daily lives
So we can steer ourselves down the winding road of our *awakening journey*
Where we arrive at vistas of inner freedom - and of loving unconditionally.

Circle of the Pillars of Awakening
(Attributes For Cultivating Inner Freedom and a Life of Mastery)

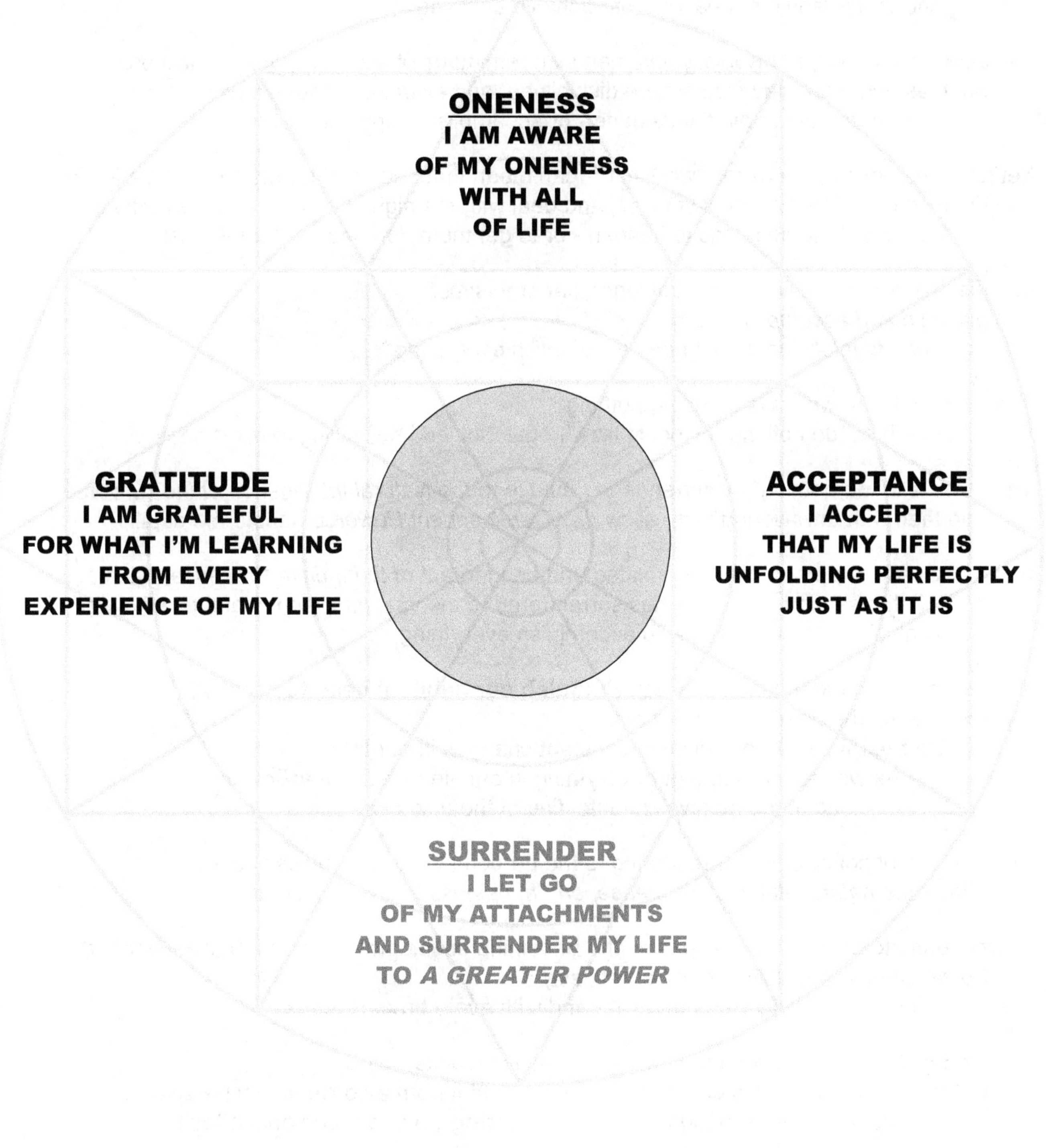

ONENESS
I AM AWARE
OF MY ONENESS
WITH ALL
OF LIFE

GRATITUDE
I AM GRATEFUL
FOR WHAT I'M LEARNING
FROM EVERY
EXPERIENCE OF MY LIFE

ACCEPTANCE
I ACCEPT
THAT MY LIFE IS
UNFOLDING PERFECTLY
JUST AS IT IS

SURRENDER
I LET GO
OF MY ATTACHMENTS
AND SURRENDER MY LIFE
TO *A GREATER POWER*

SURRENDER

I surrender to the vast Intelligence of the Universe that knows how to accomplish everything.

Within many modern cultures around the world there exists a widespread belief
    That one must work very hard "to get ahead in life"
        And that it requires great effort to achieve anything.

Of course, *the concept of working hard* can also remind us of several virtuous qualities,
    Such as one must stay focused, be disciplined, and exercise steadfastness,
        In order to get certain things done - or accomplish a specific task.

Yet for some people, the words "work hard" can mean that one must markedly struggle in life,
    Fight against "the current of what is", and deal with the high stress of certain situations
        By trying to force things to happen - or to get them done no matter the cost.

In India, there is a traditional spiritual tenet that proclaims,
    "Do little and accomplish more,
        But ultimately, do nothing and accomplish everything".

There are at least two ways of "doing nothing",
    And one is to "do nothing" by being lazy, neglectful, and not willing to exert oneself.

The other is to "do nothing" by surrendering our life to *the Natural Intelligence of the Universe,*
    And then with unwavering faith, allow *this Transcendent Power* to handle the details.

In the first case, a person can feel isolated and be ignorant of *the Infinite Presence of Love,*
    While in the second, he or she has surrendered to the vast *Intelligence* of the Universe
        That inherently knows how to accomplish everything.

The second scenario requires that we **relinquish our habitual need to control**,
    Experience the natural unfolding of life,
        Be flexible and flow with the constant changes in our life,
            As well as learn to **trust** everything in our life to *a Greater Power*
        And to the benevolent unfolding of the unknown.

The practice of consciously surrendering to the perpetual flow of *Limitless Love*
    Allows *the natural states of joy, peace, and happiness* to arise within us.

Surrendering to *Love* is like diving into, and becoming an integrated part of, *"the River of Life"*
    So we can journey downstream effortlessly
        With every activity we engage in - and with every breath we take.

Surrender can be understood from a number of viewpoints,
    But for many people, it is common to comprehend it from a conventional perspective
        Where surrender is thought of as simply **letting go** of our personal attachments.

Yet from "the Big Picture" of the Awakened Self, as we "do nothing to accomplish everything",
    Surrender is being fully aligned with *Life*, and thus aligning ourselves with the Universe,
        As if we're effortlessly riding an eternal current in *"the River of Unbounded Love".*

Circle of Surrender

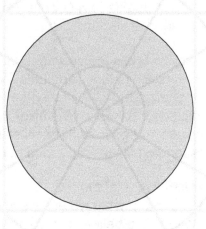

LETTING GO
SURRENDER –
MY ABILITY TO LET GO
OF MY ATTACHMENTS
REGARDING HOW I THINK
MY LIFE SHOULD BE,
AND INSTEAD,
EMBRACE WHAT IS

TRUST
SURRENDER –
MY ABILITY TO TRUST
EVERYTHING IN MY LIFE
TO *A GREATER POWER,*
AND TO THE BENEVOLENT
UNFOLDING
OF THE UNKNOWN

RELINQUISHMENT
SURRENDER –
MY ABILITY
TO RELINQUISH
MY HABITUAL NEED TO
CONTROL AND EXPERI-
ENCE THE NATURAL
UNFOLDING OF LIFE

FLOW
SURRENDER –
MY ABILITY TO BE
FLEXIBLE AND FLOW
WITH THE CONSTANT
CHANGES IN MY LIFE
AS WELL AS WITH
WHATEVER ARISES

TRUST

Today I let go of my need to control others and, instead, I trust in the perfect flow of life.

When a child learns to ride a bicycle, there's usually a parent or adult standing next to them
    Monitoring their timid forward motion - and making sure the child does not get hurt.

In order to learn this new skill, the child must *trust* that their nearby guardian
    Is ready to protect them from harm
        By eventually giving up, or letting go of, the child's strongly held fear of falling
        And focusing, instead, on the task of maintaining balance on the bike.

Developing **trust** is always about letting go of one thing
    So we can, ultimately, obtain something greater.

From a spiritual vantage, it is learning to let go of our walls of illusion, fear, and separation
    In order to move from our self-imposed prison into a sanctuary of inner freedom.

Trusting in Life is about **relinquishing the need to control the way things are**
    And thus, surrendering everything in our life to *a Greater Power (the Source of Life)*
        So we may obtain a superior kind of security.

As a child who's learning to ride a bicycle takes the courageous step
    Of **letting go** of the known world for an instant - and thus, embraces the unknown
        (In this case, embraces the challenge
            Of making brave attempts to balance on the bike),
            The possibility of discovering his or her new skill of "riding a bike"
            And its corresponding life lesson - then becomes apparent.

An important aspect of *trust* is a willingness to not know,
    In other words - being willing to abandon what we believe is the known
        (Or the illusory security of one's rigid beliefs and points of view)
        So we may experience new possibilities for the future.

In order to learn to *trust* more deeply in *Life*,
    We must be willing to give up any current unloving beliefs
        And habitual concepts of how we think things should be
            So fresh perspectives and beliefs can constantly be revealed.

Trust can also be experienced as **feeling a relative level of safety**
    From the protection of another person or group,
        Or from the perceived protection within a particular situation.

Ultimate trust is being sensitively aware of the fragility of our life
    And being so present of the inevitability that our physical life could end at any time
        That we are **willing to embrace our mortality in every moment**,
            Which helps us fully live each day with great fervor and aliveness.

We are *the children of the Universe* learning "to ride the myriad pathways of awakening"
    That offer us forward motion toward inner freedom - and the creation of a better world.

Circle of Trust

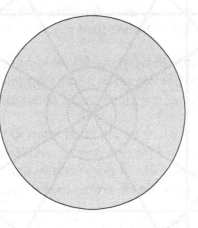

LETTING GO
TRUST –
MY EXPERIENCE
OF LETTING GO
OF THE KNOWN
- AND BEING WILLING
TO EMBRACE
THE UNKNOWN

SAFETY
TRUST –
MY EXPERIENCE
OF FEELING A RELATIVE
LEVEL OF SAFETY
FROM THE PROTECTION
OF ANOTHER OR FROM A
PARTICULAR SITUATION

**RELINQUISH
CONTROL**
TRUST –
MY EXPERIENCE
OF RELINQUISHING
CONTROL AND
SURRENDERING MY LIFE
TO *A GREATER POWER*

MORTALITY
TRUST –
MY EXPERIENCE
OF EMBRACING
MY MORTALITY
IN EVERY MOMENT
SO AS TO LIVE WITH
FERVOR AND ALIVENESS

EMBRACING THE UNKNOWN

Today I embrace the unknown by trusting unwaveringly in the unfolding perfection of life.

There is a particular group exercise performed during some transformational workshops
   That's designed to help people experience *trust* - and is described as follows.

With two people in a group, one person is blindfolded so they can't see where they're walking,
   And a second person, who is "the guide", helps direct and protect the blindfolded person
      Making sure they move safely around others throughout the workshop space.

In order for the blindfolded person to feel safe and secure,
   He or she must learn to trust, and surrender to, the protection of the other person.

From a certain perspective, we can think of our life as "a perpetual journey into the unknown"
   In which, each day, we can never truly know what may be around the next bend,
      Or what surprises may suddenly appear "out of thin air",
         Or where *The Great Mystery of Life* might take us.

So if our desire is to ultimately experience genuine inner freedom and authentic peace of mind,
   Then we must learn **to embrace the unknown** in every moment.

In a certain manner, we are all "blind" to what the future will bring us,
   Yet similar to *the trust exercise* performed in a transformational workshop,
      We each have a core of inner guidance that's constantly helping us on our way.

If our intent is *to embrace the unknown*, then we must learn to consciously live
   In **alignment with *the Source of Life*** (the *Infinite Intelligence* of the Universe),
      And we must **accept that our life is perpetually evolving**
         Toward higher expressions of order, creativity, and cooperation.

Embracing the unknown is also discovering how to **fully surrender to *a Greater Power***
   Recognizing that our inner guidance is always leading us
      To our destiny of spiritual awakening and inner freedom.

There is a metaphysical visual image of *embracing the unknown*
   That can be helpful for us to comprehend this quality.

Imagine you are standing on the bank of a small lake wanting to cross to the other side,
   However you can find no visible way to cross over the lake
      Because all you see before you is a vast surface of lightly rippling water.

Now imagine feeling aligned with *Life* in such a way that you feel a **radical trust**
   And every time you take a step across the lake,
      A large flat stone magically appears for your feet to walk upon
         As you are easily guided over the water to the other side.

To have faith that "every stone" will be there to support us when we need it
   Requires constant daily practice to develop an unwavering trust in *Life*
      And an ongoing alignment with *the Infinite Presence of Love*.

Circle of Embracing the Unknown
(Living With *The Great Mystery of Life*)

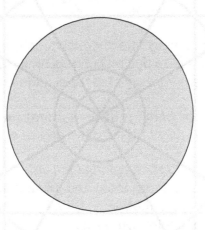

ALIGNMENT
I LIVE EACH DAY
FEELING
AN ALIGNMENT WITH
THE SOURCE OF LIFE
(THE INFINITE INTELLIGENCE
OF THE UNIVERSE)
THAT CONSTANTLY
GUIDES ME

TRUST
I LIVE EACH DAY
TRUSTING IN *LIFE* AND
KNOWING EVERYTHING
IS UNFOLDING
IN A MANNER WHICH
BRINGS GREATER
LEARNING, GROWTH,
AND DEVELOPMENT

ACCEPTANCE
I LIVE EACH DAY
FULLY ACCEPTING
THAT MY LIFE
IS PERPETUALLY
EVOLVING TOWARD
HIGHER EXPRESSIONS
OF ORDER, CREATIVITY,
AND COOPERATION

SURRENDER
I LIVE EACH DAY
SURRENDERING MY LIFE
TO *A GREATER POWER* IN
WHICH MY INNER GUIDANCE
IS ALWAYS LEADING ME
TO MY DESTINY
OF SPIRITUAL AWAKENING
AND INNER FREEDOM

BLACK HOLE

I choose forgiveness in every situation and pray for the power of grace to carry it into my heart.

With the development of the modern telescope, scientific explorations of our vast Universe
   Have led to the visual discovery of breathtakingly stunning phenomena.

One remarkable invisible phenomenon that exists throughout the Cosmos,
   Which has become a cosmological buzzword, is *the black hole*.

A *black hole* is a vortex point in space which has an enormously strong gravitational force
   Such that it pulls all objects in its vicinity into its center - even nearby rays of light.

Phenomena in the Universe that are close by, such as stars, asteroids, and fields of energy,
   Are physically drawn to *the black hole* by its huge attractive force,
      And these objects will go beyond "a point-of-no-return" called *the event horizon*,
         The location near *the black hole's* core from which nothing can escape.

Beyond this point in space known as *the event horizon* which surrounds *the black hole*,
   All things fall helplessly into its central void.

If a nearby spaceship was being drawn by this force towards the center of *a black hole*,
   It could escape from *the black hole's* pull by firing its engines in the opposite direction,
      But once it passes *the event horizon*, at that point there's no possible escape.

We can use **the visual image of *the black hole* as a metaphor for *emergence***,
   For the many ways in which we might "fall into the *grace*" of higher states of awareness.

When a person intentionally decides to seek *spiritual enlightenment*,
   He or she dedicates their life to inner freedom and, ultimately, to the service of others,
      Which could be poetically envisioned as purposely moving toward "*a black hole*",
         Where *the black hole's* center symbolizes the realization of *enlightenment*.

A person can only aim oneself toward *enlightenment* by their conscious choices and actions,
   Yet they cannot compel *enlightenment* to happen through their personal will or desire.

Enlightenment seems to require a part of life called *grace*, the mysterious quality of existence
   Which, after consciously directing oneself toward *the event horizon of* **enlightenment**,
      Allows a person to "fall", or "emerge", into a higher stage of spiritual awareness.

Similarly, letting go of control and relinquishing everything in our life to a *Greater Intelligence*
   Points to *the event horizon of* **surrender** - then through *grace*, we "fall" into *surrender*.

Another example of this is how our joyful prayers that are focused as heartfelt intentions,
   While aligned with *Limitless Love*, lead us to *the event horizon of receiving* **miracles**.

And every time we seek *forgiveness*, we recognize we can only point ourselves toward it,
   Yet as we learn and experience that only *Love* is real within every situation in our life,
      We might imagine this is like being pulled into the powerful field of "*a black hole*",
         Where we "fall into *grace*", as we pass *the event horizon of* **forgiveness**.

Circle of the Black Hole
(A Metaphor For Emergence - Ways of "Falling Into Grace")

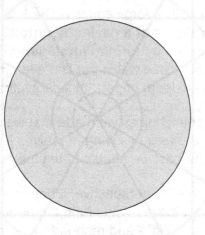

ENLIGHTENMENT
I CONSCIOUSLY LIVE
MY LIFE DEDICATED
TO INNER FREEDOM
AND SERVICE TO OTHERS
WHICH POINTS ME TO
THE EVENT HORIZON
OF ENLIGHTENMENT

MIRACLES
I ALIGN MY AWARENESS
WITH *LIMITLESS LOVE*
AND PRAYERFULLY
FOCUS MY HEARTFELT
INTENTIONS
WHICH POINTS ME TO
THE EVENT HORIZON
OF RECEIVING MIRACLES

SURRENDER
I LET GO OF CONTROL
AND RELINQUISH
EVERYTHING IN MY LIFE
TO *A GREATER*
INTELLIGENCE
WHICH POINTS ME TO
THE EVENT HORIZON
OF SURRENDER

FORGIVENESS
I PERCEIVE THAT MY LIFE
IS UNFOLDING PERFECTLY
- AND KNOW
ONLY *LOVE* IS REAL
WHICH POINTS ME TO
THE EVENT HORIZON
OF FORGIVENESS

FORGIVENESS

Within the present moment everything in my life - right now - is unfolding perfectly just as it is.

Within their distinctive traditions, most of the time-honored religions throughout the world
Speak of the power of **forgiveness** as a means of pardoning another person
And as an exonerating process to re-align one's heart with another.

For many people, a common way to define *forgiveness* is an absolution of a transgression,
In other words, a pardoning of another, a letting go of resentment toward an offender
Who has (in their eyes) wrongly enacted an "offense" against them.

Yet a more expanded view of *forgiveness* allows us to perceive these kinds of bitter events
In a completely different manner, by placing painful situations in a wider context,
And **interpreting them within a larger perspective of what is truly going on**.

It allows us to look at something that has happened and find a way to reframe it in our mind
So we can now understand it within the context of "a much Bigger Picture of reality".

From a spiritually awakened perspective, *forgiveness* is **the total acceptance**
That each of us is an integral part of a perfectly unfolding Universe
Which is flawlessly directed by *Infinite Intelligence* *(God, the Source of Life),*
And all events that take place within our life, even the hurtful experiences,
Are opportunities to learn important lessons that further our growth.

As we become aware of the personal choices we made that we didn't like or we regret making,
We can also practice *self-forgiveness* by loving ourselves just the way we are
And recognizing we did the best we could at the time regarding our past choices.

Perceiving these choices from a grander perspective, it becomes our personal responsibility
To learn to embrace and accept these events (and the people who are involved)
As "the perfect expression of life" - and respond to them as blessed opportunities
To grow spiritually - and become more loving conscious individuals.

From this expansive point of view, *ultimate forgiveness* can be seen as the realization
"There is nothing that exists in my life which is not *Love* unfolding perfectly",
So everything that has ever happened to us, even our most dreaded challenges,
Is in some sublime way, part of the exquisite blossoming of *Limitless Love.*

This simple recognition has the power to transform even the most disturbing events of our life
Through our practice of *radical forgiveness*, by taking what we previously interpreted
As harmful or destructive actions which were perpetrated on us by others,
Placing them in a much bigger context that serves our inner development,
And realizing not only do we forgive, but we've *become forgiveness.*

"A Course In Miracles" (which is a contemporary self-study spiritual training) states:
"Forgiveness is the reflection of God's Love on Earth",
Because **true forgiveness is loving every experience of life just as it is**
And is *the gift of grace* helping us see the reflection of *Perfect Love*
Which is mirrored and expressed in every aspect of our life.

Circle of Forgiveness
(From a Spiritually Awakened Perspective)

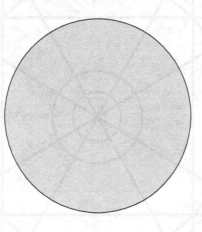

**THE REALIZATION ALL
IS *LIMITLESS LOVE***
FORGIVENESS –
THE REALIZATION THERE IS
NOTHING THAT EXISTS IN
MY LIFE WHICH IS NOT *LOVE*
UNFOLDING PERFECTLY -
FOR EVERYTHING IS A FACET
OF *LIMITLESS LOVE*

ACCEPTANCE
FORGIVENESS – THE
TOTAL ACCEPTANCE
THAT I AM AN
INTEGRAL PART OF A
PERFECTLY UNFOLDING
UNIVERSE WHICH IS
DIRECTED BY *INFINITE
INTELLIGENCE*

**EXPANDED
PERCEPTION**
FORGIVENESS –
AN EXPANDED WAY OF
SEEING THAT HELPS ME
PLACE THE PAINFUL
EVENTS OF MY LIFE INTO
A PERSPECTIVE WHERE
ONLY *LOVE* IS REAL

**UNCONDITIONAL
LOVE**
FORGIVENESS –
EMBRACING EVERY EXPERI-
ENCE OF EACH PERSON
IN MY LIFE AS PERFECT
JUST AS IT IS, AND LOVING
EVERY ASPECT OF MYSELF
JUST THE WAY I AM

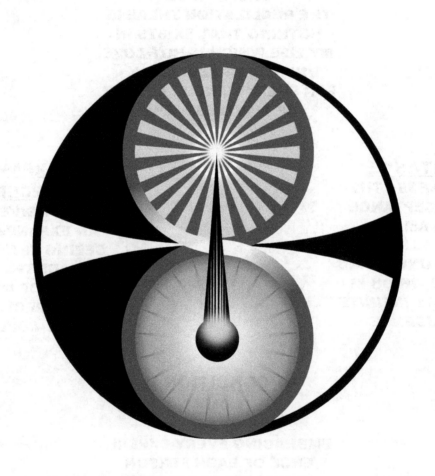

V

HEART AWARENESS PRACTICES

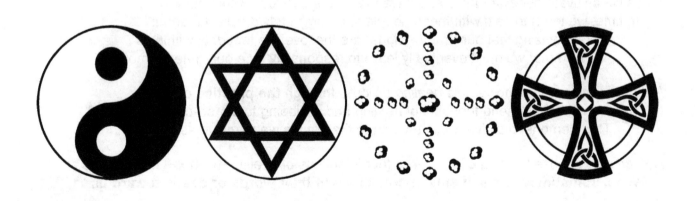

PRAYERS FOR THE "DEMONS"

People who seem to bring me difficulty are really here to help teach me to love unconditionally.

Demons are the dreadful looking creatures of mythology that can induce fear within our mind
   And, sometimes, we may think of them as certain people we regard as evil or cruel.

There are lots of horrific examples of *demonic creatures* in various Hollywood movies
   That convey tales of heroic metaphorical fantasies
      In which the hero of the story must embark on a courageous journey
         To seek the *light* - and overcome the *darkness*.

In this battle between good and evil, the hero may encounter *demons* or evil characters
   Who attempt to oppose his or her noble deeds.

Similarly within our daily lives, each of us is also on *a perpetual journey exploring good and evil*
   Where, in every moment, we must choose between aligning with *the sanctuary of Love*
      Or succumbing to *the fog of fear*.

Typically, we may think of **the "demons" in our life** as those **individuals around us**
   Who appear to bring us challenge or conflict, the people we don't like
      Or don't want to be around because they seem to make our life difficult.

We may think they are the ones that take action in opposition to us
   And so, sometimes, because of our ignorance, **we believe them to be our enemies**
      When, actually, they turn out to be our greatest messengers and teachers.

If we should encounter these people early in our life when we lack mature spiritual awareness,
   We may habitually react to them out of a programed fear -
      For up to this point, it's the only way we have learned "to survive" in this world.

Yet as we cultivate our awareness and have the courage to look within ourselves,
   In time, we learn to deal with these people in a completely different manner
      By recognizing that our "true demons" are the loveless thoughts within us
         And that we must eventually learn to responsibly face our "inner demons".

We can consciously empower this *healing process* through **the practice of prayer**
   As we intentionally send thoughts of healing and wellbeing to our so-called "demons",
      The "demons" that live within us, and to the people we perceive as our "demons".

We can also choose to **send our prayers** (our intentions of healing) **to those individuals**
   Who, sometimes, are selfishly unconscious in their words or deeds toward us.

When we choose to **pray for the people who we believe have hurt or wronged us**,
   Who we still have trouble forgiving, and begin to see each of them as a holy person,
      We access a spiritual power that can transform our habitual perceptions of them.

Just like in Hollywood fantasy movies, we can attune to a kind of benevolent *"magical power"*,
   The Power of Love, which turns our "inner demons" into "the princes and princesses"
      Who, in the realm of *Limitless Love*, are here to teach us to love unconditionally.

Circle of Prayers for the "Demons"
(A Transformative Practice)

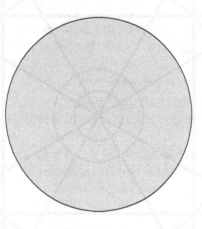

CHALLENGING
PEOPLE
I PRAY FOR
THE PEOPLE
WHO SEEM
TO BRING CHALLENGE
OR CONFLICT
INTO MY LIFE

SEEMING
ENEMIES
I PRAY FOR
THE PEOPLE WHO
OPPOSE ME,
AND WHO
I ONCE BELIEVED
WERE MY ENEMIES

THOSE WHO
HAVE HURT ME
I PRAY FOR
THE PEOPLE WHO,
I BELIEVE, HAVE
HURT ME, AND WHO
I STILL HAVE
TROUBLE FORGIVING

UNCONSCIOUS
INDIVIDUALS
I PRAY FOR
THE INDIVIDUALS
WHO ARE SELFISHLY
UNCONSCIOUS
IN THEIR WORDS
OR ACTIONS TOWARDS ME

WELLBEING OF THE HEART
I courageously follow the guidance of my heart so I may live my life with ease and grace.

It's so much easier to stay aligned with *the Source of Life* and be present in each moment
When we respond to the natural yearning within us
That's always inviting us to sustain personal balance and radiant health.

Some spiritual traditions call this natural guiding impulse *"the heart"*,
And by courageously following the benevolent longings and guidance of *the heart*,
A vibrant balance of life can be maintained.

The heart is constantly inviting us to **live each day in gratitude**
For what we're learning from every experience of our life.

For when we learn to live this way,
It's like traveling on a straight wide highway rather than a narrow winding road
In which the appreciation we feel for all we encounter in our life
Helps us experience peace of mind - more quickly and with less effort.

Living in gratitude supports our alignment with *the Source of Life,*
Helping us stay in conscious attunement with the natural current of *Life Force energy*.

Learning to be grateful for everything we experience
Also helps us "stretch the chambers of our heart"
And, thus, cultivate **greater compassion and service to others**.

Consciously living in a state of gratitude expands our ability to be mindful and aware
Allowing us to completely **experience the full spectrum of our feelings**.

The everyday events of our life provide us with many diverse emotions,
Feelings that serve as our *inner guidance system* to help us make important choices
And, therefore, it's of great benefit to embrace our emotions fully
So we can more effectively navigate through our day with ease and grace.

Our emotions are intended to be experienced and then naturally pass through us unobstructed
Like water rushing through a garden hose, flowing freely without blockage or resistance.

When we resist any part of the full spectrum of our emotions,
Such as anger, sadness, grief, or even positive emotions like joy,
We create blockages in our body that can stop the natural flow of *Life Force*
Which intends to effortlessly circulate through us.

If we should discover an emotional blockage, it's valuable to find effective ways to remove it
So we may dispel the darkness within us that hinders this natural flow,
In other words, it's a gift when we **release the shadow aspects of ourselves**.

Empowered with this awareness, our *heart* is a beacon of light that illuminates our path
So our rich spectrum of feelings can easily guide us each day
"Down the highway of life" on our ever-unfolding *journey of awakening*.

Circle of Wellbeing of the Heart
(Transformative Practices)

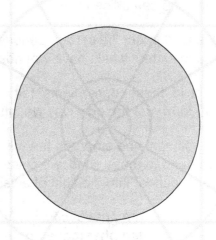

**I LIVE
MY LIFE
IN GRATITUDE**

**I AM
IN SERVICE
TO OTHERS**

**I RELEASE THE
SHADOW ASPECTS
OF MYSELF**

**I FULLY
EXPERIENCE
MY EMOTIONS**

SHADOW WORK

Today I mindfully witness my thoughts and feelings without judgment or attachment.

In our modern culture, a diamond is an object that has come to symbolize exceptional beauty,
　　The expression of great love for another, as well as the radiance of the human spirit.

In order for diamonds to be organically formed in Nature,
　　The original carbon molecules that they consist of
　　　　Need to undergo tremendous pressures in the belly of the Earth
　　　　　　Where the carbon molecules are hidden far below the surface
　　　　　　　　And, over time, these pressures transform their characteristics.

Professional diamond miners must dig tunnels deep into the ground to search for these gems
　　And when miners uncover rough diamonds, they are jagged and opaque,
　　　　And must be cut and polished to produce the exquisite forms we are familiar with.

Each one of us is like "a diamond in the rough" that yearns to be polished and transformed
　　So our inherent beauty and radiance can shine forth.

However, we have probably experienced in our life certain periods of tremendous pressure
　　And, possibly, early traumatic encounters which have wounded us in some way.

To emotionally survive as a young child, these "dark events" felt like they needed to be buried
　　Deep in "the belly of our heart", for it was the only way we intuited we could survive.

Yet in order to express our greater potential and embrace the fullness of who we really are,
　　It is essential to courageously attend to these shadowy places within us
　　　　So as to release old hidden wounds "into the light of awareness".

If we desire to "attend to these shadows", there are specific kinds of transformative practices,
　　Such as **focused breath work or intense physical exercises** that can be used
　　　　As a means to release unconscious reactive thoughts and feelings.

Many forms of **inner child work and hypnotherapy** are also valuable tools that can assist us
　　To release repressed traumatic experiences and cellular memories from the past
　　　　Which adversely influence our present everyday choices and actions.

And **expanding our awareness of what is true and learning about what really matters**
　　Can shed light on our beliefs, so we may transform the beliefs that no longer serve us.

With greater awareness, **shadow work** (i.e. releasing our unconscious destructive beliefs)
　　Does not always have to originate from some external exercise or therapy session
　　　　But eventually can become a natural daily practice of spiritual mindfulness
　　　　　　As we learn, moment to moment, to **witness our thoughts and feelings**
　　　　　　　　Without judgment or attachment.

Our *journey of awakening* can be called *a hero's journey* in which we, as its "blossoming hero",
　　Are constantly being invited by *Life* to explore the deep caverns of our heart and mind
　　　　So we may uncover and polish "the inner diamond" we have always been.

Circle of Shadow Work
(Transformative Practices)

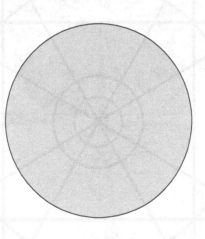

SPIRIT
SHADOW WORK –
WITNESSING, WITHOUT
JUDGMENT, THE ARISING
OF MY DAILY THOUGHTS
AND FEELINGS,
WHICH IN TURN FOSTER
GREATER SELF-LOVE
AND SELF-ACCEPTANCE

BODY
SHADOW WORK –
FOCUSED BREATH WORK
OR INTENSE PHYSICAL
EXERCISES THAT ARE
USED AS A MEANS TO
RELEASE UNCONSCIOUS
REACTIVE THOUGHTS
AND FEELINGS

MIND
SHADOW WORK –
THE EXPANSION OF
MY AWARENESS TO SHED
LIGHT ON MY CONCEPTS
AND BELIEFS
SO I CAN TRANSFORM
THE BELIEFS THAT
NO LONGER SERVE ME

HEART
SHADOW WORK –
INNER CHILD WORK
OR HYPNOTHERAPY
THAT CAN TRANSFORM
REPRESSED TRAUMATIC
EMOTIONS FROM MY
PAST WHICH INFLUENCE
MY PRESENT CHOICES

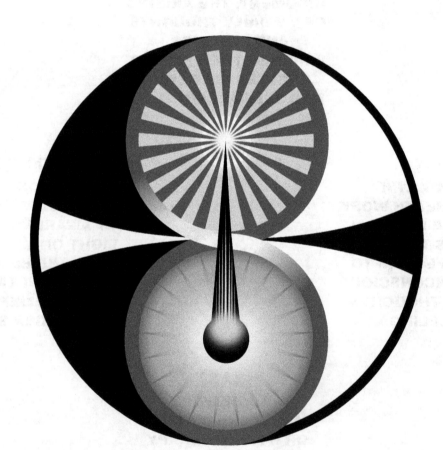

VI

ARCHETYPES OF LIFE MASTERY

RELIGIOUS ARCHETYPES

I feel a natural yearning in me that is directing me to creatively envision who I desire to become.

When engineers construct something brand new, like a tall building or a large bridge,
    They use a design that's drawn out on paper by an architect called a *blueprint*
        To provide a graphic picture of what the final structure will look like.

A *blueprint* is a visual construction tool - and if the tool is used properly,
    It can provide the means for the engineer to, most quickly and proficiently,
        Reach his or her goal of erecting the intended architectural design.

In a symbolic way, each one of us is like a construction engineer or bridge builder,
    For when we're aligned with *Life*, we can feel the nudging of a natural yearning within
        "To build another bridge" to a more developed or awakened stage of our life.

And so, similar to professional engineers, we can find great benefit
    When we use an appropriate "blueprint of our human possibilities"
        To help us achieve our intended goal of developing our higher potential.

From a spiritual perspective, **the various religious archetypes can be seen**
    As universal blueprints of possibility, or visionary patterns of human potential,
        That assist us in attaining a clear image of our visions
            So we can more easily manifest our heartfelt dreams.

These forms of "archetypal blueprints" have evolved over thousands of years
    From personal experiences of the many spiritual pioneers who lived during past ages,
        The numerous courageous men and women who have come before us
            And have devoted their lives to a pursuit of awakened living.

Their individual achievements of spiritual development have contributed to *a field of energy*,
    A collective field of human consciousness that is a demonstration of what's possible,
        And this *field* holds the wisdom of those who have dedicated their lives
            To merging with, and directly experiencing, their *Transcendent Self*.

This vast *field of energy* forms a universal blueprint of those pioneers of consciousness
    Who have attained a direct realization of their *Eternal Nature*
        And who have fully devoted their lives to helping others
            Open their hearts to *the Infinite Presence of Love*.

These pioneers are the **saints**, the **mystics**, the **sages**, and the **masters**
    (To name a few of these archetypal images),
        Which form this **collective field of what it means to be spiritually awakened**.

Deep within us is a natural guiding impulse "to build a bridge", to cross over to a better world,
    To reach a higher, more enlightened stage of awareness.

When we choose to spend time in sacred silence and authentically look deep within us,
    We can more easily discover *the visionary blueprint* for that "bridge of awakening",
        For it's always waiting within to help us be "the builder of our unlimited potential".

Circle of Religious Archetypes
(Symbolic Images to Help Me Embody My Unlimited Potential)

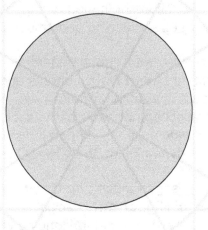

MYSTIC
ONE WHO DEDICATES
HIS OR HER LIFE
TO MERGING WITH,
AND DIRECTLY
EXPERIENCING,
THE TRANSENDENT SELF

MASTER
ONE WHO
REALIZES SPIRITUAL
MASTERY AND LIVES
A LIFE OF SERVICE
THAT'S ALIGNED WITH
THE SOURCE OF LIFE

SAGE
ONE WHO
HAS AWAKENED,
AND THUS POINTS
OTHERS TO, A DIRECT
REALIZATION OF THEIR
ETERNAL NATURE

SAINT
ONE WHO
IS DEVOTED TO SERVING
OTHERS AND TO HELPING
PEOPLE OPEN THEIR
HEARTS TO *THE INFINITE
PRESENCE OF LOVE*

THE GREAT CIRCLE OF THE ARCHETYPES

I use my creative imagination to envision myself experiencing the next level of my potential.

The Great Circle is both an ancient and modern symbolic "map of an awakened life0
    That represents the universal dynamics at play in the world and in our lives,
        And illustrates a visual flow of these essential dynamics. (see June 28th)

This iconic image helps to clarify how every person on our planet is inwardly directed
    By a natural transcendent yearning *(Limitless Love)* to expand one's **consciousness**,
        And then one's expanded consciousness is outwardly expressed as **creativity**,
            In other words - as the creative gifts and contributions within one's **life**.

These four foundational components of **The Great Circle**, which are listed separately
    (<u>Consciousness</u> and <u>creativity</u>, *Limitless Love* and <u>life unfolding perfectly</u>)
        Are all occurring as one fluid dynamic whole in the perpetual spiral of existence.

Yet in order to enhance our understanding of these universal dynamics
    And discover ways that this understanding can benefit our life,
        There's value in making distinctions of the four components of **The Great Circle**
        So we can learn their deeper meaning and influence in our daily reality.

To support this intention, we can overlay within each quadrant
    A set of archetypal images that are "universal blueprints of our human potential"
        By associating a specific set of visionary archetypes
            To each of the four distinct components of the circle
                In an attempt to create a clearer comprehension
                    Of the various dynamics of **The Great Circle**.

For the dynamic of <u>evolving consciousness</u> within **The Great Circle** (the left quadrant),
    We associate **the Archetypes of Higher Knowledge**
        In which each archetype represents a natural longing within us
            To develop our potential, awaken to *the Transcendent,*
                Correct our thinking, and reach for higher stages of awareness.

For the dynamic of <u>evolving creativity</u> (the right quadrant),
    We associate **the Archetypes of Conscious Contribution**
        In which each archetype represents a natural longing within us
            To consciously contribute our creative gifts to the wellbeing of others.

For the realm of *Limitless Love* (the top quadrant),
    We use **the Archetypes of Spiritual Awakening**
        Where these archetypes represent states of awareness on our *spiritual journey,*
            And, with time and dedication, they culminate in the Master of Freedom
                Symbolizing "one who lives a life of service that's guided by *Love*".

And finally, for the part of the circle that points us to <u>an awakened life</u> (the bottom quadrant),
    We use **the Archetypes of Life Mastery**
        Where each archetype represents key virtues, values, and qualities
            That help us cultivate inner freedom - and a life of spiritual mastery.

The Great Circle of the Archetypes

WINTER

ARCHETYPES OF SPIRITUAL AWAKENING
ALL FOUR REPRESENT MY *JOURNEY OF AWAKENING* LEADING TO MY DESTINY AS A "MASTER OF FREEDOM", A LIFE IN SERVICE GUIDED BY

LIMITLESS LOVE

AUTUMN

ARCHETYPES OF HIGHER KNOWLEDGE
EACH ONE REPRESENTS A NATURAL LONGING TO DEVELOP MY POTENTIAL AND HIGHER STAGES OF

EVOLVING CONSCIOUSNESS

SPRING

ARCHETYPES OF CONSCIOUS CONTRIBUTION
EACH ONE REPRESENTS A NATURAL LONGING TO CONTRIBUTE MY GIFTS AND EXPRESS MY EVER

EVOLVING CREATIVITY

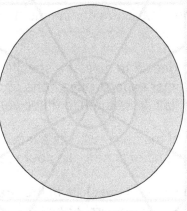

SUMMER

ARCHETYPES OF LIFE MASTERY
EACH ONE REPRESENTS THE KEY VIRTUES, VALUES, AND QUALITIES THAT HELP ME CULTIVATE INNER FREEDOM AND EMBODY MY DESTINY OF LIVING AN AWAKENED LIFE

ARCHETYPES OF LIFE MASTERY
Today I use transformative practices to help me cultivate peace of mind and inner freedom.

The country of Switzerland is known for is its master watchmakers
    Who, for centuries, have crafted some of the most exquisite timepieces.

Their watches are beautifully fashioned with expertise because many Swiss watchmakers
    Have mastered exacting skills through sustained years of dedicated study and practice.

France is famous for (among numerous other things) its fine French cuisine,
    Hosting many culinary schools where master chefs learn to hone their trade.

And when we think of highly praised and celebrated beer,
    Germany, with its master brewers, is usually one of the places which comes to mind,
        A country claiming recipes of ale that have been refined for hundreds of years.

To be a master watchmaker, a master chef, or a master brewer,
    Requires discipline, focus, perseverance, education, and a great deal of practice.

Each of these areas of distinction requires one's commitment
    To consciously develop oneself into *an expression of excellence.*

If at some time in our life we should decide to master a specific trade or skill,
    It can help us to observe what other experts have done to cultivate their abilities
        And use the inspiration we gain from them to empower our own training.

Living life fully is a grand challenge of mastery - with its exalted goals of conscious awareness,
    Of expressing ever-greater love, and of contributing our creative gifts to others.

The most important teacher to help us learn the skills of **life mastery** is our *inner guidance,*
    Yet we can also gain insight from four key archetypal images that point to our potential.

These archetypes hold the awareness of all the men and women who have come before us
    And who have demonstrated the awakened skills of life mastery we desire to embody.

The archetype of **the Enlightened King or Queen** points us to certain altruistic qualities
    Such as heart wisdom, empowering all people, service, and action guided by *Love.*

The Spiritual Magician inspires us to maintain an alignment with *the Source of Life,*
    Tap into *the Infinite Creativity* of the Universe, and manifest what *Life* directs us to do.

With daily practice, the archetypal image of **the Mystical Lover** can lead us
    To living authentically with a passion for life, being flexible, and caring for others,
        While mindfulness, responsibility, unlimited possibilities, and excellence
            Are some of the qualities of the archetype of **the Peaceful Warrior**.

If we decide to use these **Archetypes of Life Mastery** to consciously develop ourselves,
    Just like the commitment of a master watchmaker, a master chef, or a master brewer,
        It requires steady practice, focus, and perseverance to reach our intended target.

Circle of Archetypes of Life Mastery

ENLIGHTENED KING OR QUEEN
IT IS THE PART OF ME THAT CULTIVATES GENEROSITY AND HEART WISDOM, LIVES MY LIFE IN SERVICE TO OTHERS, EMPOWERS ALL PEOPLE, AND TAKES ACTION WHICH IS GUIDED BY *LOVE*

PEACEFUL WARRIOR
IT IS THE PART OF ME THAT DEVELOPS EACH DAY THROUGH THE PRACTICES OF MINDFULNESS, CONSCIOUS RESPONSIBILITY, AND BY BEING OPEN TO UNLIMITED POSSIBILITY

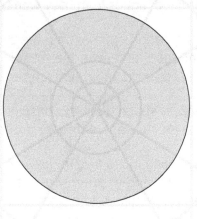

SPIRITUAL MAGICIAN
IT IS THE PART OF ME THAT ALIGNS WITH *THE SOURCE OF LIFE, THE INFINITE CREATIVITY* OF THE UNIVERSE, SO AS TO MANIFEST WHAT *LIFE* INWARDLY DIRECTS ME TO ACHIEVE

MYSTICAL LOVER
IT IS THE PART OF ME THAT LIVES AUTHENTICALLY WITH A PASSION FOR LIFE, IS FLEXIBLE TO CHANGE, QUESTIONS EVERYTHING, AND CARES FOR THE WELLBEING OF OTHERS

MYSTICAL LOVER

One way I share my love for life is by doing what I can to contribute to the wellbeing of others.

Modern discoveries of medical science have shown that our minds play an essential part
    In the physiological responses our bodies experience each day.

Behavioral scientists have carried out numerous double blind studies
    Which have demonstrated that our body registers similar immune responses
        Both when we physically undergo traumatic fearful experiences
            As well as when we only imagine within our mind
                That we're encountering these same experiences.

The dynamic power of our imagination has the potential to cause the internal part of our being
    To generate corresponding responses in our external physical body,
        Both constructive and destructive, by focusing our mind in a specific manner.

For example in sports, athletes such as *high jumpers*, use this ability of the mind
    To constructively imagine themselves going beyond their current physical limits
        By envisioning they are jumping higher than they were previously able to do.

The power of imagination can (over a period of time) help the brain and body of these athletes
    Mobilize the neural pathways needed, and even the muscular strength required,
        So as to experience greater feats than the *high jumper* has ever attained.

We may also use our faculty of creative imagination to consciously develop our inner being
    In ways that can cultivate a love for life - and a deeper compassion for others.

When we visualize ourselves participating in life fully, expressing our natural interests,
    Appreciating the good within others, and frequently questioning what we believe,
        We open new neural pathways within us to a possibility
            Of experiencing **an authentic love and passion for all of life**.

When we picture ourselves fully surrendering everything to *the Source of Life,*
    It becomes easier to be **flexible** to the changes of life, to give up our need to control,
        To let go of our attachments, and to trust in the unknown.

When we **envision how it feels to live in the most humble and authentic way we can,**
    We're more able to accept life just as it is, live boldly without fear,
        And courageously express our uniqueness and vulnerabilities.

When we imagine living a life of **kindness**, graciousness, care, and contribution to others,
    We then intentionally arouse and anchor these aspects within our inner being.

All of these transformative life-affirming qualities listed above
    Are the attributes of the visionary archetype referred to as **the Mystical Lover**.

By focusing each day on the benevolent qualities within this *archetypal template*
    Using the innate power of our creative imagination,
        We can learn to "jump" or "awaken" to a more exalted experience of freedom.

Circle of the Mystical Lover
(An Archetype of Life Mastery)

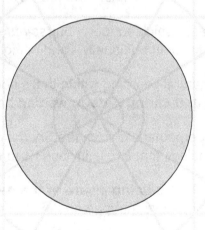

LOVE FOR LIFE
I SUSTAIN A LOVE
AND PASSION FOR LIFE,
APPRECIATE THE GOOD
WITHIN OTHERS, EXPRESS
MY NATURAL INTERESTS,
QUESTION EVERYTHING,
AND HAVE A WILLINGNESS
TO LIVE FULLY

KINDNESS
I ENGAGE IN
A COMPASSIONATE LIFE
OF KINDNESS,
LOVING CARE,
GRACIOUSNESS,
AND CONTRIBUTION
TO THE WELLBEING
OF OTHERS

FLEXIBILITY
I SURRENDER EVERY-
THING IN MY LIFE TO
THE SOURCE OF LIFE BY
BEING FLEXIBLE, GIVING
UP CONTROL, LETTING
GO OF MY ATTACH-
MENTS, AND TRUSTING
IN THE UNKNOWN

AUTHENTICITY
I LIVE MY LIFE
IN THE MOST HUMBLE
AND AUTHENTIC
WAY I CAN,
COURAGEOUSLY
EXPRESSING
MY UNIQUENESS
AND VULNERABILITIES

KINDNESS

Today I intend to be the most loving, caring, and kind person I can be in every situation.

At some point in your life you've probably listened to a particular kind of instrumental music
    That made you feel really good or inspired when you heard it,
        Because in that moment certain musical frequencies combined in a pleasing way
      So as to create an enjoyable sound which your heart responded to.

Similarly, people who resonate energetically with the quality of loving kindness
    Can help us to feel good when we're around them,
        Because there's something about who they are and how they live
      That can inspire us and remind us of our own higher potential.

It's as if their energy puts out a particular uplifting frequency
    That adjusts our "inner compass" - and points us to our true home.

Kindness is a frequency of love that radiates from the heart
    And is "a powerful song to sing" as we explore our *journey of awakening*.

It is an important foundational quality which supports our *spiritual journey*
    That points us to loving all of life unconditionally - and being in service to others.

We can think of kindness as the natural yearning within that's constantly beckoning us
    To cultivate **the most loving and caring person we can be in every moment**.

As we courageously listen to the perpetual call from *the Source of Life*, we find this yearning
    Is one of the most natural impulses that *Life* is inviting us to embody.

Kindness is a form of awareness, for it is **being aware of the needs of another**
    And taking appropriate action to serve that person in fulfilling their needs.

It's a spiritual doorway to a whole new paradigm of living
    In which we learn the gift and blessing of serving the wellbeing of others.

Kindness is also the choice to live our life with graciousness
    So that we compassionately consider the feelings of others - and honor their feelings.

Kindness is the intention to **think loving thoughts toward all people** no matter who they are,
    And even though we may not be able to take physical action in all situations,
        We can always choose to be kind with our thoughts.

Most people have heard the contemporary phrase, *"perform random acts of kindness"*,
    And this means "be kind to all people without any thought of gain for oneself".

Obviously, our world would be a much different place
    If every person on the planet responded to the natural impulse of kindness
        For we would all be radiating a powerful frequency of *Love*
            That pointed each other's "inner compass"
                To the eternal home of our *awakened selves*.

Circle of Kindness

CARING
KINDNESS –
THE NATURAL YEARNING
WITHIN INVITING ME
TO BE THE MOST LOVING
AND CARING PERSON
I CAN BE
IN EVERY MOMENT

LOVING THOUGHTS
KINDNESS –
THE HEARTFELT
INTENTION TO THINK
LOVING THOUGHTS
TOWARD ALL PEOPLE
NO MATTER
WHO THEY ARE

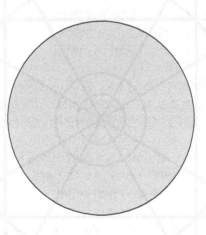

AWARENESS
KINDNESS –
BEING AWARE
OF THE NEEDS OF
ANOTHER AND TAKING
ACTION TO SERVE THAT
PERSON IN FULFILLING
THEIR NEEDS

GRACIOUSNESS
KINDNESS –
THE CHOICE
TO LIVE MY LIFE
WITH GRACIOUSNESS
SO I COMPASSIONATELY
CONSIDER
THE FEELINGS OF OTHERS

AUTHENTICITY

I live an honest, authentic, and vulnerable life while feeling each of my emotions as they arise.

Decades ago at certain festive carnivals or state fairs,
    There was a particular building called a House of Mirrors
        Which had been designed solely for one's enjoyment and entertainment.

This was a place of amusement that contained a variety of specially constructed mirrors
    Which, just for the fun of it, made a person appear very thin, or extremely fat,
        Or cleverly distorted one's true appearance in a number of humorous ways.

Yet, of course, the primary function of most mirrors we use daily
    Is to project back to us the true image of what we actually look like.

Typically in our everyday lives, we tend to unconsciously "mirror out into the world around us"
    A certain image of ourselves regarding how we want others to see us,
        And this projected image is based on the current state of our internal awareness.

If we are inwardly feeling fear or a sense of anxious isolation,
    Then the image we mirror out into our world may be distorted by our fearful thoughts
        And will, most likely, not project to others what we are actually feeling.

From a state of imbalance, we may unconsciously do this in order to protect ourselves,
    But from a bigger vantage, when we do this, we are cutting off our true essential power
        And blocking the natural flow of *Life Force energy* within us.

Yet, over time, as we learn to fully love and accept ourselves just as we are,
    We begin to project an entirely different image to others,
        One that is radiant, genuine, real, and authentic.

Authenticity can be thought of as our ability **to live an honest, open, and vulnerable life**
    In which we learn to feel the full spectrum of our emotions as they arise.

It is having the bold awareness and audacity to express our **uniqueness**
    As we share the novel offerings of our creative gifts and talents.

Loving ourselves, as well as learning to forgive ourselves for any past regrets,
    Is what makes it possible for us to live our life authentically.

Self-love enables us to **communicate courageously with the people in our life**
    And to take benevolent actions for the good of others that are guided by our heart.

To live authentically is also to consciously recognize and accept
    That the entire Universe is always unfolding perfectly just as it is
        And, thus, to **witness our life unfold naturally and spontaneously**.

At times, the world we live in seems to project many distorted images,
    Yet just imagine for a moment what our world might be like
        If each of us could "mirror back to one another" our radiant authentic self.

Circle of Authenticity

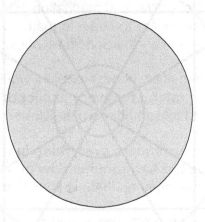

VULNERABILITY
AUTHENTICITY –
DOING MY BEST TO LIVE
AN HONEST, OPEN,
AND VULNERABLE LIFE
WHILE FULLY FEELING
MY DIVERSE EMOTIONS
AS THEY ARISE
IN EACH MOMENT

**COMMUNICATE
COURAGEOUSLY**
AUTHENTICITY –
COMMUNICATING
COURAGEOUSLY WITH
OTHERS AND TAKING
BENEVOLENT ACTIONS
TO BENEFIT OTHERS
GUIDED BY MY HEART

UNIQUENESS
AUTHENTICITY –
HAVING THE BOLD
AWARENESS
AND AUDACITY
TO EXPRESS
MY UNIQUENESS AS
I SHARE MY CREATIVE
GIFTS AND TALENTS

BE NATURAL
AUTHENTICITY –
THE ABILITY TO ACCEPT
THAT THE ENTIRE UNIVERSE
IS UNFOLDING PERFECTLY
JUST AS IT IS - AND, THUS,
TO WITNESS MY LIFE
UNFOLD NATURALLY
AND SPONTANEOUSLY

HUMILITY

I offer my creative gifts and talents to bless others from the sacred altar of a humble heart.

The image of a pious monk committed to a life of austerity living in an old stone monastery
    Is a poetic notion that can also conjure up a similar, but more contemporary image.

This might be the modest image of an ordinary simple person who has dedicated his or her life
    To cultivating spiritual awareness, being in service to others,
        And developing altruistic qualities such as living life with **humility**.

It might appear that if anyone lived in an austere monastic environment
    And dedicated themselves to prayer, meditation, and service,
        That this individual would naturally become a humble person.

But humility doesn't necessarily come from just the disciplined practice of prayer or meditation
    Or living modestly in a holy cloistered environment.

True humility comes from the direct knowing of what one's life is truly about
    Which the dedicated practices of prayer and meditation point a person's heart to,
        For authentic spiritual practices are the transformative vehicles
            That lead to one's true home - *the Sanctuary of Limitless Love.*

A sincerely humble monk, or any genuinely humble person, would live their life in such a way
    That they would constantly be **grateful for every aspect of their life**
        Perceiving everything as a blessed gift from the Universe.

It would be the type of person who **surrenders everything in their life to** *a Greater Power*
    So he or she may experience the harmonious flow of what is
        Realizing, that in this eternal moment, there is nothing to resist.

This person, through daily transformative practice, would have **developed an acceptance**
    That they are an integral part of the unfolding perfection of life.

Each new morning a truly humble person would recognize **that they are one,**
    They are intimately connected, they are sublimely merged
        With every facet of *Wholeness*, **which includes everything and everyone.**

Thus humility (from a spiritual perspective) is to be awake,
    And to authentically be awake is to love all of life unconditionally.

To be spiritually awake in this world is to <u>be grateful</u> for every situation in our life,
    To <u>surrender</u> to what is and let go of our attachments to our personal desires,
        To <u>accept</u> that our life is unfolding perfectly just as it is,
            And to <u>be aware of our Oneness</u> with all of life.

Amidst all of the glories and challenges we encounter, it appears *Life* is continually inviting us
    To be a modern monk, an urban shaman, an everyday mystic
        And, thus, to share our creative gifts and talents with the people in our life
            From the sacred altar of a humble heart.

Circle of Humility
(From a Spiritual Perspective)

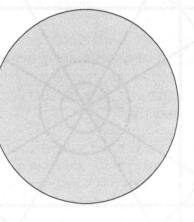

ONENESS
HUMILITY –
BEING AWARE I AM ONE
WITH EVERY FACET
OF *WHOLENESS*, WHICH
INCLUDES EVERYTHING
AND EVERYONE

GRATITUDE
HUMILITY –
BEING GRATEFUL
FOR EVERY ASPECT
OF MY LIFE AND
PERCEIVING EVERYTHING
AS A BLESSED GIFT

ACCEPTANCE
HUMILITY –
ACCEPTING THAT I AM
AN INTEGRAL PART
OF THE UNFOLDING
PERFECTION
OF LIFE

SURRENDER
HUMILITY –
SURRENDERING
EVERYTHING IN MY LIFE
SO I MAY EXPERIENCE
THE HARMONIOUS FLOW
OF WHAT IS

FLEXIBILITY

I surrender any attachments to my desires - and let go of my need to control the flow of life.

Within the unfolding of the Universe (as well as within the daily unfolding of each of our lives)
    Change is a never-ending constant that's perpetually mysterious and unpredictable.

It is "the course of change", "the variable of the unknown", that can shift the direction of our life
    By, unexpectedly, catapulting us down a completely different path,
        Or impacting us in ways that compel us to travel a brand new road of experience,
            Sometimes as quickly as in "the blink of an eye".

At times, our life can seem like a billiard ball in forward motion
    That's rolling on "the Billiard Table of Life" and heading along one fixed path,
        But then suddenly changes trajectory by hitting "the wall of the table"
            And is, therefore, sent in another direction.

Our unfolding life story (i.e. the personal drama of our life) can be likened to "the billiard ball",
    Always changing directions and heading down uncharted roads
        By bumping into the surprising circumstances of our daily reality.

Like most people, we sometimes get attached to a specific direction we want to go in
    Based on a personal desire which keeps us clinging to our preferred path,
        And we may also get agitated, fearful, or enraged,
            When we begin "to bounce in a different direction"
                As we "hit the walls of life".

At this present moment, we're each being invited by *Life* to participate in *a greater awakening*
    In which we're inwardly being asked to make a shift in our conscious awareness
        And transform from a helpless victim of ever-changing circumstances
            To *the Witnessing Presence* that observes, and flows amidst,
                The constant changes of life with flexibility and non-attachment.

When the winds of changing conditions are blowing through our personal life,
    Flexibility can be thought of as gently bending with the wind like a supple willow tree.

The Source of Life is continually guiding us to become "the Billiard Table", so to speak,
    (Where the table symbolizes our *Witnessing Presence*, our *Eternal Nature*),
        Which simply witnesses the changing experiences of our reality
            Play their part within the daily unfolding of life.

Flexibility is choosing to let go of our need to control people - or the natural flow of life,
    To adapt to the experiences of our life without resistance,
        And to be open to all possibilities while surrendering our attachments.

It is being able to **trust in the unknown by flowing with the many changes in our life**,
    A shift of awareness from focusing on our personal agenda of "the billiard ball"
        To the greater intention of "the Billiard Table" *(Infinite Intelligence)*
            While we simply observe all movements and changes,
                And, at the same time, fully enjoy "the game".

Circle of Flexibility

LETTING GO
FLEXIBILITY –
CHOOSING
TO LET GO
OF MY NEED
TO CONTROL PEOPLE
- OR THE NATURAL FLOW
OF LIFE

ADAPTABILITY
FLEXIBILITY –
BEING WILLING
TO ADAPT
TO THE EXPERIENCES
OF MY LIFE JUST
THE WAY THEY ARE
WITHOUT RESISTANCE

TRUST
FLEXIBILITY –
BEING WILLING
TO TRUST
IN THE UNKNOWN BY
CONSCIOUSLY FLOWING
WITH THE CHANGES
OF MY LIFE

OPENNESS
FLEXIBILITY –
THE EXPERIENCE
OF BEING OPEN
TO ALL POSSIBILITIES
WHILE SURRENDERING
ANY ATTACHMENTS
TO MY DESIRES

VII

HEART AWARENESS PRACTICES

PASSION FOR LIFE

Today I am willing to live a more vibrant and radiant life with passion, curiosity, and aliveness.

It can be very enlivening and inspiring to meet someone for the first time
    Who you immediately sense is a person that exudes a vibrant **passion for life**.

Being around this kind of person, you can feel the fervor regarding the way they embrace life
    And the unique manner in which they naturally vibrate
        With an enthusiasm and aliveness about everything they do and say.

Of course, there are other types of people we encounter
    Who seem to be bogged down by the everyday challenges of life,
        And it may appear for them, it's not easy to express much authentic passion
            Throughout the experiences of their day.

Yet if anyone should decide they want to feel more enthusiastic and passionate about their life,
    One way to attain this is to consciously focus their attention - on how to be passionate.

On the following page are four statements which can help us develop an awareness
    Of how to cultivate a natural passion and zest for life.

It's best to choose a specific time everyday to practice these exercises,
    Such as in the morning when you wake - or right before you go to sleep at night.

First, gently bring into your awareness a ***willingness* to live and experience life fully,**
    For the simple act of *willingness* can help set powerful forces in motion.

Next, bring into your awareness a sincere and energized gratitude for being alive,
    For our *passion for life* can emerge from **our growing experiences of loving life,**
        Loving people, and an authentic love and full acceptance of ourselves.

Then bring into your awareness **the particular areas of life you're naturally interested in,**
    The things you're deeply excited about developing and expanding within yourself
        And the specific interests you have a natural enthusiasm for.

Also bring into your awareness a healthy **curiosity to explore brand new facets of life**,
    Which can be another key that opens up even more pathways of inspiring experiences.

When we develop this awareness everyday as a conscious transformative practice,
    Over time, something "magical" begins to happen.

For greater awareness and attention can be the fuel that amplifies our "flames of passion"
    So we may intentionally live a more vibrant and radiant life.

Certainly, at our very core, we all desire to experience a long life of living on this Earth,
    Yet it's more important to live fully and passionately during the actual time we're here.

If we do this, it will be others who feel enlivened and inspired as they meet us for the first time
    And immediately sense our aliveness and genuine **passion for life**.

Circle of Passion for Life
(A Transformative Practice)

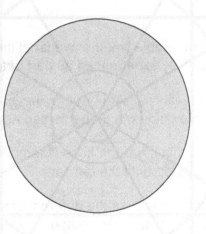

ENTHUSIASM
PASSION FOR LIFE
**EMERGES FROM
A NATURAL WILLINGNESS
TO EXPERIENCE
MY LIFE FULLY
WITH ENTHUSIASM
AND ALIVENESS**

A LOVE FOR LIFE
PASSION FOR LIFE
**EMERGES FROM
MY EVER-EXPANDING
EXPERIENCE OF
JOYOUSLY LOVING LIFE,
LOVING PEOPLE,
AND LOVING MYSELF**

NATURAL INTEREST
PASSION FOR LIFE
**EMERGES FROM
AN INTRINSIC LONGING
TO LEARN MORE ABOUT
THE THINGS I'M DEEPLY
INTERESTED IN
AND EXCITED ABOUT**

CURIOSITY
PASSION FOR LIFE
**EMERGES FROM
MY INNATE YEARNING
TO QUESTION MY BELIEFS
AND TO HAVE A HEALTHY
CURIOSITY ABOUT BRAND
NEW FACETS OF MY LIFE**

HEART AWARENESS

Today I expand my awareness of the diverse emotions that constantly pass through me.

One way to foster positive development in our life is to first intend, and then take action,
>Toward cultivating heightened conscious awareness on a daily basis.

If our intention is to sustain ongoing wellbeing and balance within our body, heart, and mind,
>Then we must learn to be mindful and vigilant in regards to our inner awareness.

In upholding vigilance concerning the *heart*, heightened awareness can be developed
>When we are in touch with, and conscious of, the many emotions
>>That we're constantly generating - and that are always passing through us.

Wellbeing of the heart can more easily be maintained
>When we're aware of the diverse feelings pulsing through our body.

When these emotions are repressed or get stuck somewhere within our body
>Due to a lack of awareness of what we're actually feeling,
>>Then imbalance can occur.

All of our emotions are natural and valuable whether we label them positive or negative,
>And each emotion wants to be fully experienced as part of the full spectrum of our life.

Our emotions are like "the moving water passing through the inside of a garden hose"
>And they flow through us to help guide our thoughts and actions throughout the day.

When the internal water passage within a garden hose is temporarily blocked,
>The nurturing of the garden will stop until the passage in the hose is re-opened.

Likewise, it's important to be mindfully aware of the different emotions present within us
>So our natural guidance system can serve us to maintain wellbeing and balance.

Occasionally during the day, stop for a moment to simply witness your emotions
>And, with an open heart, become aware of your **feelings regarding your body**,
>>So you may sense whether you accept the various aspects of your body,
>>>Or if you are unconsciously judgmental of some part of it.

Also be aware of your **positive or negative feelings about others or the events of life**,
>And if any of these feelings are generated from an unconscious habitual reaction.

Be aware of your feelings regarding **how it appears others approve or disapprove of you**,
>And sense whether or not it matters to you.

Of course, a very meaningful aspect of ***heart awareness*** is **how you feel about yourself**,
>And so sense if you accept yourself as you are, or if due to fear, you momentarily do not.

Simply bringing heightened awareness to what we're feeling each day through mindfulness
>Allows our emotions to pass through us more freely
>>So the ever-sustaining flow of *Love* can constantly nourish "the fruits of our life".

Circle of Heart Awareness
(A Transformative Practice)

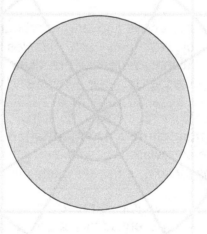

MY SELF-LOVE
I REMAIN AWARE OF MY
FEELINGS ABOUT MYSELF
SO I MAY SENSE WHETHER
I ACCEPT MYSELF JUST AS
I AM, OR IF BECAUSE
OF THE ILLUSION OF FEAR,
I MOMENTARILY DO NOT

MY BODY
I REMAIN AWARE
OF MY **FEELINGS**
REGARDING MY BODY
SO I MAY SENSE
WHETHER I ACCEPT
MY BODY AS IT IS, OR IF
I AM JUDGMENTAL OF IT

MY PERSONA
I REMAIN AWARE
OF MY **FEELINGS**
REGARDING WHETHER
OTHERS APPROVE
OR DISAPPROVE OF ME,
AND WHETHER OR NOT
IT MATTERS TO ME

ABOUT OTHERS
I REMAIN AWARE
OF MY **FEELINGS**
ABOUT OTHERS
SO I MAY SENSE
IF THESE FEELINGS ARISE
FROM AN UNCONSCIOUS
HABITUAL REACTION

CULTIVATING THE MIRACULOUS

I celebrate that the Universe is naturally "wired" to create miracles for me - and for everyone.

When professional housing contractors build new homes,
    They must first construct strong foundations on which to erect the new structures.

Through years of experience, they know that fashioning a proper foundation
    Is essential for building a well-built house.

In a similar way, if we desire "to set the stage" so we can receive more *miracles* in our life,
    In other words, if we expect to **cultivate the miraculous**,
        It's beneficial for us to prepare a proper foundation of awareness,
            Or a *miracle consciousness*, that will support our intended goal.

Miracles (in the traditional religious sense of the word)
    Are unfathomable divine events of transformation and healing
        Which seem to come from a celestial realm, from a domain beyond the known,
            From a hallowed place where it appears we have no personal control.

Yet as we continue to expand our awareness and learn what our life is truly about,
    We discover that there are many ways to *cultivate miracles* in our life
        Through a series of foundational awareness practices
            Which help us recognize the Universe is naturally "wired" for *miracles*.

Using the transformative practices
    Of **prayer**, **appreciation**, **contemplation**, and **meditation**,
        We can learn to resonate our awareness with *a morphic field of miracles*,
            Which is *the vast field of consciousness* many people simply call *Love*.

We can think of *miracle consciousness* as if it's a muscle that requires strengthening
    And, therefore, we can intentionally exercise this consciousness daily
        By making use of prayer to help keep our heart open,
            Expand our feelings of compassion and empathy,
                And send our love to others.

We can also **practice being aware to be grateful**
    For the transformative healing we intend to experience
        And, thus, knowing a *miracle* has already happened.

Another powerful practice is to **sustain an ongoing vision of certainty**
    Envisioning in the core of our being
        That *miracles* are natural - and anything is possible.

And we can, in the sanctuary of our heart through meditation or periods of silence,
    (And this is most important) align our awareness with *the Source of Life*,
        The Infinite Power of Love within us that's always at work creating *miracles*.

When "a strong foundation of an awareness that's limitless" is in place,
    We have the possibility and potential to help build a world filled with *everyday miracles*.

Circle of Cultivating the Miraculous
(In Relation to the Foundational Transformative Practices)

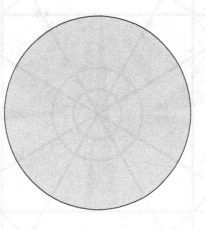

MEDITATION
TO CULTIVATE
THE MIRACULOUS,
I ALIGN MY AWARENESS
WITH *THE INFINITE POWER
OF LOVE*
IN THE SILENT SANCTUARY
OF MY HEART

PRAYER
TO CULTIVATE
THE MIRACULOUS,
I MAKE USE OF PRAYER
TO HELP KEEP MY HEART
OPEN, EXPAND MY
COMPASSION, AND SEND
MY LOVE TO OTHERS

CONTEMPLATION
TO CULTIVATE
THE MIRACULOUS,
I SUSTAIN A VISION
OF CERTAINTY IN WHICH
MIRACLES IN MY LIFE
ARE NATURAL - AND
ANTHING IS POSSIBLE

APPRECIATION
TO CULTIVATE
THE MIRACULOUS,
I GIVE THANKS
FOR MY TRANSFORMATIVE
HEALING
KNOWING A *MIRACLE*
HAS ALREADY HAPPENED

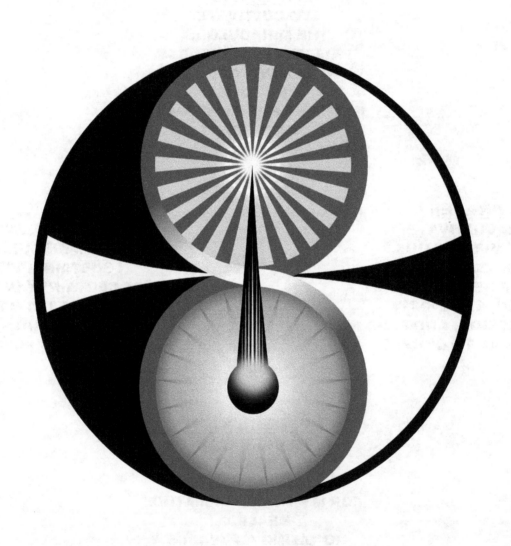

VIII

ARCHETYPES OF HIGHER KNOWLEDGE

THE GIFTS OF PAIN

The pain that I feel is also a gift in disguise which is in my life to teach me to love more fully.

When we watch an emotionally dramatic film in a theater, we may "lose ourselves" in the story
By getting totally caught up in the movie's sentiments - yet immediately after it's over,
We again remember we were simply looking at, or witnessing, a blank screen
Onto which a continuous sequence of moving images was projected.

Similarly each day, we encounter a series of internal and external experiences
That are, in a corresponding way, projected upon "the screen of our mind"
Such as our passing thoughts, our emotions, and our many physical sensations.

Sometimes, our physical sensations may be in the form of pain or discomfort,
Yet they are still temporary passing experiences, like clouds passing within a blue sky,
That we must either interpret, build a story around, or simply witness.

When we resist life the way it is - and build a personal story around our pain, we suffer,
Yet **witnessing our painful experiences and fully accepting them as they are
Offers us an opportunity to choose genuine peace of mind.**

In our everyday world, we tend to be culturally programmed by our modern society
That pain is to be covered over - and pleasure is to be sought after and held onto.

Of course no one wants to experience pain, and we must always try to alleviate it
When it enters our awareness - or when we observe it in the lives of others,
Yet pain is an essential and natural part of life that everyone encounters
And, if we remain open, pain can offer us specific kinds of "gifts".

Our pain gives us **an opportunity to learn to accept that our life is unfolding perfectly
Just as it is - without judgment or resistance**, for life simply is the way it is.

In the vast school of life, our pain can be an effective "teacher" to bring to our awareness
Any inner blockages that need to be removed so the flow of *Love* can circulate in us.

The whole Universe continues to evolve as a result of adapting to endless crisis and chaos,
And thus, is always looking for better creative solutions to solve its current challenges.

Our pain also gives us **opportunities to access new solutions and insights of creativity
As a natural response and way of dealing with the experience of pain**.

One of the greatest gifts pain has to offer us is "to bring us to our knees", so to speak,
And provide us the chance to **humbly surrender the illusions of our mind**
(Our unloving misperceptions of how we perceive the world and others)
To *the Source of Life, the Infinite Presence of Love,*
So we may consciously use our pain to learn to love more fully.

As we cultivate greater awareness of what our life is truly about - and what really matters,
Our encounters of pain can transform into benevolent gifts
That are actually in our life to teach us to love all of life unconditionally.

Circle of the Gifts of Pain

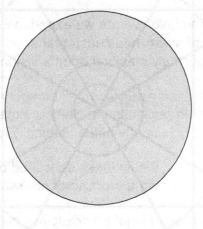

LOVE
**MY PAIN GIVES ME
AN OPPORTUNITY
TO SURRENDER
THE ILLUSIONS OF MY MIND
AND THEN CONSCIOUSLY
USE MY PAIN
TO LEARN TO LOVE
MORE FULLY**

THE WITNESS
**MY PAIN GIVES ME
AN OPPORTUNITY
TO WITNESS EACH OF MY
THOUGHTS, EMOTIONS,
AND SENSATIONS
WITHOUT ATTACHMENT
SO I MAY EXPERIENCE
GENUINE PEACE OF MIND**

ACCEPTANCE
**MY PAIN GIVES ME
AN OPPORTUNITY
TO ACCEPT
THAT MY LIFE IS
UNFOLDING PERFECTLY
JUST AS IT IS
- FOR LIFE SIMPLY IS
THE WAY IT IS**

CREATIVITY
**MY PAIN GIVES ME
AN OPPORTUNITY
TO ACCESS
NEW SOLUTIONS AND
INSIGHTS OF CREATIVITY
AS A NATURAL RESPONSE
TO DEALING
WITH THE PAIN**

EXTRAORDINARY MOMENTS OF AWARENESS

I recognize that every moment of this day has the possibility to be extraordinary.

For most of us, life is rich with both blessings as well as its occasional disturbing challenges
Since, obviously, we sometimes encounter various experiences that bring pain
Yet, fortunately, we also meet ample opportunities for much joy and happiness.

As we grow and learn how to face our challenges directly with courage and responsibility
Instead of fearfully running from them - or trying to cover them up,
We find there can be a *gift* in choosing to dive straight into our painful emotions.

When we're able to do this, the personal experience of fully embracing our pain
Can, sometimes, unexpectedly reveal to us an epiphanal moment of sublime **peace**.

Through *a sudden and spontaneous moment* of embracing *complete acceptance of what is*
(In other words - of fully accepting our experience of life just as it is without resistance),
We gracefully open ourselves to "a transcendent portal of possibility",
"A doorway to **ecstasy**", and a communion with *the Sacredness of Life.*

These brief periods of revered communion where we experience Oneness can be described
As **extraordinary moments of awareness**, instantaneous glimpses of awakening,
A personal epiphany surprisingly cracking open a vision of *an expanded reality.*

Epiphanies of this kind are hallowed moments when all thought stops,
Our mind becomes fully at rest, a realization of Unity is experienced,
And the one *Ultimate Reality* is briefly and ecstatically revealed.

Within these fleeting moments of *grace*, within these sanctified portals of eternity,
Shine the illuminating rays of hope and a promise of renewal.

Through *grace*, we are given a glimpse of what it's like to live *an awakened life* - for example:
To live in <u>gratitude</u> for what we're learning from each of our experiences,
To <u>surrender</u> everything to a *Greater Power* and let go of our attachments,
To <u>accept</u> that our life is unfolding perfectly just as it is,
And to be aware of our <u>Oneness</u> with all of life.

These are the spiritual attributes, or paths, that we're constantly being invited to travel
Which eventually lead us to *the sacred sanctuary within*
Where human suffering can be consciously transformed into inner freedom.

We are given the possibility of being transformed by these moments of higher consciousness,
By these **altered states** of expanded awareness,
In which our experience of ecstatic union
Suddenly attunes us to a vast ***Field of Infinite Creativity.***

Ultimately, as we grow spiritually and experience more frequent *glimpses of awakening,*
We discover these *spontaneous extraordinary moments* start to blend together
As they weave a tapestry of expanded awareness which begin to merge as one,
Until, at some point, we come to realize - "there are no ordinary moments".

Circle of Extraordinary Moments of Awareness
(Epiphanal Glimpses of Awakening)

ALTERED STATE
A MOMENT
OF AN ALTERED STATE
OF CONSCIOUSNESS
IN WHICH
I SPONTANEOUSLY
EXPERIENCE A STATE
OF BLISSFUL UNION

**INSPIRED
CREATIVITY**
A MOMENT
OF SACRED ALIGNMENT
WITH A VAST *FIELD
OF HIGHER AWARENESS*
THAT ATTUNES ME
TO INSPIRED
CREATIVITY

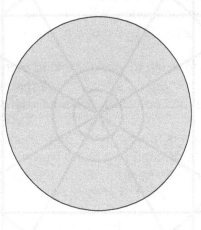

ECSTASY
A MOMENT
OF SUDDENLY REALIZING
COMPLETE ACCEPTANCE
OF WHAT IS
THAT GENERATES IN ME
DEEP ECSTASY
AND AN AWARENESS
OF ONENESS

SUBLIME PEACE
A MOMENT
OF PROFOUND SURRENDER
IN WHICH I FULLY
EMBRACE THE EXPERIENCE
OF MY PAIN - THAT
UNEXPECTEDLY REVEALS
TO ME SUBLIME PEACE

EXPERIENCES OF EPIPHANY

My search for the true, the good, and the beautiful is also about discovering who I really am.

Many of the revered mystics and sages from the numerous spiritual traditions of the world
(From Buddhism to Christianity - and from Taoism to Islam, to name a few)
Have given us written accounts about their direct mystical experiences
Of exploring a vast transcendent reality that they discovered within them.

When we take time to study the sacred writings of these mystics and sages
Which portray their intuitive leaps of spiritual understanding
And exalted insights into the interior realms that transcend the human mind,
They inform us of three primary types, or distinctions, of epiphany
(In other words, of *extraordinary moments of awareness*):
The epiphany of **truth**,
The epiphany of **goodness**,
And the epiphany of **beauty**.

The ancient mystics wanted to know *Absolute Truth*
And so they engaged in a deep inquiry into what truth is,
Which led to an abundant array of questions about the greater nature of reality.

In the fullness of time, this search for truth inspired the kind of inquiry and questioning
That, over thousands of years, produced specific systems of investigations into reality
Which gradually **matured into common form as the many fields of science**.

The fundamental purpose of science is to search for, and discover, the truth of what is
(Which is the knowledge and understanding of the true nature of reality)
And then to explain the intricate secrets of how the patterns of Nature work,
Which, for some, also include the study of a *Transcendent Unified Field*.

The search for goodness, in other words - for how to best live in harmony with one another,
Revealed a natural moral compass that abides within the heart of every person.

Over time, the longing to determine what is essentially "good" inspired a series of explorations
Regarding the best ways to live together, in families, communities, nations, and globally,
As well as how to effectively and fairly govern these societies,
Which eventually **led to the various distinctive forms of philosophy**.

The fundamental search for what is beautiful also emerged from an instinctive impulse,
A yearning to create a more satisfying life and to creatively express one's feelings
By putting into form what communicates joy, pleasure, and an inner fulfillment,
Which ultimately **became the myriad expressions of art**.

The existential quest within all people to find each of these individual **epiphanal experiences**
Was recognized by the mystics as identical to one's quest to realize one's *True Nature*
And to be aware of a Oneness with all of *Life*, referred to as **transcendence**.

In other words - our perpetual search for the true, the good, and the beautiful is the same
As our *spiritual journey - our journey of awakening* to discover who we really are.

Circle of the Experiences of Epiphany

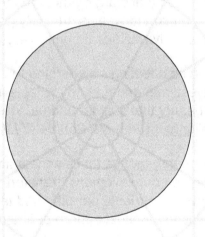

SPIRITUAL
THE EPIPHANY OF
TRANSCENDENCE
CAN EMERGE FROM
MY "MYSTICAL
PRACTICES" AND FROM
ECSTATIC MOMENTS
OF PROFOUND UNION

PHYSICAL
THE EPIPHANY OF
TRUTH
CAN EMERGE FROM
MY "SCIENTIFIC
INQUIRIES" IN WHICH
I EXPERIMENT WITH
BETTER WAYS TO LIVE

MENTAL
THE EPIPHANY OF
GOODNESS
CAN EMERGE FROM
MY "PHILOSOPHICAL
INVESTIGATIONS"
INTO HOW BEST
TO LIVE WITH OTHERS

EMOTIONAL
THE EPIPHANY OF
BEAUTY
CAN EMERGE FROM
MY "ARTISTIC
EXPRESSIONS" IN WHICH
I ACCESS MY INNATE
FLOW OF CREATIVITY

ARCHETYPES OF HIGHER KNOWLEDGE
There is a yearning in me that constantly invites me to create the person I envision I can be.

It's a fact of science that every person (whether they're aware of it or not)
  Is constantly encountering various invisible forces of universal energies
    Which harmlessly and unnoticeably pass right through their physical bodies.

For example, there is a force of gravity from Earth that's always pulling on each of us
  As well as a subtle force of magnetism that's ever streaming through our bodies
    Which is produced by huge layers of molten lava deep within the Earth
      Spinning around a solid iron core that generates a massive magnetic field.

We are also subject to the cyclic gravitational effects of the orbiting Moon
  And numerous kinds of *cosmic rays* that pass undetected through our body
    Which benignly beam down on our planet from the distant depths of space.

And in a similar way, there is a natural *Impulse of Universal Energy* called *Transcendence*,
  An invisible force vibrating within us that's urging us to reach for something greater
    In an attempt to explore and expand what is humanly possible,
      And this impulse perpetually radiates though every cell of our being.

This innate impulse activates within us a feeling - a yearning to:
  1) Discover what is <u>true</u>, 2) investigate and embody what is inherently <u>good</u> in life,
    3) Be more aware of the <u>beauty</u> that's all around us,
      And 4) maintain an <u>alignment</u> with *the Source of Life*.

There is also a *Universal Impulse of Immanence* that's constantly vibrating through us
  Which is urging us to move beyond our limitations, transform our unloving beliefs,
    Express our unique creativity, contribute our gifts and talents,
      And live a life that helps to manifest a more peaceful world.

The interweaving of these two intrinsic impulses *(Transcendence and Immanence)*
  Generates four streams, or patterns of archetypal qualities,
    Which all people, in time, can learn to embody and express in their lives.

From the influence of these two impulses, we sense a natural desire to use effective ways
  To maintain an alignment with *the Source of Life* so we may truly serve others,
    And this primary pattern of human development is called **the Awakened Mystic**.

These impulses also enliven in us a yearning to foster heart wisdom
  So as to manifest the most harmonious, <u>good</u>, and meaningful ways to live together,
    And we will refer to this moral stream of energy as **the Awakened Philosopher**.

The yearning to live life as an expression of <u>beauty</u> is the impulse of **the Awakened Artist**,
  And the longing to dedicate our life as a living experiment to discover greater awareness
    Of the <u>true</u> nature of reality is the universal template of **the Awakened Scientist**.

These four archetypal patterns, whether we're yet mindfully aware of them or not,
  Are constantly flowing through us inviting us to create the person we envision we can be.

Circle of the Archetypes of Higher Knowledge

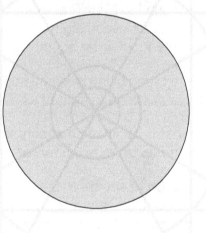

AWAKENED MYSTIC
IT IS THE PART OF ME THAT USES EFFECTIVE WAYS TO MAINTAIN AN ALIGNMENT WITH *THE SOURCE OF LIFE* SO I CAN TRULY BE OF SERVICE TO OTHERS

AWAKENED SCIENTIST
IT IS THE PART OF ME THAT DEDICATES MY LIFE AS A LIVING EXPERIMENT SO I MAY GAIN GREATER AWARENESS OF THE *TRUTH* (WHAT IS BELIEVED TO BE UNDENIABLY TRUE)

AWAKENED PHILOSOPHER
IT IS THE PART OF ME THAT FOSTERS HEART WISDOM SO I MAY ESTABLISH THE MOST HARMONIOUS, *GOOD*, AND MEANINGFUL WAYS TO LIVE WITH OTHERS

AWAKENED ARTIST
IT IS THE PART OF ME THAT CULTIVATES ABUNDANT WAYS TO ENJOY AND EXPERIENCE "LIFE AS AN ART - AND AS A CREATIVE EXPRESSION OF *BEAUTY*"

AWAKENED ARTIST

Today I consciously live my life as a creative expression of beauty with everything I do.

Most children find it easy and fun to get out their paper, crayons, and colored pencils
And freely express their raw creativity through their unpretentious drawings.

Of course all children don't have the same degree of artistic talent,
But they all seem to share a basic intrinsic desire to creatively express themselves,
Fashion something new, and manifest their unique notion of beauty into form.

For various reasons, adults sometimes lose this vital connection with their innate creativity
When life gets bogged down with the mundane concerns of living,
Yet a desire to express one's natural artistry can always be rekindled.

As we cultivate more elevated levels of awareness by connecting with what really matters,
By expanding our understanding of what our life is truly about,
And by becoming more open vehicles for *Life Force energy* to flow through us,
We begin to develop a heightened sensitivity to our environment
And may notice new subtleties such as colors becoming more vivid,
The shapes around us becoming more pronounced,
And new patterns of order becoming more obvious.

When we're truly aligned with *Life*, the organic patterns and intricate relationships of Nature
Can seem as if they're magically appearing in front of us everywhere we go.

The archetype of **the Awakened Artist** is an image that can be used to expand our creativity
By helping us **learn to live our life as *an expression of beauty* with all that we do**.

It assists us to **be a creative expression of the heart, the transcendent, and the sublime,
In all the ways we're guided to contribute our unique gifts to the world**,
Reminding us we're all an integral part of one unfolding spiral of consciousness.

From a visionary point of view, to be **an Awakened Artist**
Is to **live our life with the awakened perception that everything we do
Is a creative expression of "life as art"**.

Everything in our homes, in our places of work, in our cities, and what we wear on our body,
Hold the possibility of becoming a novel expression of beauty.

Moreover, to be **an Awakened Artist** is to mindfully use our life to **express into form
The glorious future that we imagine is possible for all people**,
A vision of our world's potential expressed into practical forms of artistic living.

But to embody these expanded qualities usually requires greater awareness, an open heart,
Determination, and vigilance to develop our individual potential,
As well as maintaining an alignment with *the Source of Life*.

Ultimately, as a true **Awakened Artist**, we discover there is beauty to be creatively expressed
In every step we take, in every breath we breathe, and in everything we do.

Circle of the Awakened Artist
(An Archetype of Higher Knowledge)

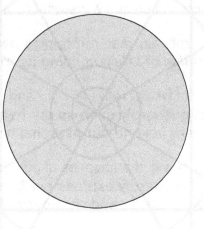

BEAUTY
I CHOOSE
TO LIVE MY LIFE
EACH DAY
AS AN EXPRESSION
OF BEAUTY
WITH EVERYTHING
I'M GUIDED TO MANIFEST

EXPRESSION
I CHOOSE
TO LIVE MY LIFE
WITH THE AWAKENED
PERCEPTION THAT
EVERYTHING I DO IS
A CREATIVE EXPRESSION
OF "LIFE AS ART"

CREATIVITY
I CHOOSE
TO BE A CREATIVE
EXPRESSION
OF THE HEART,
THE TRANSCENDENT,
AND THE SUBLIME,
IN EVERYTHING I DO

IMAGINATION
I CHOOSE
TO EXPRESS
INTO CREATIVE FORM
THE GLORIOUS FUTURE
THAT I IMAGINE
IS POSSIBLE
FOR ALL PEOPLE

THE NATURAL IMPULSE OF CREATIVITY

The Natural Creative Impulse that I feel in me is constantly inviting me to fully love all of life.

If you were to take time to keenly observe the myriad wonders of Nature
    Everywhere you look you would see a strong impulse to express endless creativity.

For example, within a tiny acorn is an innate creative impulse
    To break through its outer casing, push through the moist darkness of soil,
        Reach for the nurturing light of the Sun, and grow skywards into a tall oak tree.

A baby bird upon hatching from its egg
    Feels the natural drive to eat, nourish its frail body, and grow strong
        So it can eventually leap from the nest and freely soar through the heavens.

Male peacocks are continually evolving ever more intricate and colorful feathers
    Which adorn their bodies and are used to attract a mate.

Of course, we humans have also been blessed to feel this **natural impulse of creativity**,
    And this yearning expresses itself in unique ways within our <u>body</u>, <u>heart</u>, and <u>mind</u>.

There is an intrinsic drive to **outwardly express our <u>mind's</u> natural yearning**
    To do what *the Creative Impulse of Life* is guiding us to do or accomplish.

If we spend time listening to the quiet whispers within our heart,
    We may sense an inner call to **outwardly express our <u>heart's</u> yearning to give**
        And be in service to others beyond our personal needs and concerns.

As we pay close attention and attune with the energies of our physical body,
    We may feel an innate drive to **outwardly express our <u>body's</u> natural yearning**
        To productively move our bodies - and connect with our environment.

Each impulse is an aspect of our primary drive to **express our <u>*True Nature's*</u> yearning**
    To fully love all people - and all of life.

The artistic expressions of dance, painting, music, and other art forms,
    Or the urge to create architectural masterpieces, or to climb a majestic mountain,
        Contain no important function that supports and benefits
            The inborn drive regarding our instinctual physical survival.

These creative expressions are not fundamentally necessary for our survival,
    Yet we produce them in response to a **natural creative impulse**
        That drives us forward toward our pursuit for more **awareness** and cooperation,
            Greater **service** to others, expanded connection with our **inner guidance**,
            And a ceaseless longing to **fully love all of life**.

As we cultivate a commitment to passionately express our unique creativity,
    We find that at the same time, we are moving in sync with *the Song of the Universe*
        Which resounds deep within us, constantly inviting us to dance to its *melodies*
            And rapturously sing its *sacred song of Limitless Love*.

Circle of the Natural Impulse of Creativity

LOVE
THE INNATE DRIVE
TO OUTWARDLY EXPRESS
MY *TRUE NATURE'S*
YEARNING
TO FULLY LOVE
ALL PEOPLE
AND ALL OF LIFE

BODY AWARENESS
THE INNATE DRIVE
TO OUTWARDLY
EXPRESS MY BODY'S
NATURAL YEARNING
TO CREATIVELY MOVE
MY BODY - AND CONNECT
WITH MY ENVIRONMENT

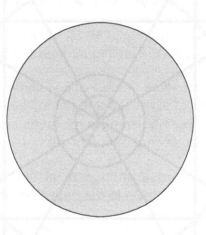

INNER GUIDANCE
THE INNATE DRIVE
TO OUTWARDLY
EXPRESS MY MIND'S
NATURAL YEARNING
TO DO WHAT *THE
CREATIVE IMPULSE OF
LIFE* GUIDES ME TO DO

SERVICE
THE INNATE DRIVE
TO OUTWARDLY EXPRESS
MY HEART'S NATURAL
YEARNING
TO GIVE TO, AND SERVE,
THE WELLBEING
OF OTHERS

BEAUTY

I keep my heart open so I can experience more of the natural beauty that's all around me.

Physical beauty is to be found everywhere around us, both in Nature and in our modern world,
>Yet, of course, we must "open our eyes" if we want to see it
>>For experiencing the abundant beauty of the planet is in the eye of the beholder
>>>And requires us "to open the eyes of the heart".

Beauty can be thought of as our recognition that a high level of natural order or pattern
>Has been expressed and observed within some facet of the physical world,
>>**A natural order that inspires us and brings pleasure to our senses**.

So, for example, if we decide one day we would like to experience more beauty in our life,
>One way to accomplish this is to learn "to expand the appreciative edges of our heart".

As we find ways to deepen our gratitude, expand our awareness of what really matters,
>And live in the present moment where all true experiences of beauty reside,
>>Our world becomes more alive with colors, shapes, sounds, and perceptions.

One person may look at a common clump of dirt and not think it's very beautiful
>Because he or she is seeing it from the limited perspective that it's simply *ordinary*.

Yet another person could look at this same sample of soil under a high-powered microscope
>And observe an amazing world of aliveness and natural beauty,
>>An entire community of incredibly inventive microbes and bacteria
>>>Living together in a magnificent dance of harmony and mutual creation.

If you were to view a terrorist from a remote vantage point, such as a TV news program,
>From this distance, you might not be able to recognize his or her intrinsic beauty.

But if you could take the time to get to know this person and genuinely empathize with their life,
>You may perceive a very different perspective of an individual attempting and struggling
>>To free him or herself from fear, just as in our own way, we all do the best we can
>>>To free ourselves from our personal illusions of limitation and fear.

When we can look intimately into the *heart* of another with a wider circle of compassion,
>We create a greater opportunity to experience the inherent beauty within them.

As we view our world from this "Bigger Picture" and from a more empathetic perspective,
>We're able to observe more of the pattern and beauty that constantly exists around us.

Beauty can also be seen as **the perception of the sublime** that comes from being aware
>Of "the higher waves of our emotional spectrum" - such as joy, happiness, or peace.

The more awakened awareness we've achieved from our conscious inner development,
>The more beauty we are able to experience in our life.

The more loving service we offer others, the more natural it is to open our heart even further
>And, therefore, **the more beauty within life we're able to enjoy each day.**

Circle of Beauty

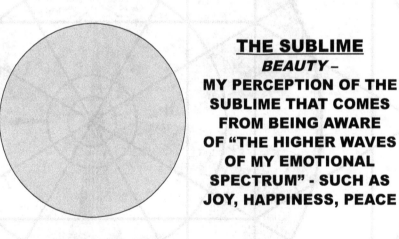

PLEASURE
BEAUTY –
**THE INHERENT QUALITY
OF AN OBJECT
OR AN ENVIRONMENT
THAT INSPIRES ME
AND BRINGS
PLEASURE
TO MY SENSES**

JOY
BEAUTY –
**THE ATTAINMENT
OF TRANSCENDENTJOY
THAT COMES
FROM VISUALLY
DELIGHTING IN
CERTAIN KINDS OF
PLEASING EXPERIENCES**

THE SUBLIME
BEAUTY –
**MY PERCEPTION OF THE
SUBLIME THAT COMES
FROM BEING AWARE
OF "THE HIGHER WAVES
OF MY EMOTIONAL
SPECTRUM" - SUCH AS
JOY, HAPPINESS, PEACE**

NATURAL ORDER
BEAUTY –
**THE RECOGNITION
THAT A HIGH LEVEL
OF NATURAL ORDER
OR PATTERN
HAS BEEN EXPRESSED
WITHIN SOME FACET
OF THE PHYSICAL WORLD**

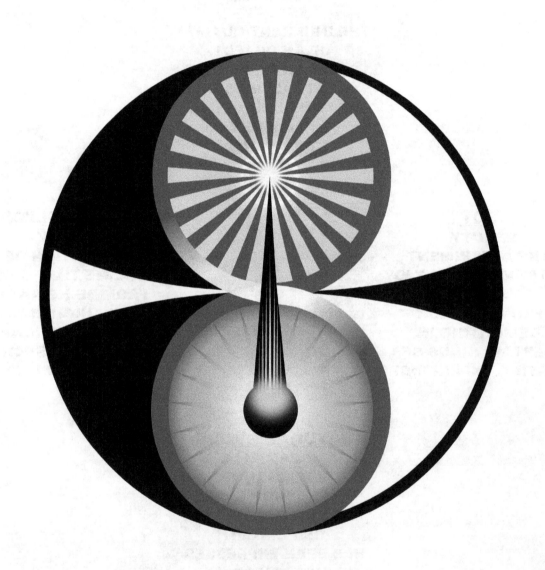

IX

HEART AWARENESS PRACTICES

AUGUST 6
<u>AWAKENING THE INNER ARTIST</u>

Focusing my energy on what I'm passionate about helps me to cultivate my creative potential.

There may be periods of time during your life in which you notice
That, for whatever reason, *"the creative artist within you"* seems to be absent or stifled.

If this occurs, there's an innate impulse within you yearning to re-access your natural creativity
And to achieve that, there are three choices you can make to transform the situation.

First, you simply choose to be **willing** to change or develop yourself in relation to your situation,
Second, you choose an **intention** to focus greater creativity in some area of your life,
And third, you choose to take a specific action by **practicing** a specific art form.

Initially, if we make a decision to **be willing to change our self-limiting beliefs**
About the things in our life we believe we cannot do,
This choice can help us open to countless possibilities of our creative potential.

Yet we don't need to know exactly how this change will happen,
Since we only need *to be willing* for it to transform into something new and expressive.

The simple act of surrendering to the unknown - and being willing to trust in the mystery of life
Sets powerful forces in motion.

Next, we can decide to **set a clear intention for our creative goal**,
Whether we choose to engage in a particular art form, or a hobby, or a strong desire,
And then focus each day on our heartfelt vision of what we intend to create.

In order to strengthen our intention, we can visualize powerful images within our mind's eye
Of all the various ways we would like to express more of our unique form of creativity.

Finally, we can choose to generate the time, energy, and commitment necessary
So that we **take action toward our goal - and put our intention into actual practice**.

Daily or weekly practice is an important component of inner development,
And so it's of great benefit for us to be consistent with our discipline.

You could choose a special form of creativity that passionately enlivens your *inner artist*
Such as painting, sculpting, dance, creative hobbies, building furniture,
Or it could be as simple as planting a few flowers in your yard,
Finding a sport to share with friends, learning to play a musical instrument,
Or even redecorating your home.

When we align **willingness**, **intention**, and **practice** in order to **awaken our *inner artist***,
We open our heart to the natural yearning in us to see, touch, hear, and communicate
More of the intrinsic beauty and creativity that *Life* wants to express through us.

Choosing an individual creative art form to practice
Is like initially priming an old-fashioned water pump with a little water
In order to get the natural flow of creativity to stream forth in all facets of our life.

Circle of Awakening the Inner Artist
(A Transformative Practice)

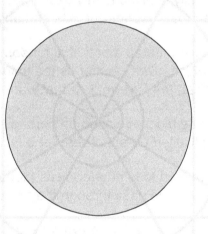

SOUND
+ MUSIC
+ SINGING
+ DRUMMING
A YEARNING
TO EXPRESS BEAUTY
THROUGH
THE CRAFTING OF SOUND

FORM
+DANCE
+ SCULPTURE
+ ARCHITECTURE
A YEARNING
TO EXPRESS BEAUTY
THROUGH
THE DESIGN OF FORM

LANGUAGE
+ POETRY
+ STORIES
+ LITERATURE
A YEARNING
TO EXPRESS BEAUTY
BY SHAPING
LANGUAGE

COLOR
+ ART
+ PHOTOGRAPHY
+ FLOWER GARDENS
A YEARNING
TO EXPRESS BEAUTY
BY WEAVING COLORS
AND PATTERNS

CULTIVATING AN OPEN HEART

Today I keep my heart open so I may feel the Universal River of Life flow through me.

The Infinite Source of Life can also be poetically expressed as *the Universal River of Life*
   That perpetually flows through "the open canyons of our hearts",
      For it is the unlimited stream of *Life Force energy* that animates and nourishes
         All people and every living thing on Earth.

But, for various reasons, should "the canyons of our heart get blocked"
   By "the boulders of illusion" we habitually self-create with our fearful thoughts,
      Then "the mighty *River of Life Force*" can no longer flow through us unimpeded.

For most of the diverse creatures that live instinctually within the wilds of Nature,
   The Universal River of Life is experienced through them as an effortless movement
      Because they have not, as humans have, developed an egoic mind
         That can, consciously or unconsciously, impede this natural flow.

We, as Homo sapiens, have gradually evolved highly developed minds
   Which, in time, have produced many wonderful gifts and abilities to benefit our planet.

Yet our mental development has also created a potential for some pathological characteristics
   Due to our power of choice, which gives each of us the unique ability to choose
      To either align with, or resist, *the River of Life* that wants to circulate within us.

The natural flow of *Life Force* can be blocked based on certain kinds of choices we make,
   Choices that are derived from limited perspectives - or a lack of conscious awareness.

Lack of awareness (ignorance) can lead to inferior choices that are like kinks in a garden hose
   Which don't allow the flow of water to pass through the hose.

When we remove the "kinks" by cultivating a loving awareness using transformative practices
   Such as the practice of **prayer**, **appreciation**, **contemplation**, or **meditation**,
      We can deepen our awareness of how to consciously cultivate an open heart.

A powerful way to keep *the Universal River of Life* streaming through our heart
   Is **to pray for the health and wellbeing of the people in our life**.

Being conscious of **living life with an attitude of gratitude** in every situation that arises
   Is also a valuable way to foster an open heart.

Furthermore, when we are mindfully aware of the quality of our thinking,
   We can more easily **choose thoughts that are life-affirming and self-empowering**.

And to sustain an open heart, we can **take time throughout the day to pause in silence**
   So as to strengthen and maintain our alignment with *the Source of All That Is*.

The River of Life, which is *Limitless Love* (the unbounded *Life Force* within the Universe),
   Can more easily be felt flowing through us with its nourishing and radiant energy
      When we're able to consciously keep our heart wide open.

Circle of Cultivating an Open Heart
(Transformative Practices)

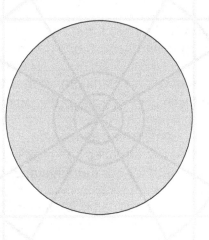

MEDITATION
TO CULTIVATE
AN OPEN HEART,
I TAKE TIME
THROUGHOUT THE DAY
TO PAUSE IN SILENCE
AND ALIGN WITH *LIFE*

PRAYER
TO CULTIVATE
AN OPEN HEART,
I PRAY FOR
THE HEALTH
AND WELLBEING OF
THE PEOPLE IN MY LIFE

CONTEMPLATION
TO CULTIVATE
AN OPEN HEART,
I REMAIN
MINDFULLY AWARE
OF THE QUALITY
OF MY THINKING

APPRECIATION
TO CULTIVATE
AN OPEN HEART,
I CONSCIOUSLY
LIVE MY LIFE
WITH AN ATTITUDE
OF GRATITUDE

AFFIRMATIONS FOR PRIMARY EMOTIONAL NEEDS

I feel safe, loved, empowered, and connected with the beauty and goodness within all of life.

If you pour a full glass of water through your open fingers,
　　It won't feel like an effective tool to be used for carving,
　　　　At least not for carving a wooden object - or for sculpting a clay statue.

Sculptors make use of special tools like chisels, rasps, and small hammers
　　To help them form the contours of their artistic masterpieces.

Yet if a steady flow of water runs over a flat rocky surface in the same location for a long time,
　　It will begin to carve a winding groove (and potentially a canyon) through the solid rock.

The constructive transformation of our personal awareness requires constant choices,
　　Sometimes choices to travel a much different path than one we've previously traveled.

There are basically two kinds of choices we make every day - conscious and unconscious,
　　Depending on the level of our awareness and our acuity of mindfulness.

As humans, our invitation from *Life* is to learn to bring awareness to our choices
　　And to shift from habitually living in an *unconscious* manner to one that is *conscious*.

An awareness tool we can use to support this transformation is the practice of *affirmations*
　　Which can help us cultivate a more developed expression of ourselves.

Certain affirmations, used as a daily transformative practice,
　　Are like waves of water which steadily run over "the rock of our habitual thinking"
　　　　And, over time, carve a new path for our thoughts and feelings to travel.

As evolving human beings, we all have *primary emotional needs* that we strive to attain
　　In order to experience greater wellbeing, harmony, and peace.

All of us have an intrinsic yearning throughout our lives to feel <u>safe</u>, <u>loved</u>, <u>empowered</u>,
　　And <u>connected</u> with the goodness and beauty within all of life.

So if we desire to deepen the experience of these feelings,
　　We can use affirmations "to form a new groove" regarding the way we feel and respond,
　　　　Such as the **four affirmations for our primary emotional needs** listed below
　　　　　　That can be utilized each day as a powerful practice.

I feel safe in the protective arms of *Life*,
　　I feel loved by the entire Universe,
　　　　I feel empowered by all of creation,
　　　　　　I feel connected to the heart of Nature.

When we consistently use these affirmations,
　　"The River of Life" can slowly carve another kind of "canyon within our heart",
　　　　One that makes a receptive path for <u>safety</u>, <u>love</u>, <u>empowerment</u>, and <u>connection</u>
　　　　　　To consciously flow into "the new grooves of our life".

Circle of Affirmations for Primary Emotional Needs
(A Transformative Practice)

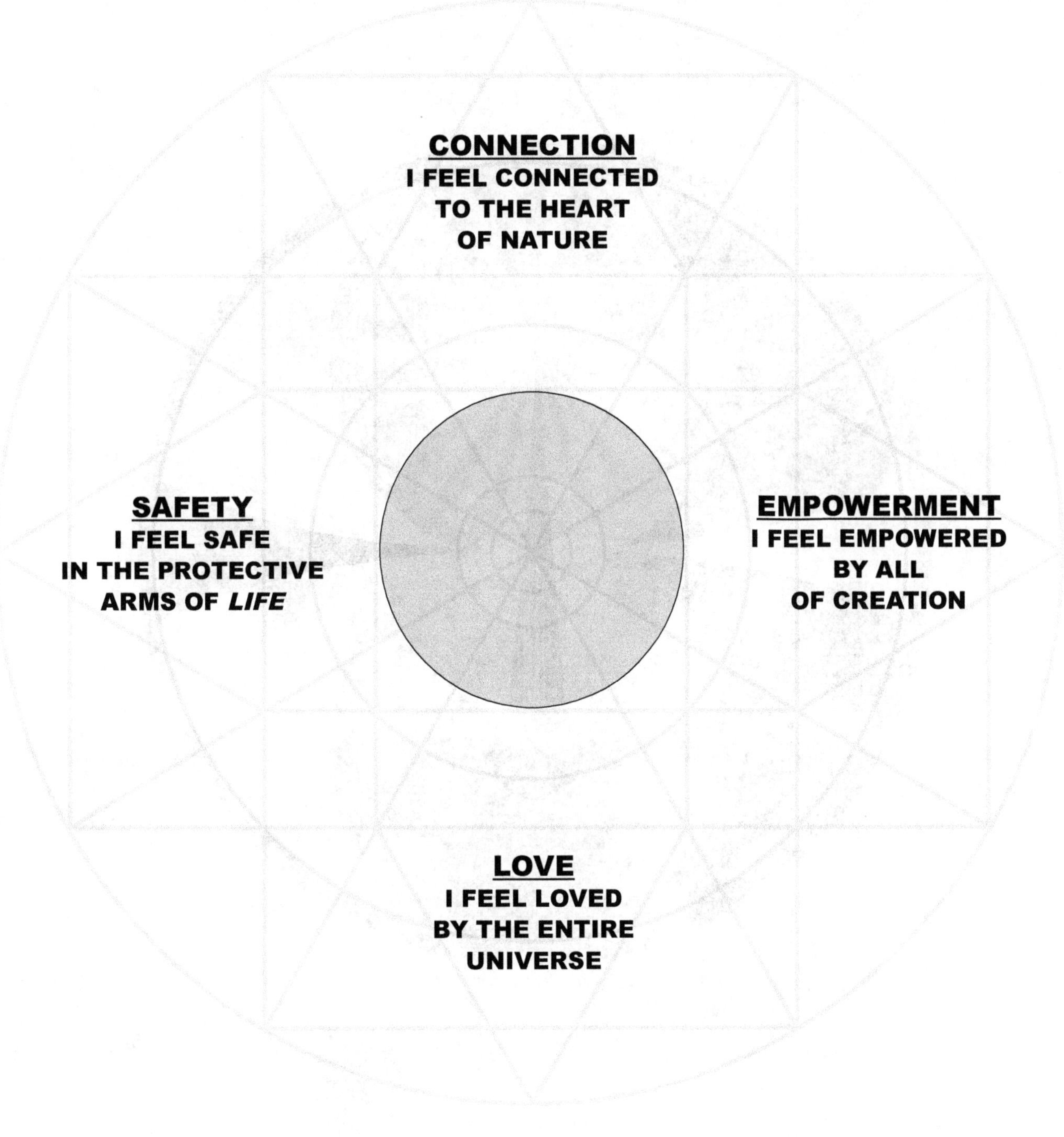

CONNECTION
I FEEL CONNECTED
TO THE HEART
OF NATURE

SAFETY
I FEEL SAFE
IN THE PROTECTIVE
ARMS OF *LIFE*

EMPOWERMENT
I FEEL EMPOWERED
BY ALL
OF CREATION

LOVE
I FEEL LOVED
BY THE ENTIRE
UNIVERSE

X

THE EVOLUTIONARY PERSPECTIVE

GIFTS FROM AN EVOLUTIONARY PERSPECTIVE
Embracing a "Big Picture perspective" helps me to cultivate compassionate service to others.

When a business executive working in a tall multi-floor office building
    Is feeling frustrated or overwhelmed by the challenges of the moment,
        He or she might take a needed break from the business at hand
            To ascend to the roof of the building
                And look out over the city streets below
                    In order to get a larger perspective of the situation.

To experience a much bigger vantage, a hiker can climb to the peak of a tall mountain
    And gaze out from there into the panoramic landscape,
        Which can sometimes help to place the meaning of life in a wider context.

Going a bit further outward, we have all seen the stunning images of planet Earth
    Which were photographed by astronauts from orbiting spacecrafts,
        And have experienced the shift in perspective
            That comes from looking at our home planet from space,
                Seeing a world without dividing fences, borders, or national flags.

Now, let's go even farther out by visualizing for a moment that you are an intuitive scientist,
    Someone who has developed a strong insightful imagination such as Albert Einstein,
        And then simply project your inner awareness to "the center of the Universe".

From this "supreme vantage point"
    (Using this expanded perspective and your imagined intuitive sensibilities)
        You could then observe a 360-degree vista of our vast evolving Universe
            And intuit there's a *Natural Intelligence* seeking ever-greater development
                Of diversity, inclusion, and cooperation which **awakens the joy**
                    Of even further personal development.

From this mammoth view you might also realize that every individual facet of creation
    Is an integral part of a whole unified system, one perpetually evolving Universe,
        Which then inspires you to maintain an alignment with *the Source of Life*
            And contribute to evolution with **responsible and integrous actions**.

Someone mindfully taking in this "Big Picture perspective" could perceive a clear vision
    Of the personal thoughts and actions which support life - and also those which do not,
        And this larger vision can motivate one to **transform an old way of living life**
        Into an awakened life that serves the wellbeing of others.

And from this expansive vantage where one can more fully understand the larger purpose
    And interdependent relationships of *the evolutionary perspective of life*,
        One might discover a deep sense of empathy for others
            And a **greater compassion for all of the myriad creatures on Earth**.

Each day, *Life* is constantly presenting us with an invitation to go to "the roof of our world",
    The place where we embrace a larger perspective of what's truly important,
        The sacred place within us where we consciously experience who we really are.

Circle of Gifts From An Evolutionary Perspective

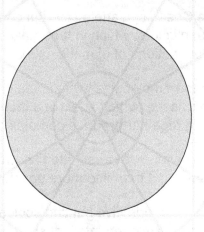

INTEGRITY
**REALIZING EVERYTHING
IS AN INTEGRAL PART OF
A PERPETUALLY EVOLVING
UNIVERSE EMPOWERS ME
TO ALIGN WITH *LIFE*
AND LIVE WITH INTEGRITY
+*GIFT – CREATES A VISION
OF LIVING WITH INTEGRITY***

DEVELOPMENT
**KNOWING THAT ALL
OF EVOLVING LIFE HAS
A NATURAL IMPULSE
TO LEARN INSPIRES ME
TO FURTHER DEVELOP
MY OWN POTENTIAL
+*GIFT – AWAKENS A JOY
TO DEVELOP MYSELF***

TRANSFORMATION
**EMBRACING "THE BIG
PICTURE" PROVIDES ME
CLARITY CONCERNING
MY THOUGHTS WHICH
SUPPORT LIFE - AND
THOSE WHICH DO NOT
+*GIFT – MOTIVATES ME
TO TRANSFORM MYSELF***

COMPASSION
***THE EVOLUTIONARY
PERSPECTIVE* HELPS ME
FEEL EMPATHY
FOR ANOTHER - AND LIVE
A COMPASSIONATE LIFE
THAT SERVES OTHERS
+*GIFT – CULTIVATES IN ME
COMPASSIONATE SERVICE***

EVOLUTION OF COMPASSION

The Natural Intelligence within me is constantly inviting me to cultivate greater compassion.

If you throw a pebble into a still pond, it produces a series of waves on the water's surface
In the form of many concentric circles - first one, then another, then three, four, etc. -
That travel outward from the center of the impact until it covers the entire pond.

"The Big Picture perspective" that *a science-based knowledge of evolution* provides us with
Can be likened to expanding concentric circles on the surface of a pond
Which get larger over time, for as we learn more about the science of evolution,
This understanding can help us cultivate greater compassion for all of life.

As we invite into our open mind "the larger vantage of *the evolutionary perspective*"
And comprehend more of the universal dynamics that affect our life,
We can, more easily, discover how we and all other sentient beings
Are integral parts of this "Big Picture of life" evolving together on Earth,
And thus learn to truly understand how interconnected we are.

If we look at *the macro view* of the Cosmos, planets are vital components of solar systems,
Solar systems are parts of star clusters, which in turn make up massive galaxies,
And galaxies shape the foundations of gigantic galaxy clusters.

At *the micro view* of reality, atoms form molecules, which then create individual cells,
Which are part of living organic tissue, which again is a facet of larger organ systems,
And these systems working together produce complex organisms.

Single-cell organisms, over billions of years, evolved into fish, which morphed into mammals,
Which eventually led to primates, and then into more developed creatures like humans.

Social groups also evolved, for example, primitive hunting societies led to agricultural societies,
Which, over long periods of time, developed into industrial and information societies,
And potentially will lead our world, one day, to "a more enlightened society".

The above progressions provide context from which we can see where we humans came from,
How we are all connected as one global family, and where humanity might be headed.

From this grand vantage, we can deepen our understanding
That **the circle of unfolding compassion** within *the heart of humanity*
Is also expanding in a natural evolving progression from **family**, to **community**,
To **nation**, and, with time, will eventually embrace **the entire world**.

We live in a momentous time in which each of us has an important responsibility
To cultivate, within ourselves, greater compassion and empathy for others
So we may together create an experience of greater peace on Earth.

"The first pebble of human compassion was metaphorically thrown into the pond long ago"
And its concentric waves have been traveling outward upon the vast Ocean of Life,
Yet it is you and I, and all who choose to love with every choice we make,
That keeps the ripples of compassion growing ever-larger.

Circle of the Evolution of Compassion

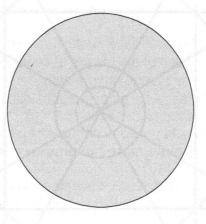

ONENESS
ULTIMATELY,
"INFINITE COMPASSION"
IS THE NATURAL
YEARNING TO REALIZE
AN AWARENESS
OF ONENESS WITH EVERY
FACET OF EXISTENCE

FAMILY
INITIALLY, COMPASSION
MAY BE EXPRESSED AS
A NATURAL YEARNING
FOR THE CONCERN
AND WELLBEING
OF ONE'S
IMMEDIATE FAMILY

WORLD
IN TIME WITH GREATER
DEVELOPMENT,
COMPASSION
MAY EVOLVE INTO
A NATURAL YEARNING
TO BE IN SERVICE TO
ALL SENTIENT BEINGS

COMMUNITY
THEN, COMPASSION
MAY EVOLVE INTO
A NATURAL YEARNING
TO BE IN SERVICE
TO EVER LARGER
COMMUNITIES, REGIONS,
OR ONE'S NATION

THE FRACTAL NATURE OF EMERGENT EVOLUTION

I am a small but integral part of the Universe that's learning to love all of life unconditionally.

Most people have seen the intriguing image of a *hologram,*
    Possibly in a scene from a science fiction movie or TV show,
        Or by enjoying the educational exhibits of a contemporary science museum.

One specific form of a hologram is a photographic image
    Which has been recorded on a flat holographic plate
        That produces a three-dimensional image when a light source is projected on it.

A unique aspect of a hologram (which provides us with a metaphor for *emergent evolution)*
    Is that when you break the initial holographic plate into smaller fragments
        And shine a focused light source like a laser on just one of the smaller pieces,
            It will display the entire image of the original hologram -
                Only the image will be slightly weaker in intensity.

If you were to keep breaking the holographic plate fragments into smaller and smaller pieces,
    Every time a light is projected on one, the entire original image will always be there.

Some progressive contemporary scientists have postulated that "the Universe is holographic",
    And what is meant here is that each of the stages of evolution throughout the Cosmos
        Retains the totality of the evolutionary information
            Of all the previous stages of development, but with additional variations.

This universal phenomenon of retaining previous patterns of information from stage to stage
    Can also be referred to as **the fractal nature of emergent evolution.**

Our Solar System was formed from the dynamic forces operating within the Milky Way Galaxy,
    And these evolutionary forces are constantly seeking greater creativity and cooperation.

The Earth is a fractal expression, a similar pattern formed from a supernova explosion
    And retains all of the previous evolutionary information since the birth of the Universe.

From the emergence of the Earth, evolution formed another fractal by producing biological life,
    Which eventually developed into **humans**, repeating a similar pattern of the living Earth.

Like the fragments of a holographic plate which retains all the information of the original image,
    The emergence of **the self-reflective mind** also holds all of the information
        It has received from Earth, our Solar System, our Galaxy, back to the beginning.

We each have access to boundless information within us, yet we also are but a mere fragment,
    A small but integral piece of *a holographic Universe*, a unique individual fractal
        That contains all the vast information and creativity of our ever-evolving Cosmos.

Due to science, many are now aware of *The Grand Cosmic Story, The Great Story of Evolution,*
    And those who embrace this evidence-based *evolutionary perspective* recognize
        That the vast living Universe is naturally ***awakening*** to an awareness of itself
            So, over time, every person on Earth can learn to love unconditionally.

Circle of the Fractal Nature of Emergent Evolution
(In Relation to the Awakening Human)

THE EVOLUTION OF PLANET EARTH
THE EARTH, AS WELL AS OUR ENTIRE SOLAR SYSTEM, EVOLVED FROM A MASSIVE SUPERNOVA AND, OVER TIME, THE EARTH *AWAKENED* INTO A LIVING ORGANISM

THE EVOLUTION OF THE AWAKENED HUMAN
MODERN HUMANS ARE EVOLVING TOWARD NEW EMERGENT STAGES OF *AWAKENING*, REPEATING THE FRACTAL PATTERNS OF ALL LIVING SYSTEMS

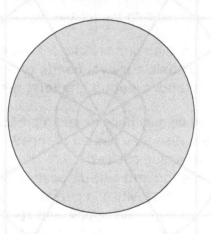

THE EVOLUTION OF EARLY HUMANS
PRIMITIVE HUMANS EVOLVED FROM THE EARLY BIOLOGICAL LIFE OF PLANET EARTH, REPEATING A SIMILAR FRACTAL PATTERN OF EMERGENT *AWAKENING*

THE EVOLUTION OF THE SELF-REFLECTIVE MIND
THE HUMAN MIND EVOLVED AND BECAME SELF-REFLECTIVE, *AWAKENING* ANOTHER REPEATING EMERGENT FRACTAL PATTERN

EVOLUTION OF CONSCIOUS CREATIVITY

I maintain an alignment with Life so that my daily choices help contribute to a better world.

There are many exquisite flowers in Nature that blossom in a very slow manner
    Employing a lengthy process which requires numerous days or even weeks
        To completely unfold its petals from the flower's bud into the full light of the Sun.

With each new dawn, the animating *Life Force* within one of these flowers
    Pushes its petals outward in an incremental fashion every day
        Until the full blossoming of the flower has occurred.

The evolution of human creativity can be seen as similar to this type of flower
    Given that the creative expressions of Nature have evolved over millions of years,
        Yet in the case of us modern humans, it has required many thousands of years
            For the flowering of our current expressions of creativity to be realized.

The human mind with its unique ability to cultivate conscious choices
    Has developed the creative power to help positively shape the future of the world
        When those choices are aligned with *the Infinite Intelligence of Life.*

As the first humans evolved long ago, their primary choices were instinctual
    And were used to help fulfill the **basic survival needs of the people,**
        For example - producing food, creating shelters, procreation, etc.

When early humans further evolved as they became more proficient at their ability to survive
    (Gaining added leisure time because their basic daily needs were satisfied),
        They began to consciously pursue choices
            To expand self-knowledge and self-discovery, which over many eons,
                Led to the expanded creativity and personal expressions
                Of the sciences, arts, philosophy, and spirituality.

These forms of inquiry, combined with our current evidence-based knowledge of evolution,
    Are now leading many people to a profound new awareness
        Of the importance and responsibility to make **the conscious creative choices**
            That will further the positive progression of evolution
                (I.e. the wellbeing of an ever-evolving Earth and all of its creatures),
                Choices that are aligned with *the Natural Intelligence of Life.*

As each of us continues to expand our awareness,
    We are, collectively, just beginning to explore the importance of what it means
        To consciously choose to transform our own egoic nature
            So, together, we create opportunities for "a collective intelligence"
                (I.e. "a collective intelligent field of consciousness")
            To guide our further shared development.

"The creative flowering of humanity" has an intrinsic yearning
    To display all of its "petals to the light of ever-expanding awareness"
        As *Life* constantly invites us to develop greater personal awareness
            Of the power and responsibility in every single choice we make.

Circle of the Evolution of Conscious Creativity
(In Relation to the Power of Choice)

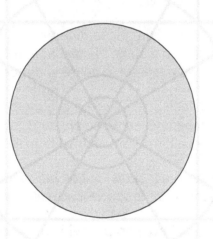

THE CREATIVITY OF "CO-INTELLIGENCE"
THE CHOICES TO TRANSFORM PERSONAL EGO CREATING OPPORTUNITIES FOR "COLLECTIVE INTELLIGENCE" TO GUIDE OUR COLLECTIVE EVOLUTION

FUNCTIONAL CREATIVITY
THE CHOICES WHICH HELP FULFILL BASIC SURVIVAL NEEDS
+ PRODUCING FOOD
+ CREATING SHELTER
+ PROCREATION

THE CREATIVITY OF CONSCIOUS EVOLUTION
CONSCIOUSLY MAKING THE CREATIVE CHOICES TO FURTHER THE POSITIVE PROGRESSION OF EVOLUTION

THE CREATIVITY OF SELF-DISCOVERY
THE CHOICES WHICH HELP EXPAND SELF-KNOWLEDGE
+ THE SCIENCES
+ THE CREATIVE ARTS
+ PHILOSOPHY
+ SPIRITUALITY

EVOLUTION OF GOOD AND EVIL

Everything I perceive and experience in the world is a perfect expression of Limitless Love.

If you were to pick up an ordinary rock and observe it, it would appear to be one solid object,
    Until you take this same rock and examine it under a high-powered microscope
        And find it's made of different molecules amassed from many chemical elements.

Based on the evidential knowledge which comes from *atomic structure chemistry*,
    It's understood that all of the various elements of the rock are comprised
        Of atoms made up of electron fields surrounding a central nucleus.

Furthermore from quantum physics, we know the nucleus consists of sub-atomic particles
    And yet these sub-atomic particles are not actually solid
        Because they're made of universal energy which is blinking in and out of reality,
            Appearing and disappearing again, returning back to *The Unified Field*.

So at a quantum realm, the physical rock you may hold in your hand is not really "solid" at all
    And at the level of the outer material world, can be said to be "an illusion of the mind".

Just like an ordinary rock can be "seen" from these different vantage points,
    Our concepts of "good and evil" can also be viewed from numerous perspectives
        That change over time as we continue to develop our cognitive awareness.

We live in a world of duality where each positive force is always balanced by its opposite,
    In which there appears to be a benevolent force we call "good" or "God" or *"Light"*,
        And an opposing force we call "evil", which also has been given many names.

We may think "good and evil" are solid concepts, but as humanity evolved over eons of time,
    The meaning it gave to the concept of "good versus evil" gradually evolved as well.

In certain stages of human evolution, **God was perceived as being opposed by the "world"**
    Because some forces in the world were seen as creating the obstacles to daily survival.

In primitive times, the definition of "good" was anything that supported the community's survival
    And "evil" was anything that caused physical danger to any member of the tribe.

As humanity and religion evolved - and as **a new concept of God versus Satan** emerged,
    The meaning of "good" changed into "choosing to abide by God's commandments",
        And "evil" was modified to mean "choosing to oppose God's divinely given laws".

In today's world, the concept of God versus Satan has transformed into **God versus the ego**,
    As "good" depicts integrous action that supports Nature and life-affirming evolution,
        And "evil" is any loveless action that opposes Nature or natural evolution.

Quantum physics has shown at one level of reality, the solidity of a rock is simply "an illusion",
    And at another level of reality, the rock is actually radiant universal energy.

Maybe **the evolution of good and evil** will ultimately reveal that "evil", from an absolute view,
    Is simply an illusion that does not exist, and everything in the Universe *is Limitless Love*.

Circle of the Evolution of Good and Evil

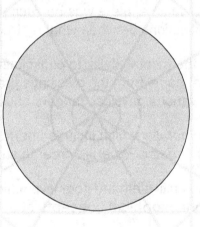

GOD = ALL THAT IS
(AWAKENED HUMANS)
GOOD – IS EVERYTHING
THAT IS WITHIN ALL
DIMENSIONS OF LIFE IN
ALL LEVELS OF REALITY
EVIL – DOES NOT EXIST
FOR LIFE SIMPLY IS -
AND ONLY LOVE IS REAL

GOD VS. WORLD
(PRIMITIVE HUMANS)
GOOD – IS ANYTHING
THAT SUPPORTS THE
COMMUNITY'S
ONGOING SURVIVAL
EVIL – IS ANYTHING IN
THE WORLD CAUSING
PHYSICAL DANGER

GOD VS. EGO
(MODERN THOUGHT)
GOOD – IS INTEGROUS
ACTION THAT SUPPORTS
NATURE AND LIFE-
AFFIRMING EVOLUTION
EVIL – IS ANY LOVELESS
ACTION THAT OPPOSES
NATURE OR EVOLUTION

GOD VS. SATAN
(EARLY RELIGIOUS)
GOOD – IS EVERY CHOICE
TO LIVE AND ABIDE
BY GOD'S DIVINE LAWS
AND COMMANDMENTS
EVIL – IS CHOOSING
TO OPPOSE GOD'S
DIVINELY GIVEN LAWS

EVOLUTION OF MORALITY

I choose to live my life with integrity so my actions contribute to the wellbeing of others.

In order for the seed of any fruit tree to develop into its full expression of maturity,
It must naturally progress through a number of growth stages.

First, the seed must produce a small shoot that breaks through the soil into the light of day
So it can grow a healthy trunk, small branches, and eventually an abundance of leaves.

Then the plant must generate a bud and flower on many of its branches,
And finally, as an extension of the flowers, the fruit will begin to mature until fully ripe.

In a similar way, **the evolutionary growth of morality** has been like the development of a tree
In that morality has also matured through numerous stages of human development,
But instead of decades for a tree, morality required thousands of years to evolve.

During the pre-human developmental era when early hominids were evolving,
Awareness was instinctual and primarily focused on the survival needs of its species,
So of course, at that primitive time, there was no such thing as *morality*
For there were no distinctions between what is "true" and what is "untrue".

As humans evolved and acquired the mental ability to consciously make simple moral choices,
They claimed ideas that "good" came from the blessings granted by an all-powerful god
And "evil" came from the various physical dangers caused by demonic beings.

Some groups began developing a *morality* which included performing **religious rituals**
(That they believed pleased *a Greater Power)* in order to survive the evils of the world.

Over time, as humans continued to cultivate more cognitive abilities,
They proposed ever-greater **philosophical concepts** about how to best live together.

Certain philosophical ideas defined "right" as proper forms of human conduct and behavior,
And "wrong" was defined based on their agreements of inappropriate forms of behavior,
Which shifted one's *moral actions* from the focus on some god outside oneself
To actions oriented toward self - and the choices one makes to be "good".

Today with **awareness of *the evolutionary perspective***, many are growing into a new stage
In which the definition of morality is changing to mean something much more refined.

From a more awakened perspective, a new concept of morality defines "good" and "right"
As the actions we consciously make that serve life-affirming evolution for all of life,
And "evil" and "wrong" as every action which does not support life.

In other words, this means to be a moral person today who is spiritually awake and aware
Is to focus our actions on integrously serving the wellbeing of others and all of life,
While shifting our focus away from self-centered needs and agendas.

We are constantly being invited by *the Source of Life* to grow towards *higher visions of morality*
And to turn our gaze to the unfolding of greater cooperation taking place on our planet.

Circle of the Evolution of Morality

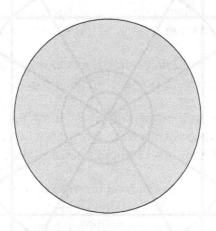

EVOLUTIONARY PERSPECTIVE
(CONSTRUCTIVE AND DESTRUCTIVE)
CONSTRUCTIVE – THAT WHICH SERVES LIFE-AFFIRMING EVOLUTION
DESTRUCTIVE – THE DAILY CHOICES WHICH DO NOT SUPPORT LIFE

INSTINCTUAL AWARENESS
(PRE-HUMAN TRUTH)
TRUE – EVERY PART OF REALITY IS SIMPLY JUST AS IT IS
UNTRUE – DOES NOT EXIST, SINCE ONLY WHAT IS TRUE EXISTS

PHILOSOPHICAL CONCEPTS
(RIGHT AND WRONG)
RIGHT – PROPER FORMS OF HUMAN CONDUCT AND BEHAVIOR
WRONG – AGREEMENTS OF INAPPROPRIATE FORMS OF BEHAVIOR

TRADITIONAL RELIGIOUS
(GOOD AND EVIL)
GOOD – THE BLESSINGS GRANTED BY AN ALL-POWERFUL GOD
EVIL – THE VARIOUS DANGERS CAUSED BY DEMONIC BEINGS

EVOLUTION OF JUDGMENT

I constantly listen to my inner guidance so each day, I make the most life-affirming choices.

The basic electronic functioning within all computers runs on a simple binary system
    Made of "one's" and "zeros" in which for every operation within a computer,
        Either a numerical "one" or "zero" must be selected.

We can think of this process as similar to a person on a journey coming to a fork in the road
    And finding it necessary to choose whether to continue traveling either "right" or "left".

In both of these examples, in order to progress further along "the adventure",
    One of two possible choices must be selected.

We live in a binary Universe, a world of duality, consisting of a vast array of polar opposites
    In which we must constantly choose throughout each day
        Either to contribute to the "expansion" of the Earth - or to its "contraction".

All creatures on our planet have developed mechanisms that allow them to be receptive
    To a natural and ubiquitous impulse of *Infinite Intelligence*
        Which animates and directs every facet of the evolution of life.

These mechanisms, or *forms of judgment*, enable them to continuously engage new choices
    That can potentially contribute to the planet's positive expansion and evolution.

Reptiles and amphibians have evolved in ways in which they make simple kinds of ***judgments***
    Based on a physical response within their <u>body</u> that instinctually discerns
        Whether some aspect of their reality should be brought closer - or pushed away.

As mammals evolved, their new faculties enabled them to make more complex ***judgments***
    Based on a wide range of <u>emotions</u> that determines
        Whether some aspect of their reality should be supported - or opposed.

Furthermore, some advanced mammals with more evolved brains like apes and hominids
    Developed refined <u>thought</u> processes that helped them choose
        Whether some aspect of their reality should be either accepted - or rejected.

We humans have cultivated all three of these mechanisms of judgment to higher degrees,
    Which includes **instinctual**, **emotional**, and **mental** forms of judgment.

Due to various reasons, many people have become disconnected from their *True Nature*
    Shifting their focus from an innate instinct, attuned emotions, and aligned thought,
        To a habitual obsession with their self-centered personal attachments,
            Which is an aspect of the human psyche that's currently pathological.

As we learn, through mindfulness, to reconnect with these natural mechanisms of *judgment*
    By consciously being aware of the instinctual sensations within our <u>body</u>,
        By fully feeling the spectrum of <u>emotions</u> that intuitively directs our decisions,
            And by aligning our <u>thoughts</u> with *the Source of Life*,
            We will be guided to make choices that are life-affirming.

Circle of the Evolution of Judgment

NON-JUDGMENT
(AWAKENED BRAIN)
**THE REALIZATION,
FROM AN ABSOLUTE
PERSPECTIVE,
THAT EVERY ASPECT
OF MY LIFE IS
UNFOLDING PERFECTLY
JUST AS IT IS**

**INSTINCTUAL
JUDGMENT**
(REPTILIAN BRAIN)
**THE PHYSICAL RESPONSE
WITHIN MY _BODY_ THAT
INSTINCTUALLY DISCERNS
WHETHER SOME ASPECT
OF MY REALITY SHOULD
BE BROUGHT CLOSER
OR PUSHED AWAY**

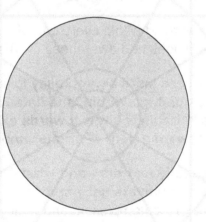

**MENTAL
JUDGMENT**
(NEO-CORTEX BRAIN)
**THE _THOUGHT_ PROCESS
I USE IN WHICH
I CONSCIOUSLY CHOOSE
WHETHER SOME ASPECT
OF MY REALITY
SHOULD BE ACCEPTED
OR REJECTED**

**EMOTIONAL
JUDGMENT**
(MAMMALIAN BRAIN)
**THE WIDE RANGE
OF MY _EMOTIONS_
WHICH INTUITIVELY
DETERMINES WHETHER
AN ASPECT OF
MY REALITY SHOULD BE
SUPPORTED OR OPPOSED**

CULTIVATING HEART WISDOM
I frequently take time to be quiet, so I may listen to the guiding wisdom within me.

If you were to take a handful of fresh potent vegetable seeds
    And randomly throw them in a nearby open field, they may or may not take root.

Depending on soil conditions, temperature, and the availability of water and light,
    The seeds may die, or if they do live, may not reach their full vibrant potential.

But if you were to scatter the same handful of seeds
    In a prepared garden enriched with good fertile soil and cultivated the garden properly
        By nourishing it with adequate nutrients and ample water,
            You would, most likely, produce an abundance of healthy plants.

Similarly, if we truly desire to live our life with greater wisdom,
    (I.e. - intend to live our life with aligned insight that helps us make life-affirming choices)
        Then we must learn how to consciously cultivate this wisdom
            Within "the fertile garden of our inner being".

There is an intelligent impulse or yearning within every one of us that's constantly inviting us
    To develop, each day, a more heightened awareness of what really matters.

This yearning can be likened to "a seed that's always ready to sprout in the right environment",
    So **when we take time to be quiet, go within, and listen for guidance,**
        This "seed" will naturally begin to grow towards expanded awareness
        And direct our life toward a path of greater understanding.

Greater understanding of what really matters - and what our life is truly about
    Can inspire and activate us to cultivate daily spiritual practices
        Like meditation, mindfulness, contemplation, and brain-heart coherence,
            Which help weed out our loveless thinking
                And point us to a more compassionate perspective of the world.

These spiritual practices assist us in "preparing the fertile soil of our life experience"
    By training us to embody the qualities of surrender, acceptance, and gratitude,
        And these awakening qualities are "the inner nutrients"
            That produce the future harvest of our ever-developing consciousness.

Then in the appropriate season and at the proper time,
    Our life experiences combined with our greater understanding
    Establish and anchor *heart wisdom* into our awareness.

Life has given us "an abundance of potent seeds", the seeds of our vast creative potential,
    Which have the possibility to develop into "a plentiful harvest of new insights".

Do we want "to throw these seeds randomly into a field without purpose"
    Through our absence of conscious attention, our apathy, and our lack of awareness,
        Or do we want "to cultivate these seeds in the garden of intentional living"
            Through daily transformative practice?

Circle of Cultivating Heart Wisdom

HEART WISDOM
MY LIFE EXPERIENCES
COMBINED WITH
MY GREATER
UNDERSTANDING
ESTABLISH AND ANCHOR
HEART WISDOM
INTO MY AWARENESS

UNDERSTANDING
THERE IS AN INNATE
INTELLIGENCE IN ME
THAT GUIDES MY LIFE
AND NATURALLY
DIRECTS ME TOWARD
A PATH OF GREATER
UNDERSTANDING

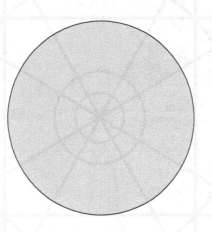

LIFE EXPERIENCE
DAILY SPIRITUAL
PRACTICES DEVELOP
AN AWARENESS IN ME
IN WHICH I EXPERIENCE
A DEEPENING OF SUR-
RENDER, ACCEPTANCE,
AND GRATITUDE

PRACTICE
GREATER UNDERSTANDING
INSPIRES AND ACTIVATES
ME TO CULTIVATE DAILY
SPIRITUAL PRACTICES,
SUCH AS MINDFULNESS,
THAT HELP ME REMOVE
ANY LOVELESS THINKING

XI

ARCHETYPES
OF SPIRITUAL
AWAKENING

ARCHETYPES OF SPIRITUAL AWAKENING

I am on a journey of awakening in which I'm learning the gift of serving the wellbeing of others.

For over four billion years, certain forms of life on Earth have explored the evolutionary journey,
    A journey that has progressed through countless levels of species development.

Yet based on our current scientific knowledge of evolution's epic arc of unfoldment,
    Scientists have observed that there are specific monumental points along this journey
        When various phases of evolving life made a sudden leap during its development,
        A mysterious *emergence* into a whole new form of physical expression.

After two hundred million years of continuous evolution on our planet,
    Homo sapiens may possibly, in time, achieve another of these *sudden emergent leaps.*

This "leap" may occur due to *a collective shift within humanity* from living <u>self-centered lives</u>
    Which are based in fear - and habitually focused on self-power, control, and approval,
        To shifting to, and living, <u>world-centered lives</u> that are focused on serving others.

A world-centered person is one who has developed the awareness to support the collective,
    Who has compassion and care for others, is grateful for life, and serves the good of all.

Regarding the definition we are using, it's also a person who has discovered an inner gateway
    To a direct experience of *the Transcendent (the Infinite Presence of Love).*

In order to bring more understanding to our *spiritual journey,*
    We can use certain symbolic images such as **the Archetypes of Spiritual Awakening**,
        To help us envision how our *journey of discovery* naturally unfolds and develops.

A novel way to describe a self-centered person, yet also one who yearns to awaken,
    Is to use the phrase - **the Young Awakening Self**
        Which represents one who has not yet matured into higher stages of awareness
        Yet has begun to feel an inner yearning to awaken one's spiritual force.

A world-centered person can be referred to as **the Compassionate Heart** (a Servant of Love),
    Or one who has learned to serve the wellbeing of others,
        Whereas **Infinite Presence** is a universal way to portray *the Transcendent Self,*
        Our *True Nature* which is eternal and unbounded.

Humanity has the potential to undergo an *emergent shift* into a unique elevated awareness
    Through each person ultimately becoming a conscious master of one's own life.

This kind of mastery is one's dedication to the realization or union
    Of <u>the Compassionate Heart</u> fully merged and integrated with *Infinite Presence.*

So to embody this sacred integration, we must learn to experience our life as *a living paradox,*
    To live each day in the service of others - and also be aware we are one with all of life.

The Archetypes of Spiritual Awakening can help shine "the light of awareness" on our path,
    The path of our *spiritual journey* that leads to our destiny as a **Master of Freedom**.

Circle of Archetypes of Spiritual Awakening
(My Spiritual Journey of Personal Transformation)

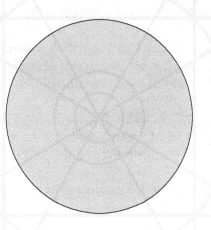

**MASTER
OF FREEDOM**
MY AWARENESS AS I LIVE
AN AWAKENED LIFE
OF INNER FREEDOM - AND
LOVE UNCONDITIONALLY
+ MY <u>COMPASSIONATE
HEART</u> FULLY MERGED
WITH *INFINITE PRESENCE*

**YOUNG
AWAKENING SELF**
THIS IS MY LEVEL
OF AWARENESS WHEN
I AM SELF-CENTERED,
FOCUSED ON APPROVAL,
ATTACHMENT, CONTROL,
SELF-POWER, OR FEAR,
YET YEARN TO AWAKEN

**INFINITE
PRESENCE**
*"THE ONE", THE SOURCE
OF LIFE, UNIVERSAL
CONSCIOUSNESS, GOD,
INFINITE INTELLIGENCE,
LIMITLESS LOVE, THE
TRANSCENDENT SELF,
MY ETERNAL NATURE*

**COMPASSIONATE
HEART**
MY LEVEL OF AWARENESS
AS I CONSCIOUSLY LIVE
A WORLD-CENTERED LIFE
THAT IS COMPASSIONATE,
CARING, GRATEFUL
FOR LIFE, AND IN SERVICE
TO THE GOOD OF ALL

AUGUST 18
COMPASSIONATE HEART

Today I shine "the light of spiritual awareness" into the sanctuary of my heart.

If you would like to produce visibility in a room that's completely dark
  Then you could easily transform the space by turning on a lamp or lighting a candle.

Yet rather than trying to remove the "darkness" from the room (which of course is impossible),
  You can, instead, transform the area by simply shining "light" into it.

In a similar way, when we intend to remove "the dark fearful aspects" of our inner being,
  Such as competition, selfishness, or the habitual need to be in control,
    We can shine into the sanctuary of our heart - "the light of awareness".

It is the radiance of our higher awareness that shines into the dark shadows of our inner self
  That, in time, can bring transformation and healing to every area of our life.

When light transforms a darkened room
  We are able to clearly see what has been present in the room all along
    But which we could not previously see without its illumination.

As we learn what truly matters and radiate this expanded awareness into our heart and mind,
  It becomes so much easier to sustain an alignment with *the Natural Intelligence of Life*
    And consciously cultivate a life of inner freedom.

Our alignment with *Life* gives us greater clarity of the impulses that further our development,
  For example - to be **grateful** for what we're learning from everything we experience,
    For all of our blessings, and for the perfect unfolding of our life.

This *Intelligence* also invites us to learn to **be caring and kind** to all the creatures of the world
  And love the people in our life unconditionally.

This alignment empowers us to respond to the natural yearning within
  That invites us to feel empathy and **compassion** for the suffering of all sentient beings
    And to generously do what we can to alleviate their pain.

And it reveals to us the blessings of being in **service** to the wellbeing of others
  As we deepen our recognition that every form of creation is an expression of one Unity.

These are the primary qualities within the visionary archetype of **the Compassionate Heart**,
  Which can also be referred to as "the Servant of Love".

We have all embarked on an ever-unfolding journey of transforming our lives
  Through the expansive illumination of "the light of spiritual awareness",
    And this "light" is perpetually inviting us to live as a Servant of Love
      (One who dedicates his or her life to the compassionate service of others).

If we use the archetype of **the Compassionate Heart** as "a light we shine into our life",
  It can help illuminate the awakening path we intend to travel
    And the radiant life we intend to create.

Circle of the Compassionate Heart
(A Servant of Love)

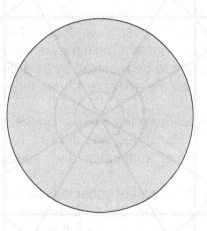

SERVICE
I LIVE MY LIFE
IN SERVICE TO OTHERS
RECOGNIZING
THAT EVERY PERSON
AND FORM OF CREATION
IS AN EXPRESSION
OF ONE UNITY

GRATITUDE
I AM GRATEFUL
FOR WHAT I'M LEARNING
FROM EVERYTHING
I EXPERIENCE, FOR ALL
OF MY BLESSINGS,
AND FOR THE PERFECT
UNFOLDING OF MY LIFE

COMPASSSION
I FEEL EMPATHY
AND COMPASSION
FOR THE SUFFERING OF
ALL SENTIENT BEINGS,
AND GENEROUSLY
DO WHAT I CAN TO
ALLEVIATE THEIR PAIN

**INTRINSIC NATURE
TO CARE**
I AM LEARNING
TO BE CARING AND KIND
TO ALL THE CREATURES
OF THE WORLD - AND TO
LOVE THE PEOPLE IN MY
LIFE UNCONDITIONALLY

THE INTRINSIC NATURE TO CARE

I am aligned with Limitless Love, - and thus, being caring towards others is my intrinsic nature.

In our modern world, we are all exposed to constant radio, TV, and cell phone frequencies
    Which, simply stated, are "invisible fields of focused energy and information"
        That radiate out in every direction sent from various electronic transmitters.

These frequencies are continually traveling through the air, permeating our cities and homes,
    And are invisibly moving through the physical cells of our bodies.

Of course, we don't hear radio and TV stations or phones directly through our physical bodies,
    Because our bodies don't have the necessary kind of electronic receivers
        Required to finely tune ourselves to those specific frequencies.

Yet if we were to use a standard radio that has a proper *tuning mechanism*
    And adjusted the radio's receiver to the frequency of our favorite music station,
        We could then enjoy the many songs played by the station's DJ.

One's intrinsic nature to care for another person, or for any facet of life,
    Can be likened to *an invisible field of energy, an unseen field of consciousness,*
        And, as a metaphor, is like a constant radio frequency that's being broadcast
            Which is always available to be received by us at any time
                If we have developed the ability to attune ourselves to its frequency.

This *impulse of consciousness* comes from *the Field of Limitless Love (Infinite Intelligence)*
    That's perpetually guiding and directing us, and all people,
        Towards greater expressions of contribution and service to others.

When most people are young and their level of conscious awareness is first being formed,
    They, generally, have not yet developed *"the tuning mechanisms"* required
        To hear this natural longing vibrating through them
            Until they cultivate certain life experiences that expand their awareness.

The tuning mechanisms or *personal attributes* for developing conscious care for others
    Come **from our empathy which helps us feel what another is experiencing,**
        From opening our heart with compassion for another's needs,
            And from the inherent yearning to relieve another's suffering.

The intrinsic nature to care can also arise due to **a concern for others**
    That's awakened from the ever-expanding awareness of our meaning of life
        Which continues to evolve from our personal inquiry regarding what truly matters.

Furthermore, caring can emerge out of our daily experiences
    That provide **a more inclusive perspective resulting from a deeper connection**
        With others - or the world - or with who we really are.

The Field of Universal Love is constantly sending out its "frequencies of compassion"
    And when we're able to consciously attune ourselves to its heartfelt transmissions,
        Being more caring toward others is one of its "natural songs".

Circle of the Intrinsic Nature To Care

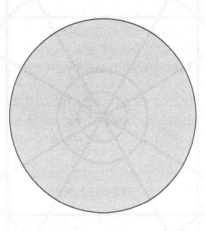

COMPASSION
CARING DEVELOPS
AS I OPEN MY HEART
WITH COMPASSION
AND RESPOND
TO MY NATURAL LONGING
TO RELIEVE
THE SUFFERING OF OTHERS

EMPATHY
CARING DEVELOPS
OUT OF MY
SINCERE EMPATHY
FOR SOMEONE
THAT HELPS ME FEEL
WHAT THEY ARE
EXPERIENCING

MEANING
CARING DEVELOPS
FROM GIVING MEANING
TO MY LIFE THAT
EVOLVES AND EXPANDS,
WHICH CREATES IN ME
A DEEPER CONCERN
FOR OTHERS

CONNECTION
CARING DEVELOPS
OUT OF A LARGER CIRCLE
OF INCLUSION RESULTING
FROM A DEEPER CONNECTION
WITH OTHERS
- OR THE WORLD
- OR WITH WHO I REALLY AM

COMPASSION

I stay aligned with Life, keep my heart open, and celebrate compassion flourishing within me.

As children grow up and begin the search for what life is truly about,
    Their process of discovery involves various stages of psychological development.

First, there's a very early developmental stage in which an infant believes that its identity
    Is the same as its identity with its mother - and its surrounding physical world,
        For it has not yet determined clear distinctions between self and its outer reality.

During a further stage, young children are "programmed to believe" that they are separate
    From the rest of their perceived world, including their mother,
        And begin a period in which they are only concerned with their personal needs.

As children continue to develop, they're taught to be consciously aware of the needs of others
    And they learn to embrace more inclusive moral concerns beyond themselves.

In a similar manner, as we each learn to express greater maturity
    Through a lifetime of myriad experiences and personal development,
        We commonly notice that the feelings of greater compassion for others
            Start to naturally increase and become a more important part of our life
                Which, in time, can grow within our heart like an unfolding flower.

Yet in order for our *circle of compassion* to blossom more fully,
    This "noticing" requires that we develop beyond our child-like self-oriented ways
        By staying aligned with *Life*, opening our heart, and learning what truly matters.

The attribute of compassion is **an innate yearning to restore wellbeing and peace of mind
    To the lives of those who suffer and undergo pain**.

It can be thought of as **an intention to rekindle the spark of joy into the hearts
    Of those who are struggling** with the demanding challenges of living in this world.

Compassion is the natural longing that inwardly invites us
    To **be in service to the wellbeing of others - and all of life**.

It is **a natural desire within the heart to help others experience greater freedom**,
    Which includes physical, emotional, and spiritual freedom.

Compassion can be likened to a beautiful jewel at the bottom of a shallow transparent pond,
    And when the water in the pond is still and crystal clear,
        Then the radiant jewel can be visible to everyone.

But when the pond is agitated and turbulent, and the water is full of dirt and mud,
    Then "the radiance of the jewel" cannot be enjoyed by anyone.

So when we quiet our mind, keep our heart open, and stay aligned with *the Source of Life*,
    "The jewel of compassion" that abides within constantly invites us
        To share its vibrant beauty with more and more of our world.

Circle of Compassion

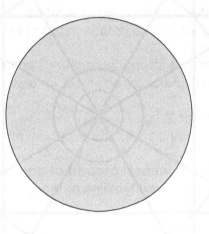

PEACE
COMPASSION –
**MY INNATE YEARNING
TO RESTORE WELLBEING
AND PEACE OF MIND
TO THE LIVES
OF THOSE WHO SUFFER**

SERVICE
COMPASSION –
**MY NATURAL
LONGING TO BE
IN SERVICE TO THE
WELLBEING OF OTHERS
- AND ALL OF LIFE**

JOY
COMPASSION –
**MY INTENTION
TO REKINDLE
THE SPARK OF JOY
INTO THE HEARTS
OF THOSE IN PAIN**

FREEDOM
COMPASSION –
**THE NATURAL DESIRE
WITHIN MY HEART
TO HELP OTHERS
EXPERIENCE
GREATER FREEDOM**

EMPATHY

I keep my heart open which helps me empathize with the feelings and experiences of others.

You have probably heard some variation of the following contemporary question,
    "Can you walk in the shoes of another person?"

The above question means **can we imagine what it's like to be another person,**
    Or try to sense what someone else is thinking,
        Or attempt to feel what someone else is feeling?

This is *empathy*, which can be thought of as the awareness we experience
    In which we intuit the feelings or thoughts of another.

When you witness a theater play that's well acted,
    You may find yourself totally immersed in the play's drama
        And experience an emotional attunement with a particular character,
            An awareness of being **in harmony** with the character's inner being.

You may laugh, or cry, or encounter a wide range of feelings,
    And for a moment, seem to become the person in the play.

For a brief time, you may experience a strong "resonance" with another human being,
    Even if the person is a fictional character acted out on a stage.

In our everyday lives, we do a similar thing
    When we're able to deeply empathize with the experiences of another person.

As we're able to **internally feel the common ground of another**
    And be sensitive and empathetic to the feelings or thoughts they encounter,
        We widen our *circle of compassion.*

And perhaps because of a sudden moment of insight - or an epiphany of spiritual awareness,
    We may find ourselves experiencing a profound feeling of Oneness with another.

When this happens, the arcane spiritual thought that *"we are one with all of humanity"*
    Transforms from an almost incomprehensible philosophical concept
        To an actual heartfelt experience of deep personal communion.

Empathy is "a vehicle of the heart" that can open us to an embodied experience
    Of our Oneness with another human being, even for a fleeting instant.

It can be likened to an icebreaker ship in the artic ocean
    Cracking open northern routes through thick sea ice
        And brand new territory where ocean vessels could not journey before.

The experience of *empathy* can expand our *circle of compassion* further and wider
    Until we're able to, metaphorically, "walk in the shoes of every person"
        And compassionately open our heart
            So we can learn to embrace "the entire ocean of humanity".

Circle of Empathy

INTUITION
EMPATHY –
THE AWARENESS
I EXPERIENCE
IN WHICH I INTUIT
THE FEELINGS
OR THOUGHTS
OF ANOTHER

FEELING
EMPATHY –
THE SENSITIVITY
I EXPERIENCE IN WHICH
I FEEL THE FEELINGS OR
THOUGHTS OF ANOTHER,
FROM SHARING
COMMON EXPERIENCES

IMAGINATION
EMPATHY –
IMAGINING
HOW IT WOULD BE
TO EXPERIENCE
THE FEELINGS
OR THOUGHTS
OF ANOTHER

RESONANCE
EMPATHY –
RESONATING
IN HARMONY
WITH THE FEELINGS,
THOUGHTS
OR EXPERIENCES
OF ANOTHER

149

AUGUST 22
GENEROSITY

Today I deepen my awareness of how I can compassionately give, and be of service, to others.

A half a billion years after the initial formation of Earth, the first cellular forms of life emerged
  As they inexplicably attained the essential creativity to manifest "the miracle of life".

Then these primal life forms used the next four billion years to evolve from simple cells
  To complex cells, to multi-celled organisms, to larger creatures,
    And eventually to self-conscious animals.

Similarly, our human species has been evolving in a comparable process of unfolding stages,
  Or what is referred to as *the fractal nature of emergent evolution*, (see Aug. 11th)
    A process that has accelerated within humanity in the last ten thousand years
      And is now producing a stage where many people on our planet
        Are becoming more aware of the need to co-create cooperatively
          Rather than competitively.

**Generosity can be thought of as an act of compassionately giving to another
  In order to help, uplift, or cooperate with them in some fashion.**

Our personal expression of generosity can continue to expand as we learn to live each day
  Within larger and larger circles of compassion.

It is similar to the evolution of life on Earth that slowly discovered, over time, how to manifest
  Larger circles of diverse and more cooperative evolutionary forms and relationships.

Humanity has been engaged (through the trials of development) on a long evolutionary journey
  Of enlarging its *circles of compassionate concern* from <u>the individual (or the self)</u>,
    To one's immediate <u>family</u>, and next to one's <u>clan or tribe</u>,
      Then to one's <u>region, state, or nation</u>, and finally to <u>the entire world</u>.

Through this unfolding development, we have learned (and are still discovering)
  The myriad benefits of **offering service to another so as to support their wellbeing**,
    Which, surely, can be experienced as an important aspect of generosity.

We can also think of generosity as **kindly sharing our abundance with others
  And empowering others with our time and energy**.

Ultimately, "the Big Picture of generosity" that every person's *heart* is destined to awaken to
  Includes a recognition that all of humanity is intimately connected as one Circle of Life.

From this perspective, the generosity of compassionately giving to another
  Is the same as giving to ourselves, since in truth - we're all united as "one global tribe".

Thus, with this discovery comes the personal realization that generosity is *a natural expression
  Of the evolution of life on Earth becoming one global village in service to one another.*

So when we are engaged in small acts of generosity towards others,
  We're also assisting *Life's* natural yearning to fulfill its blossoming into one world family.

Circle of Generosity

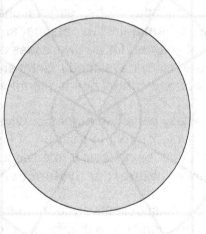

SHARING
GENEROSITY –
BEING AWARE
OF HOW I CAN
KINDLY SHARE
MY ABUNDANCE
WITH OTHERS

SUPPORT
GENEROSITY –
BEING AWARE
OF HOW I CAN
OFFER SERVICE
TO ANOTHER
SO AS TO SUPPORT
THEIR WELLBEING

GIVING
GENEROSITY –
BEING AWARE
OF HOW I CAN
COMPASSIONATELY
GIVE TO OTHERS
IN ORDER TO HELP
OR UPLIFT THEM

EMPOWERMENT
GENEROSITY –
BEING AWARE
OF HOW I CAN
EMPOWER ANOTHER
WITH MY TIME
AND ENERGY

VARIOUS FORMS OF ARCHETYPES OF SPIRITUAL AWAKENING

Mastery of inner freedom is natural, for it is every person's destiny - and thus, it is my destiny.

For many people climbing to the top of a tall mountain can seem like a massive undertaking,
 But those who have done it tell us it basically comes down to "one step after another".

At times, even the thought of achieving *spiritual mastery* can seem like an impossible feat,
 Yet as we open our heart and expand our understanding of what our life is truly about,
  We find it's the most natural thing to do, and that everyone is destined to attain it.

For each of us to realize this, seemingly, elusive quest for *mastery of inner freedom*,
 There are essential choices we must make, vital paths of the heart we must travel,
  And certain challenges we must face along our journey "one step after another".

The evolution of Homo sapiens has now progressed for over two hundred thousand years
 Which initially included a long and difficult period
  Of learning effective ways to physically survive in a hostile and dangerous world.

In order for early humans to overcome many of their survival challenges,
 It became necessary for them to form a unique persona, an individualized egoic nature,
  The part of the psyche that yearned for an awareness of an individuated self
   So as to manifest more highly developed mental and emotional capacities
    And gain the power and control needed to thrive successfully.

Over time, this egoic self (which initially benefited human survival) acquired dysfunctional traits
 That no longer supported the evolutionary progression of further growth for our species,
  And this fear-based facet of our being is now referred to as **the egocentric self**,
   Our unconscious lower nature, our dysfunctional self-centered ego.

For our species to survive today, we must collectively learn to transform our fear-based nature
 And discover how to maintain an alignment with *Life* that's focused on serving others.

This next phase of our *journey of awakening* can be referred to as **the worldcentric self**,
 In other words, **our compassionate higher nature**, or **living as a Servant of Love**.

As we continue to investigate the mystery of our authentic identity (**our *True Eternal Nature*)**
 And dive into the central core of our being by entering the sanctuary of silence within,
  We can become aware of, and directly experience,
   Our Transcendent Self, the illumination of Limitless Love.

"The sky" has been described by poets in many ways using numerous words and phrases,
 Such as *the firmament, the arch of heaven, the atmosphere*, and *the blue yonder*.

In a similar way, spiritual traditions from around the world have used many diverse ways
 To describe a person who attains *spiritual liberation* or *enlightenment*,
  Or what we are calling in these contemplative narratives, a **Master of Freedom**.

For example, a truly liberated person can be referred to as **the Fully Awakened Self,**
 One who loves all of life unconditionally, or **one who experiences inner freedom**.

Circle of the Various Forms of Archetypes of Spiritual Awakening

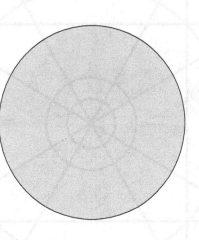

MASTER OF FREEDOM
+ ONE WHO LIVES A LIFE OF INNER FREEDOM
+ ONE WHO LOVES UNCONDITIONALLY
+ THE FULLY AWAKENED SELF

YOUNG AWAKENING SELF
+ ONE'S UNCONSCIOUS LOWER NATURE
+ ONE'S DYSFUNCTIONAL SELF-CENTERED EGO
+ THE EGOCENTRIC SELF

INFINITE PRESENCE
+ ONE'S TRUE ETERNAL NATURE
+ LIMITLESS LOVE
+ THE TRANSCENDENT SELF

COMPASSIONATE HEART
+ ONE'S COMPASSIONATE HIGHER NATURE
+ ONE WHO LIVES LIFE AS A SERVANT OF LOVE
+ THE WORLDCENTRIC SELF

XII

HEART AWARENESS PRACTICES

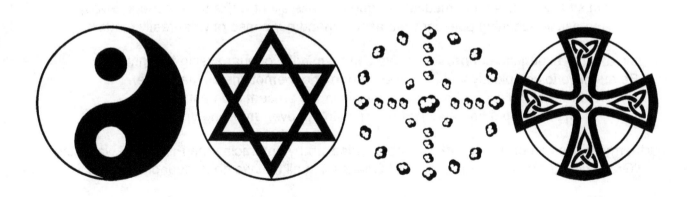

NURTURING THE FEMININE NATURE

As a means to cultivate my wellbeing, I nurture the vital part of me that is my feminine nature.

For thousands of years, many of the traditional world religions have been primarily focused on
Cultivating a person's <u>internal</u> virtues which are mostly about becoming a better person,
Or helping a spiritual seeker attain a direct realization of God *(the Transcendent)*,
And these *interior* experiences are associated with one's **feminine nature**
Referring to *Being*, <u>receptivity</u>, <u>presence</u>, and one's <u>heart wisdom</u>.

In contrast to many of the world's religions, most of the sciences have been focused on
Gaining knowledge and evidence-based truth of our <u>external</u> world, the world of Nature,
And understanding the natural laws of the Universe (how *exterior* reality works),
Which can be thought of as associated with one's **masculine nature**
Referring to *Becoming*, <u>service in action</u>, and <u>manifesting intention</u>.

The new paradigm of *evolutionary spirituality* is about merging, integrating, and embodying
These two seemingly paradoxical facets of the <u>internal</u> and <u>external</u> realms as one,
Or from another perspective, it's about the blending of a more refined expression
Of one's feminine nature united with a more refined masculine nature.

Our feminine nature is the part of us that inwardly yearns to be <u>aligned with *the Source of Life*</u>,
Is <u>receptive</u> to *the Impulse of Creation* (what desires to be birthed into form through us),
And is <u>open</u> so we may be attuned with the unique vision and mission for our life.

Both the feminine nature and masculine nature within ourselves
Must constantly be nurtured to cultivate ongoing personal balance and wellbeing,
But for a moment, just focusing on our feminine aspect, there are many practices
We can use each day to **nurture the feminine nature** within us.

For example, in order to sustain **an alignment with *Being*** (with *the Infinite Presence of Love*),
We can sit quietly in Nature, meditate frequently, take silent walks to center ourselves,
And ask life-defining questions, so as to expand our sense of what really matters.

To gain a richer experience of **presence**, we can be mindful of our passing thoughts,
Be attentive to completely feel the full spectrum of our emotions as they arise,
Be aware of the aliveness in our body within the present moment,
And develop a courageous openness to the ever-unfolding unknown.

Furthermore, we can **connect with our heart wisdom** by embracing the Pillars of Awakening
(Gratitude, surrender, acceptance, and Oneness) in all that we do throughout the day.

And in order to **be receptive to the vision** that wants to be expressed through us
We can maintain an alignment to the guiding *Intelligence* that's always available within.

The feminine nature within us is constantly evolving to higher levels of awareness,
And as our feminine nature develops further
Through our alignment with *Life*, our mindfulness, and our daily practice,
Our *masculine nature* is ready to serve the *feminine* part of us
By manifesting in the world our highest visions of what is possible.

Circle of Nurturing the Feminine Nature
(Transformative Practices)

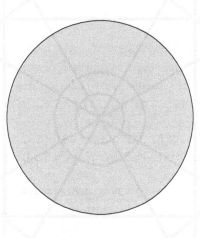

**ALIGNMENT
WITH *BEING***
+ MEDITATE FREQUENTLY
+ SIT QUIETLY IN NATURE
+ TAKE SILENT WALKS
   TO CENTER MYSELF
+ ASK LIFE-DEFINING
   QUESTIONS

PRESENCE
+ LIVE FULLY IN THE
   PRESENT MOMENT
+ BE MINDFUL
+ COMPLETELY FEEL
   ALL MY EMOTIONS
+ BE OPEN TO THE
   UNKNOWN

**RECEPTIVITY
TO THE VISION**
+ ESTABLISH A CLEAR
   INTENTION
+ RECEIVE MY VISION
+ TUNE INTO GUIDANCE
+ CELEBRATE THE
   PROCESS OF GROWTH

**CONNECTION WITH
HEART WISDOM**
+ LIVE IN *GRATITUDE*
+ *SURRENDER* TO LOVE
+ *ACCEPT* MY LIFE JUST
   AS IT IS
+ BE AWARE OF MY *ONE-
NESS* WITH ALL OF LIFE

NURTURING THE MASCULINE NATURE

As a means to cultivate my wellbeing, I nurture the vital part of me that is my masculine nature.

When humans first appeared on Earth as a new species approximately two million years ago,
    Their primary purpose was simply to survive and thus, at that point in evolution,
        Their primal feminine nature was innately aligned with *Life* to fulfill this purpose.

The primal masculine nature in early humans instinctively served this core feminine purpose
    By doing everything it could possibly do to use its survival skills to achieve its mission.

Apparently this ancient masculine nature did an effective job because Homo sapiens endured,
    While many other kinds of early human species did not survive.

As humans evolved further, this innate feminine nature aligned with "a more expanded vision",
    "A vision of securing a stronger emotional and psychological influence over others"
        In order that their entire tribe could better survive in their harsh and hostile world.

Once again, the innate masculine nature within these evolving humans was willing to serve
    This new "vision" and "heart wisdom" of the feminine nature with its ever-growing skills.

And even now during modern times, our masculine nature is still that evolving aspect within us
    That longs to serve the "vision" and "heart wisdom" of our intrinsic feminine nature,
        And is the creative force that yearns to **bring into manifested form**
            The most expanded vision or inner revelation of the feminine within.

Yet over time, a part of the ever-changing masculine nature has become imbalanced,
    And like the feminine, **the masculine nature needs to be nurtured** to maintain health.

Our masculine nature can be nurtured by **following our inner guidance**
    So we can learn to respond to the natural yearning within us to develop our potential,
        To question and refine our beliefs,
            To discover how to embrace life's spiritual paradoxes,
                And to cultivate ever-greater perspectives of what really matters.

Our masculine nature can also **learn to serve the feminine nature**
    By using our unique gifts to manifest *the visions of the feminine* that long to take form,
        Developing our ability to stay organized and focused,
            And boldly taking risks to express new facets of our creativity.

And one of the most important responsibilities of our masculine nature is to **love ourselves**,
    To unconditionally love the person we are, to love and accept our life just as it is,
        And to care for the ever-changing needs of our heart, mind, and body.

We are constantly being invited by *the Creative Impulse within all of existence*
    To maintain an alignment with *the Source of Life,*
        To do everything we can to integrate our **internal realm** with our **external realm**,
            And to merge our **feminine nature** with our **masculine nature**
                So we may be guided each day regarding what gifts and talents
                We are to contribute to the wellbeing of others.

Circle of Nurturing the Masculine Nature
(Transformative Practices)

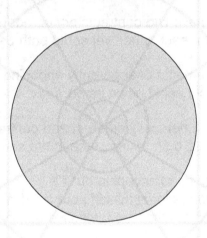

FOLLOW GUIDANCE
+ DEVELOP MY CREATIVE
GIFTS AND TALENTS
+ QUESTION EVERYTHING
+ EMBRACE THE SPIRITUAL
PARADOXES OF LIFE
+ CULTIVATE GREATER
PERSPECTIVES OF
WHAT REALLY MATTERS

**SERVE THE
FEMININE NATURE**
+ LIVE FROM MY HEART
+ ABIDE BY MY OWN
HEART WISDOM
+ STAY ALIGNED WITH
THE SOURCE OF LIFE
+ TRUST IN THE
UNKNOWN

MANIFEST VISION
+ BRING THE FEMININE
VISION INTO FORM
+ STAY ORGANIZED
AND FOCUSED
+ TAKE NEW RISKS TO
EXPRESS CREATIVITY
+ CELEBRATE ATTAIN-
MENTS OF MY GOALS

SELF-LOVE
+ LOVE MYSELF
UNCONDITIONALLY
+ LOVE AND ACCEPT MY
LIFE JUST AS IT IS
+ CARE FOR THE NEEDS OF
HEART, MIND, AND BODY
+ USE TRANSFORMATIVE
PRACTICES DAILY

PARADOX SURRENDER PRAYER

Today I cultivate the intuitive faculty in me that helps me embrace life's existential paradoxes.

How can life on Earth shift through <u>cycles of order and chaos</u>, yet at the same time
  (As some Eastern traditions suggest), there is <u>perfection everywhere in the Cosmos</u>?

How can we live in a phenomenal world of <u>unfolding linear time</u>, yet in the same instant
  (As metaphysics suggests), there is also <u>infinite eternity where time does not exist</u>?

How, in the material realm of physicality, can <u>darkness and evil exist together with the light</u>,
  Yet at the same time within the absolute realm of existence
    (As many religions have suggested for thousands of years), <u>there is only *Light*</u>?

How, in the relative world of manifested form, is it that <u>the future has not yet happened</u>,
  Yet in the infinite reality of *The Unified Field* (as quantum mechanics suggests),
    <u>All events within the Universe, including past, present, and future,</u>
      <u>Are taking place simultaneously in the eternal now</u>?

All of the statements listed above have two contradictory components
  That are radically different from each other, yet could both be a part of our existence?

In order for us to include both statements of apparently opposing aspects of reality,
  We must learn to embrace a concept known as *paradox*.

Paradox is, of course, when two diametrically different and contradictory concepts of reality
  Both appear to be true - and are both taking place at the same time.

Typically, paradox is not an easy thing to accept in our life
  For it goes against the common rational thinking our mind is used to
    And requires us to develop another more intuitive faculty within our being.

Yet it very well may be an important key to help us access
  "A unique portal" of ever-expanding awareness and accelerated consciousness.

If we want to learn how to embrace paradox in our life, then we must find ways to feel it,
  So on the following page is **a transformative practice** with four statements,
    A short affirmative prayer we can use to assist us in "opening this portal".

This practice helps us "absorb the mystery" of surrendering everything to *the Source of Life*
  While at the same time know, in some unfathomable way, *we <u>are</u> one with the Source*.

Most children are at a level of mental and spiritual development
  In which comprehending paradox is difficult.

Many mystics spend their lives attempting to transcend the seeming limitations of the mind
  And discover a transcendent realm where paradox is natural.

Yet we are all "children of the Universe" constantly learning, so we might one day recognize
  That we're becoming Awakened Mystics, or what we can also call Masters of Freedom.

Circle of the Paradox Surrender Prayer
(A Transformative Practice)

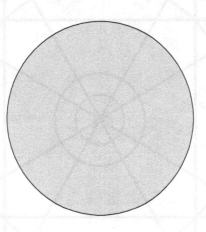

THE TRANSCENDENT
I FULLY LET GO
INTO
THE SANCTUARY
OF *THE TRANSCENDENT*,
AND YET, IN SOME
MYSTERIOUS WAY,
I AM ONE WITH
THE TRANSCENDENT

LIMITLESS LOVE
I GIVE MY LIFE
AND ALL THAT I AM
TO *THE INFINITE
PRESENCE OF LOVE*,
AND YET, IN SOME
INEXPLICABLE WAY,
I AM ONE
WITH *LIMITLESS LOVE*

SOURCE OF LIFE
I SURRENDER
EVERYTHING
TO *THE SOURCE
OF LIFE*,
AND YET, IN SOME
UNFATHOMABLE WAY,
I AM ONE
WITH *THE SOURCE*

**INFINITE
INTELLIGENCE**
I COMPLETELY YIELD
TO *THE INFINITE
INTELLIGENCE
OF THE UNIVERSE*,
AND YET, IN SOME
INCOMPREHENSIBLE WAY,
I AM ONE
WITH *THE UNIVERSE*

XIII

ARCHETYPES OF CONSCIOUS CONTRIBUTION

SPHERES OF CONTRIBUTION

I give to my community by cultivating integrous relationships, equality, and cooperation.

If you've ever been to a high school or college track meet
    Then you have probably experienced the excitement of a competitive relay race.

In sports, *a relay race* is an event in which four individual runners from each team take turns,
    Each running sequentially one quarter of the race
        And then handing off a baton to the next runner
            Until the fourth and last runner on the team
                Tries to take the baton across the finish line to victory.

In order for the relay team to win the competition,
    Every person on the team must be physically strong and in great shape,
    And must also be responsible to maintain his or her strength.

Similarly in our everyday life, if we desire to live in a more cooperative and harmonious world,
    Then we must discover ways to personally contribute to its manifestation
        By, first, being responsible to **maintain our own state of wellbeing**
        So we're truly able to contribute to, and serve, others.

Like the individual runners of a relay race
    Who each add their skills and strength to the betterment of the whole,
        We're much more able to **contribute to healthy functional families**
        When we are in a balanced state of health and wellbeing.

We, as strong balanced individuals, can more easily give what our families truly need,
    Which, surely, is to feel safe and protected, feel nurtured and loved,
        Feel supported and empowered, and feel connected with life and one another.

Naturally, healthy families can more easily serve the larger community around them
    By positively **contributing to the co-creation of a functional productive community**
    And cultivating integrous relationships, equal opportunities, and cooperation.

A solid functional family is, again, like one of the key runners in a relay race
    "Handing off the baton to the next runner" which, here, represents the larger community.

Then, of course, it becomes even more obvious
    That strong robust communities that are working together
        With a spirit of harmony and cooperation
            Make it easier for those community members
                To **be in service to the larger sphere of the entire world**.

We are all contributing members of "the human race"
    Learning to further develop our radiant minds, hearts, and bodies
        So we can "hand the baton" to a loving and empowered family,
            Then to a vibrant community,
                While "the race" heads toward the awakened vision
                    Of creating a sustainable and peaceful world.

Circle of the Spheres of Contribution

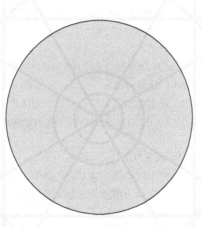

CONTRIBUTION TO ONESELF
I CONTRIBUTE TO
THE CARE OF MY
PERSONAL WELLBEING
AND HAPPINESS
SO I'M TRULY ABLE
TO SERVE OTHERS

CONTRIBUTION TO THE WORLD
I CONTRIBUTE
MY CREATIVE GIFTS
AND TALENTS TO THE
WELLBEING OF OTHERS
SO I MAY HELP BUILD
A BETTER WORLD

CONTRIBUTION TO FAMILY
I CONTRIBUTE TO
MY FAMILY AND "LOVED
ONES" BY HELPING THEM
FEEL SAFE, LOVED,
EMPOWERED,
AND CONNECTED TO *LIFE*

CONTRIBUTION TO COMMUNITY
I CONTRIBUTE TO
MY LOCAL COMMUNITY BY
CULTIVATING INTEGROUS
RELATIONSHIPS,
EQUAL OPPORTUNITIES,
AND COOPERATION

CONTRIBUTION TO COMMUNITY

I give of my time, talents, and creativity to help others live a more peaceful and fulfilling life.

Many migratory birds instinctually fly in formation on an annual journey toward northern lands
Collectively responding to their primal impulse to propagate the next generation.

Emperor penguins, in the freezing winters of Antarctica,
Huddle together in a large pack to keep them, and their eggs, warm and protected
Instinctually taking turns standing at the sub-zero edge of the outer circle.

A swarm of bees viscerally works together - as if they intuitively sense each individual bee
Has an important part to play in the overall wellbeing and maintenance of the hive,
And communally, they function within an integrated group awareness.

The intricate colonies of ants also thrive and prosper
Because of an innate silent communication with one another
That links them together for the common good of the collective.

Each of these animal species listed above is innately attuned to the rhythms of Nature
And is instinctually aligned with *the Natural Intelligence* that governs all of life.

Because of their intrinsic connection with *Infinite Intelligence*,
They all respond to an impulse within them
To collectively unite in a natural expression of community
So they can contribute to building greater harmony and cooperation.

And there are numerous indigenous tribes from around the world
Which still follow the ancient traditions of living their lives aligned with Nature
And continue to express this innate *impulse of community*.

Yet generally in our world, large industrial cultures and so-called "modern civilized societies"
Have unconsciously lost much of their inborn connection to this natural impulse,
And, over time, many people have become dysfunctionally self-centered
And obsessively focused on individual personal needs and concerns.

In our present era, there's a longing to reconnect with, and rekindle, this *impulse of community*
As each of us discovers how to sustain an alignment with *the Source of Life*.

The *impulse of community* inwardly directs us **to give of our time, talent, and creativity**
So together, we may all live a more peaceful, equitable, and fulfilling life.

It also motivates us to serve others by helping to lessen the tasks of everyday life
Through sharing common work and resources collectively.

This impulse enlivens participation in creating a system of fair agreements and laws,
And in contributing to community celebrations that honor and revere life.

Metaphorically, we are all in a process of learning to consciously "fly in harmonious formation"
Aligned with *the Source of Life* on our migratory path towards ever-greater cooperation.

Circle of Contribution to Community

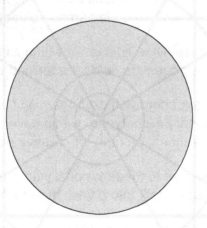

GENEROSITY
I GIVE OF MY TIME,
TALENTS,
AND CREATIVITY
SO OTHERS
MAY LIVE A MORE
PEACEFUL, EQUITABLE,
AND FULFILLING LIFE

SHARING
I SERVE OTHERS
BY HELPING TO LESSEN
THE TASKS
OF EVERYDAY LIFE
THROUGH SHARING
COMMON WORK
AND RESOURCES

AGREEMENTS
I CONSCIOUSLY
PARTICIPATE
IN CREATING A SYSTEM
OF FAIR AGREEMENTS
AND LAWS
WHICH HELPS BUILD A
STRONGER COMMUNITY

CELEBRATION
I CONTRIBUTE TO,
AND PARTICIPATE IN,
COMMUNITY
CELEBRATIONS THAT
HONOR AND REVERE
VARIOUS ASPECTS
OF COLLECTIVE LIFE

ARCHETYPES OF CONSCIOUS CONTRIBUTION
Today I consciously align my awareness with all that is good and beautiful in this world.

Rupert Sheldrake, a contemporary biologist, plant physiologist, and author
    Wrote a book, *"A New Science of Life"*, about his theory of *morphic field resonance*.

He postulated that every form of life is invisibly connected to *a radiant field of energy*
    Which outwardly organizes and structures its unique creative expression,
        And that all members of one particular species each attune with, and influence,
            The vibrational patterns of their species' distinct collective field of energy
                Which he referred to as *a morphogenetic field.*

A species' *morphogenetic field* is constantly evolving and undergoing changes with time
    As an individual species evolves and gains new information about its environment.

When a critical mass within a species develops to the emergent stage of *an evolutionary leap,*
    Its *morphic field* expands due to the increased awareness from a group of its members
        And, thus, through the interconnectedness of *morphic field resonance,*
            The rest of the species will make the same evolutionary leap.

The more conscious and aware an evolving species is within its actual development,
    The more unique types of *morphogenetic fields* are formed to parallel that awareness.

All human beings are connected to numerous *morphogenetic fields* of various types,
    And some fields contain "visionary archetypes" within collective human consciousness
        That generate specific vibrational patterns of creative possibility and potential.

By purposefully aligning our awareness to these visionary archetypes (or fields of potential),
    We can enter, through "a veiled portal", into a vast invisible library of higher knowledge.

In order to expand our spiritual awareness and support our heart's intentions,
    We can make a choice to align ourselves to, and utilize, the fields of consciousness
        Of the numerous spiritually awakened masters who have lived before us
            And have contributed to the wellbeing of our world.

There are many **healers** from previous ages who have created a powerful "field of service"
    By helping others align their awareness with the unlimited source of all healing power
        And attune their mind, heart, and body with their *Eternal Nature.*

There is a "field of past **visionary leaders**" holding the consciousness of all that really matters,
    Inventive creativity, as well as a profound understanding of who we really are.

And there are "fields of former **teachers** and **storytellers**" who have contributed to humanity
    Their heightened awareness, enlightened inspiration, and compassion for others.

When we take the time to become still and go within, and intentionally align our awareness
    With the specific *morphogenetic fields* of the **Archetypes of Conscious Contribution**,
        It can help us access and embody within our life, a wealth of insight and creativity
            From these **visionary healers, leaders, teachers, and storytellers**.

Circle of Archetypes of Conscious Contribution

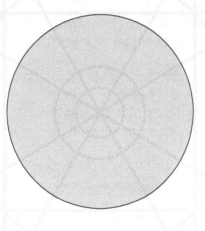

VISIONARY LEADER

IT IS THE PART OF ME THAT HELPS OTHERS EXPAND THEIR AWARENESS OF HOW TO BE A TRUE LEADER - AND TO EMBRACE LIFE AND ITS CHALLENGES FROM A MORE INCLUSIVE PERSPECTIVE AND VISION

VISIONARY HEALER

IT IS THE PART OF ME THAT HELPS OTHERS ATTUNE THEIR MIND, HEART, AND BODY WITH THEIR *ETERNAL NATURE* AND ALIGN WITH THE UNLIMITED SOURCE OF ALL HEALING POWER

VISIONARY TEACHER

IT IS THE PART OF ME THAT TEACHERS OTHERS THROUGH EXAMPLE TO ALIGN WITH *THE SOURCE OF LIFE*, LEARN WHAT LIFE IS TRULY ABOUT, FOSTER BEAUTY, AND SERVE OTHERS

VISIONARY STORYTELLER

IT IS THE PART OF ME THAT SHARES WITH OTHERS EMPOWERING STORIES WHICH ARE INSPIRED FROM "A BIG PICTURE PERSPECTIVE" SO AS TO EXPAND AWARENESS OF WHAT REALLY MATTERS

AUGUST 30
VISIONARY STORYTELLER

I consciously create, and fully live, the most benevolent and loving story of life I can imagine.

At the most fundamental level of our existence
    The external reality we experience each day is based on our internal consciousness.

In other words - the perceptions by which we perceive and respond to our everyday world
    Are directly influenced by our awareness and distinctive content of our current beliefs
        (Both conscious and unconscious) that we hold to be true about our life.

By cultivating our conscious awareness and letting go of our unloving concepts of reality,
    Over time, our consciousness expands as we acquire and act on new beliefs.

With more life-affirming beliefs, we develop a whole new interpretation of our external reality
    Which results in our outer life experience *mirroring* these inner changes.

All people are constantly "telling themselves a story" about what they believe to be true
    And then - *Life* out-pictures and mirrors that "story" as their perceptual experience.

As our "inward story" changes as we mature, our outward experiences of reality also change
    Giving us opportunities to encounter whole new portals of possibility regarding our life.

Since the dawn of language, mythic storytellers have created novel styles of stories
    Which they would use to inspire and teach,
        And to direct the inquisitive minds of their listeners
            Toward sacred places of personal growth and inner development.

For example, "the stories of particular visionary archetypes" have the ability to point us
    To our deepest and innermost connections with various aspects of life.

Of course today, "stories" come in numerous forms, such as fictional books, memoirs, poems,
    Songs, theatre, film, an abundance of Internet videos, as well as other sources.

When certain **storytellers inspire us to develop more of our unlimited potential**
    And contribute our creative gifts and talents to the wellbeing of others,
        Their "stories" express an alignment with a natural *Transcendent Impulse* of life.

A Visionary Storyteller is one who shares stories that empower others to embrace life
    With more inclusive perspectives of what really matters.

It is the archetypal image of one who **tells stories so as to develop higher awareness**
    And consciously cultivate a deeper meaning and purpose of life.

Ultimately all stories, at their fundamental core, are really about one essential human story,
    And this is ***The Great Story* of awakening to a life of loving unconditionally**.

Humanity is now in the process of emerging to a higher level of awakened consciousness,
    And each of us, as **a Visionary Storyteller**, has an important and unique role to play
        In doing our best to live the most benevolent and loving story we can imagine.

Circle of the Visionary Storyteller
(An Archetype of Conscious Contribution)

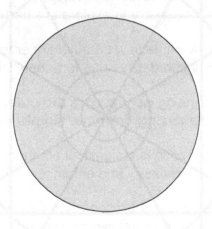

**SHARE
INSPIRATION**
I SHARE "STORIES"
THAT INSPIRE PEOPLE
TO DEVELOP
THEIR POTENTIAL
AND CONTRIBUTE THEIR
CREATIVE GIFTS TO THE
WELLBEING OF OTHERS

**DEVELOP
AWARENESS**
I TELL "STORIES"
THAT ASSIST OTHERS
TO DEVELOP
HIGHER AWARENESS
AND CULTIVATE
A DEEPER MEANING
AND PURPOSE OF LIFE

**INCLUSIVE
PERSPECTIVES**
I EXPRESS "STORIES"
THAT EMPOWER OTHERS
TO EMBRACE LIFE
WITH MORE INCLUSIVE
PERSPECTIVES
OF WHAT REALLY
MATTERS

**CELEBRATE
LIFE**
I DO WHAT I CAN TO SERVE
OTHERS BY OFFERING
"STORIES" THAT ARE
EMPOWERING, UPLIFTING,
AND WHICH CELEBRATE
THE MANY GLORIOUS
FACETS OF LIFE

CELEBRATION

Every moment that I experience has the possibility of becoming a unique celebration of life.

In some of the wild forests throughout the world, a natural impulse of joy is expressed
In the various forms of wolf puppies frolicking together as they play over dead tree logs,
The cubs of bears wrestling with one another in utter fun amidst tall grasses,
Or young chimpanzees rolling together and amusing themselves.

All of these playful younglings are species from a category of animals referred to as mammals
And the active explorative characteristic of *play* has had an important role
In the evolution of emotional development for most species of mammals.

As far as scientists can tell from our current knowledge,
Before the evolutionary appearance of mammals on Earth,
Other animals, such as multi-celled organisms, fish, amphibians, and reptiles,
Did not express much, or any, of this emotional characteristic of *play*.

These diverse non-mammal forms of life have not developed
The higher level of awareness necessary to explore this particular aspect of reality.

When mammals finally did appear, a whole new paradigm of emotional development evolved
That required this quality of *play* in order to bring forth new facets of evolutionary form.

Play is, essentially, "the act of celebrating life" - and it's **the outer creative expression
Of feeling the enjoyment, or blessing, from the simple wonder of being alive**.

For us contemporary humans, *celebration* is a significant component
For helping expand our inner awareness - and enhance our wellbeing.

Most people have experienced *play* and *celebration* when they were young and growing up,
Yet some adults tend to lose this emotional awareness over time as they age.

Many psychologists have asserted that adults also require *celebration* and *play*
To support and assist the healthy unfolding of their ongoing psychological development.

The higher the level of conscious awareness that evolves in a particular species,
The more *play* and *celebration* become important components
In that species' overall growth, development, and wellbeing.

***Celebration* can also be thought of as the honoring and acknowledgement
That each person or creature is an integral part of a much greater Circle of Life.**

**It is the external manifestation of an inner awareness
That venerates deep reverence for life
And is an active demonstration of affirming life's empowering qualities**.

As humans continue to evolve and, in time, awaken to an entirely new paradigm of expression
In which each person discovers an authentic recognition of his or her *True Nature*,
Then **every moment has the possibility of becoming *a unique celebration of life***.

Circle of Celebration

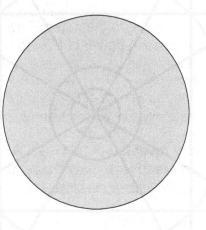

HONORING
CELEBRATION –
THE HONORING AND
ACKNOWLEDGEMENT
THAT EVERY PERSON
IS AN INTEGRAL PART
OF A MUCH GREATER
CIRCLE OF LIFE

REVERENCE
CELEBRATION –
THE EXTERNAL
MANIFESTATION OF
AN INNER AWARENESS
THAT VENERATES
DEEP REVERENCE
FOR LIFE

AFFIRMATION
CELEBRATION –
THE ACTIVE
PLAYFUL
DEMONSTRATION
OF AFFIRMING
THE EMPOWERING
QUALITIES OF LIFE

BLESSING
CELEBRATION –
THE OUTER CREATIVE
EXPRESSION OF FEELING
THE ENJOYMENT,
OR BLESSING,
FROM THE WONDER
OF BEING ALIVE

INSPIRATION

I maintain an alignment with the Source of Life and thus, I naturally align my heart to inspiration.

When an electrical cord that's attached to a lamp
    Is unplugged from an electric wall socket, which is the source of its power,
        Then obviously no current is able to flow through the wire
            To bring luminance to the lamp.

But if you were to simply reconnect the cord to its power source and turn on the switch,
    Then the lamp could shine radiantly once again.

Likewise, the attribute of **inspiration** works in a similar fashion
    For **when we're consciously aligned with *the Source of Life*,**
        We connect our heart to the vast current of *the Field of Infinite Creativity*.

As we do this, we become like a hollow flute that *the Breath of Life* effortlessly flows through
    Playing its "sacred music into our open vessel"
        So as to share its boundless melodies of inspired creativity.

Our creative inspiration is directly connected to the natural flow of our breath,
    Which is an expression of the animating power of *Life Force energy* (also called *Chi*).

For when we're breathing fully and deeply,
    And we align our awareness with *the Breath of Life (the Infinite Presence of Love)*,
        Then creative inspiration naturally moves through us unimpeded.

Inspiration is the natural ingenuity revealed in us when we attune our mind
    With the flow of the unlimited creative energy that's always present,
        Which is also referred to as *the infinite creative energy of life*.

It can be thought of as **the revelation and insight we sense**
    When our consciousness is in resonance with the *Source of all creativity*.

Another way of thinking about inspiration is that it's **the inventiveness that comes to us**
    When we align our awareness with *Infinite Intelligence*,
        The Natural Intelligence within each of us
            That's constantly urging us to develop our boundless potential.

There are many time-tested methods (or transformative practices)
    We can use to maintain and feel an alignment with *the Source of Life.*

Experiencing silence, meditation, contemplation, mindfulness, service to others,
    And living in a state of gratitude
        Are some of the foundational practices that help keep us aligned.

Then, when we are consciously "plugged into" *the Source of Limitless Love*,
    "The current of inspiration" is available to flow through us
        So the radiance of our *inner light* may shine brighter each day
            And so we may joyously contribute our creative gifts to the world.

Circle of Inspiration

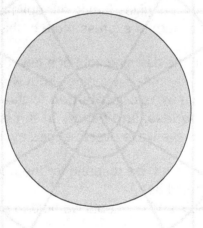

CONNECTION
INSPIRATION –
**THE INSIGHT I INWARDLY
RECEIVE WHEN
I CONNECT MY HEART
TO THE VAST CURRENT
OF *THE FIELD*
OF *INFINITE CREATIVITY***

ALIGNMENT
INSPIRATION –
**THE INVENTIVENESS
THAT COMES WHEN
I ALIGN MY AWARENESS
WITH *THE NATURAL
INTELLIGENCE*
WITHIN ALL OF LIFE**

ATTUNEMENT
INSPIRATION –
**THE NATURAL
INGENUITY REVEALED
IN ME WHEN I ATTUNE
MY MIND TO THE FLOW
OF UNLIMITED
CREATIVE ENERGY**

RESONANCE
INSPIRATION –
**THE REVELATION
I SENSE WHEN
MY CONSCIOUSNESS
IS IN RESONANCE
WITH THE *SOURCE*
OF ALL CREATIVITY**

HOPE

Today I accept my life just as it is - yet at the same time, I imagine myself creating a better future.

During former days (well before the advent of TV, radio, film, and computer technology)
When catastrophic times were upon the hearts of humanity
Such as periods of war, plagues, droughts, or starvation,
Storytellers and bards would tell uplifting stories around warm campfires
To inspire people to embrace the possibility of a brighter day
And a more hopeful tomorrow.

Inspiring stories were often used in times of great distress or anguish to assist people
In accessing **an ability to envision their current challenging situation**
Somehow shifting towards greater peace and harmony.

These storytellers attempted to encourage people who were beginning to lose hope
By helping them discover **the capacity to accept life just as it is,**
Yet at the same time, imagine themselves creating a better future.

Hope can be thought of as a quality that gives fuel to our optimistic beliefs,
And with daily practice, we can learn to express more of this empowering quality.

Each morning when we wake up to the dawning light of a new day,
We, consciously or unconsciously, make a choice about what we choose to think,
Such as whether we believe we're **contributing to the constant unfolding**
Of greater *truth*, *goodness*, and *beauty* in our world,
Or whether we believe we're overwhelmed by life's problems.

Every day, within our subconscious mind, we respond to "the personal story" we tell ourselves
About how we think our life should be
Based on our current beliefs and concepts we hold to be true.

Yet the grandest story of all, one that possesses a shining promise of hope for all people,
Is what has been called *"The Great Story* of an Infinitely Intelligent Universe".

It's a story that's shared by all of humanity, which points us to both the perfection of our lives,
As well as our development, and helps us learn to love and accept our life just as it is.

"The Universe Story" reminds us where we came from, how we evolved and progressed,
And the natural process of discovery that every form of life must go through,
Which includes the necessity of using the challenges of chaos and disturbance
To help catapult us to new and higher levels of awareness and growth.

It also gives us a vision of where we're possibly headed with the hope that we can one day
Learn to **feel and express gratitude for all we're learning from each life experience**
Which includes our most disturbing and difficult situations.

This grand story of intelligent evolution is essentially (at a fundamental level) "our own story"
And it gives us entrance to a vast portal of new and magnificent possibilities for our life
By pointing each of us to our ultimate destiny of learning to live an awakened life.

Circle of Hope
(In Relation to the Pillars of Awakening)

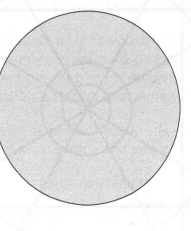

ONENESS
HOPE –
THE ABILITY
TO ENVISION MY CURRENT
CHALLENGING SITUATION
SHIFTING TOWARDS
GREATER LEVELS
OF PEACE AND HARMONY

GRATITUDE
HOPE –
THE ABILITY
TO FEEL AND EXPRESS
GRATITUDE DURING
THE DIFFICULT
AND DISTURBING
EXPERIENCES OF MY LIFE

ACCEPTANCE
HOPE –
THE ABILITY
TO ACCEPT MY LIFE
JUST AS IT IS,
WHILE ALSO IMAGINING
MYSELF CREATING
A BETTER FUTURE

SURRENDER
HOPE –
THE ABILITY TO LET GO
OF MY ATTACHMENTS
AND YET BE RECEPTIVE
TO EXPERIENCING
GREATER TRUTH,
GOODNESS, AND BEAUTY

"THE UNIVERSE STORY"

Embracing an evolutionary perspective of life empowers me to help co-create a better world.

At some time in your life you have probably had the heartfelt experience of going to a theater
Where you watched an inspirational movie which deeply touched you
And noticed that when you left the theater after the film was over,
You were walking taller, your shoulders were held a little higher,
And you sensed "a big smile in your heart".

Usually when this happens, it's because you resonated with the uplifting story in the film
And it made you feel good about some aspect of your life - thus your body responded.

Also reading an excellent novel, or classic literature, can sometimes do a similar thing,
And we may find ourselves feeling so emotionally connected to the story's characters
That we don't want the book to end.

These types of evocative stories tend to move us and touch a place deep within
That can inspire us to be better people,
And reach something inside us that brings out the finest we have to give.

They are the kind of stories that have **the power to profoundly transform us,**
Encourage us to open our heart so we may live a more compassionate life,
Develop our unexpressed potential and innate creativity,
And be a more responsible and integrous citizen of the Earth.

"The Universe Story", also called "The Great Story of an Infinitely Intelligent Universe",
Is the type of *science-based story* that can inspire us to help create a better world.

There's a natural and intrinsic impulse within each of us
Which is constantly inviting us to expand our conscious awareness
So that as we become open to learning about this magnificent epic story,
It can motivate us to cultivate the best of who and what we can be.

"The Universe Story of Intelligent Evolution" can also open our heart
To feel a larger capacity for compassion - and to be in service to others
By biologically demonstrating how all people are united as one global family
And are each an integral part of the same Circle of Life.

As this evolutionary story is more frequently taught in schools to children across our planet,
Its cosmic perspective can encourage them to <u>develop</u> their creative potential,
Make responsible and <u>integrous</u> choices, positively <u>transform</u> their lives,
And help build a more <u>compassionate</u> and peaceful world.

This universal story holds the promise to bring all nations, all ideologies, and all cultures
Towards a growing awareness that we are all truly connected,
For science has clearly shown us we're all descendants from one family tree.

Embracing and understanding "The Great Story" gives the children of the Earth the opportunity
To walk taller with their shoulders a bit higher, while feeling "a big smile in their hearts".

Circle of "The Universe Story"
(The Benefits of an Evolutionary Perspective)

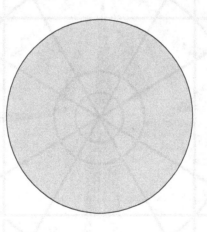

INTEGRITY
"THE UNIVERSE STORY
OF INTELLIGENT
EVOLUTION" POINTS ME
TO <u>ONE INTERCONNECTED</u>
<u>CIRCLE OF LIFE</u> IN WAYS
THAT ENCOURAGE ME
TO MAKE RESPONSIBLE
AND INTEGROUS CHOICES

DEVELOPMENT
"THE UNIVERSE STORY
OF INTELLIGENT
EVOLUTION" INSPIRES
ME TO LEARN WHAT MY
LIFE IS TRULY ABOUT,
EXPAND MY AWARENESS,
AND DEVELOP MY
UNLIMITED POTENTIAL

TRANSFORMATION
"THE UNIVERSE STORY
OF INTELLIGENT
EVOLUTION" HELPS ME
BE AWARE OF ALL THAT
I DO TO SUPPORT LIFE,
AND MOTIVATES ME
TO TRANSFORM MYSELF
WHEN I DO NOT

COMPASSION
"THE UNIVERSE STORY
OF INTELLIGENT
EVOLUTION" HELPS ME
OPEN MY HEART
TO A GREATER CAPACITY
FOR COMPASSION,
EMPATHY, AND BEING
IN SERVICE TO OTHERS

XIV

HEART AWARENESS PRACTICES

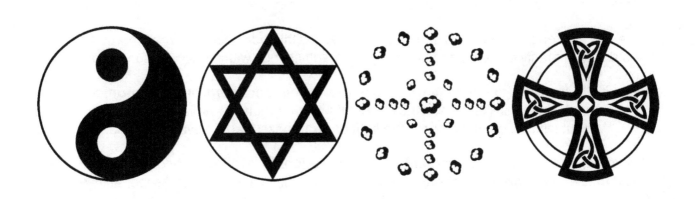

CONSCIOUS SPIRITUAL PARTNERSHIP

Today I honor and celebrate the holiness and magnificence within every person in my life.

In the seventeenth century, alchemists attempted to discover the arcane mysteries of life
By using a mortal and pestle to blend certain obscure materials into novel compounds
And then placed their prepared substances in a clay container called a *crucible*
Where the mixture was heated with great hope to reveal something new.

If we agree that *the purpose of life* is to develop our creative potential, expand our awareness,
And learn to love others more fully - so we may consciously live a life of inner freedom,
Then one dynamic arena that can serve this goal is *the crucible of relationships*.

Our relationships present us with opportunities to deepen our awareness of what really matters
By together forming "a vessel of the heart" where we blend our beliefs and perspectives
While examining and re-evaluating (if necessary) what we believe to be true.

In relationships (especially our primary intimate relationship) we encounter various situations
In which we're given the chance to cultivate a greater vision of our Fully Awakened Self
By acting as mirrors for one another so we may consciously refine our awareness
And transform any unhealthy or loveless aspects that impede our growth.

Within *the shared covenant of spiritual partnership* there is a sacred agreement
That we will do our best to keep our heart open, aid one another's spiritual unfolding,
And use the mutual resources and creativity within the relationship
To offer our unique gifts and talents toward contributing to a better world.

If we desire to cultivate *a conscious spiritual partnership*, we can choose to practice each day
A series of transformative exercises that support the healthy growth of our relationship.

First, we **honor and celebrate *the holiness* in each other** - and give our sacred alliance
To *the Presence of Love* so our union more easily benefits one another and the world.

We use this awareness practice of seeing *the holiness* within our closest intimate partner
As a way to practice seeing and honoring *the magnificence* within each person in our life.

It is especially important to **cultivate honest, empowering, and integrous communication**,
For communication is like the electric current flowing through the walls of our home
Without which we can't turn on "the light of awareness that removes the dark".

Furthermore, it's essential to **be present for, and emotionally available to, one another**
And to use any challenge that may arise as an opportunity to grow ever deeper in love.

It's also vital to regularly be in service to one another - and **share daily expressions of love**,
Which can be likened to nurturing a flower garden with a bounty of water and nutrients,
For when a garden is nourished, it prospers - and when it's not, it withers.

Developing *a conscious spiritual partnership* is like being alchemists - in which we both decide
To mix into "the hallowed living crucible of our spiritual awareness" a solid commitment
To exalt one another with the promise - *"our enduring love is what truly matters"*.

Circle of Conscious Spiritual Partnership
(Transformative Practices)

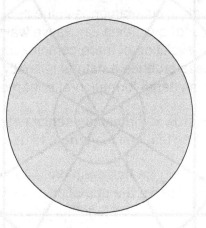

**HONORING
THE BELOVED**
I HONOR AND CELEBRATE
THE HOLINESS
WITHIN MY PARTNER AND
GIVE OUR RELATIONSHIP TO
THE PRESENCE OF LOVE SO
OUR UNION BENEFITS ONE
ANOTHER - AND THE WORLD

**BEING
PRESENT**
I AM PRESENT FOR,
AND EMOTIONALLY
AVAILABLE TO,
MY PARTNER - AND
I USE ANY CHALLENGE
AS AN OPPORTUNITY TO
GROW DEEPER IN LOVE

**HONEST
COMMUNICATION**
I CULTIVATE HONEST,
EMPOWERING,
AND INTEGROUS
COMMUNICATION
FINDING THE COURAGE
TO BE VULNERABLE
AND SELF-REVEALING

**EXPRESSIONS OF
LOVE AND SERVICE**
I AM DEPENDABLY IN
SERVICE TO MY PARTNER
AND SHARE DAILY
EXPRESSIONS OF MY LOVE
SO AS TO CONTINUOUSLY
"NURTURE THE GARDEN
OF OUR RELATIONSHIP"

INTIMACY

Today I am committed to be honest, authentic, and vulnerable with the people I love.

Intimacy requires **honesty**, which is our ability to share the truth - and courageously reveal
The shadow or hidden aspects of our inner being to another person.

It also calls for **vulnerability**, the ability to feel safe and trust another enough that we're willing
To expose wounded areas of our life to them - without feeling we're being judged.

From "the Big Perspective", intimacy is the expression of **greater union** between "two bodies",
Which is another way of saying there's a more connected relationship between them.

The vast Universe seems to be perpetually progressing towards greater measures of intimacy
By discovering ever-more creative ways for "its individual bodies to bond or connect",
And this requires that the diverse expressions of the Cosmos constantly remove
Any blockage or resistance which obstructs them moving closer together.

Individual carbon atoms found ways to "bond" together by forming ordered-lattice structures
Which eventually became rough uncut diamonds in the belly of the Earth,
Multi-celled organisms "bond" by finding innovative ways to work collectively
In order to further the evolution of more complex organisms,
And flocks of geese produce a natural intimacy as they soar as one
"Bonding" in an aerial formation of patterned grace.

Typically, we define intimacy in regards to the human sentimental communion of two lovers
And the honesty and vulnerability that can lead them to deeper states of union.

Yet we might also perceive that evolving life has been creating *simple forms of intimacy*
For millions of years, when we observe the primal intimacy in a band of chimpanzees
Or in a pack of wolves that are bonded together and emotionally entwined.

But at the level of human awareness, intimacy is our ability to let go of identifying ourselves
With our individual separate self and, thus, cultivate an experience of our *True Self*
By being authentic and real as we bond with another - emotionally or spiritually.

Intimacy can be thought of as our ability to fully surrender in each moment
In order to be **completely present** and open to what we're really feeling
So we may bravely expose the most raw and true parts of our being to another.

There seems to be a natural impulse at the core of every expression within the Universe
That yearns for *greater intimacy* so as to merge in deeper union with "its partners"
And cooperate with its environment more effectively.

We may not normally think of it in this way, but from *the cosmic perspective*,
The Universe is always reaching for, and creatively moving toward, *greater intimacy.*

So maybe in the distant future, when our own Milky Way Galaxy collides and merges
With our closest neighbor, the Andromeda Galaxy, in about a billion years from now,
This will be another form of the Universe becoming *ever more intimate with itself.*

Circle of Intimacy
(A Transformative Practice)

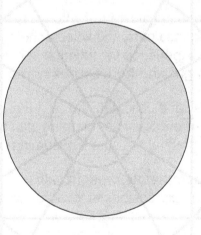

HONESTY
INTIMACY –
MY ABILITY
TO HONESTLY
AND COURAGEOUSLY
REVEAL THE SHADOW
OR HIDDEN ASPECTS
OF MYSELF
TO ANOTHER

PRESENCE
INTIMACY –
MY ABILITY
TO FULLY SURRENDER
IN EACH MOMENT
IN ORDER TO BE
COMPLETELY PRESENT
AND OPEN WITH
ANOTHER PERSON

GREATER UNION
INTIMACY –
MY ABILITY TO REMOVE
SOME BLOCKAGE
OR RESISTANCE IN ME
SO I MAY TRULY BOND
EMOTIONALLY
AND FEEL CLOSER
WITH ANOTHER

VULNERABILITY
INTIMACY –
MY ABILITY TO FEEL SAFE
AND TRUST ANOTHER
ENOUGH THAT
I AM WILLING TO EXPOSE
THE WOUNDED AREAS
OF MY LIFE TO THEM
WITHOUT FEELING JUDGED

SEPTEMBER 6
SACRED SEXUALITY

Today I consciously choose to be present, keep my heart open, and fully relax in each moment.

If you have ever watched a skilled concert violinist passionately perform a solo
During an allegro section of a famous classical symphony,
You would, most likely, notice how completely present the performer is,
How natural he or she makes the performance appear,
How relaxed and easy the musical piece is offered,
And how much *heart* seems to be in every note.

A concert violinist of this high caliber
Can make playing the violin look like an easy and natural experience.

In a similar way, the shared experience of **sacred sexuality** is meant to be easy and natural
For it is the sublime celebration of being fully present with our cherished partner,
It is the vulnerable opening of our heart to our beloved's outpouring of love,
And it is the most genuine and relaxed union between two lovers.

If we think of *sacred sexuality* as an intrinsic part of who we are
And envision it as if it were a gentle nurturing voice echoing deep within us,
Then it would invite us to experience the intimate sensuous dance with our mate
As **the most natural gift and holy expression of our mutual love**.

It might feel as relaxed as a gentle wind delicately dancing through autumn leaves,
Or as flowing as the mighty current of a river merging with the ocean,
Or as magnificent as the gradual but sure blossoming of a beautiful red rose.

Sacred sexuality invites us to **be completely present** with
Both our partner's and our own expressions of love - as well as any emotions that arise,
Much like the unbounded sky above that's perpetually ever-present
To every passing cloud, raging storm, or crystal clear day.

Sacred sexuality also invites us to **constantly relax our body and mind**
Into the sensual stimulations of our partner's love.

The relaxation of *sacred sexuality* can be thought of as "resting in the calm eye of a hurricane"
Where there's complete trust and safety at the center of every breath
No matter the stimulating winds of sensual delight
That surrounds us in the sweeping moments of ecstatic passion.

And *sacred sexuality* invites us to be consciously aware
To **keep opening our heart to our shared love no matter what feelings may arise**.

This kind of love-centered opening can lead two lovers into a direct experience of *the Divine*,
A profound union with *Ultimate Reality*, a deep communion with *the Essence of Life*.

In **sacred sexuality**, we are like two master musicians merged as one,
Intertwined in a playful erotic duet within a symphony of *Love*,
While intuitively playing "the finely tuned instrument of our Beloved".

Circle of Sacred Sexuality

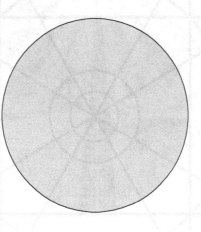

PRESENCE
SACRED SEXUALITY
INVITES ME TO BE
COMPLETELY PRESENT
WITH BOTH MY PARTNER'S
AND MY OWN EXPRESSIONS
OF LOVE - AS WELL AS ANY
EMOTIONS THAT ARISE

NATURAL
SACRED SEXUALITY
INVITES ME TO SEE THE
INTIMATE SENSUOUS
DANCE WITH MY
PARTNER AS THE MOST
NATURAL EXPRESSION
OF OUR MUTUAL LOVE

RELAXATION
SACRED SEXUALITY
INVITES ME
TO CONSTANTLY RELAX
MY BODY AND MIND
INTO THE SENSUAL
STIMULATIONS
OF MY PARTNER'S LOVE

OPENING
THE HEART
SACRED SEXUALITY
INVITES ME TO BE AWARE
TO KEEP OPENING MY
HEART TO MY PARTNER'S
LOVE NO MATTER
WHAT FEELINGS ARISE

XV

NAVIGATING THE JOURNEY OF *THE GREAT CIRCLE*

THE GREAT CIRCLE OF A CONSCIOUS AND BALANCED LIFE

Today I align with the Source of Life, learn what is true, create more beauty, and serve others.

Many spiritual teachers have stated that *the Universal Laws of Love* are simple to understand,
  Yet they are not always easy to live and apply in one's daily life.

There's an important distinction between something "simple" - and something that's "easy",
  For there are many examples in life of things that are simple at their very nature,
    But are not necessarily easy to attain or carry out.

For example, chess is an international game in which the playing rules are basically "simple"
  And most people can learn the rules of chess in thirty minutes or so,
    But it takes a lifetime to truly learn its intricate strategies, its clever maneuvers,
      And it's not "easy" to become an expert at this game
        Without many years of dedication and practice.

Reading piano music from the written scores of the great masters is fundamentally "simple"
  For the basic instructions of reading the notes from a musical page is straightforward,
    But the actual performance of written music is not "easy" for most beginners
      And takes a long time of committed work to become proficient at this skill.

The primary dynamics of life can be simply illustrated in "the spiritual map of an awakened life"
  Known as **The Great Circle**, yet truly living an awakened life of compassionate service
    Requires the daily commitment of developing a conscious, balanced awareness.

Within **The Great Circle**, there are two quadrants that display our inner and outer realities,
  The evolution of consciousness depicted in the left quadrant by the word **"learning"**,
    And the evolution of creativity depicted on the right by the word **"creating"**.

Also within **The Great Circle**, two vertical quadrants display *"The One"* and *"The Many"*,
  That is, the formless *Source of All That Is* represented in the upper quadrant as **"aligning"**,
    And the perfect unfolding of form, denoted in the lower quadrant as **"serving"**.

These four powerful words illustrate "a much simpler version" of **the Great Wheel of Life,**
  Yet usually require an entire lifetime to master what these words are pointing to.

In our everyday world, it typically takes a good amount of practice to do anything well
  And this includes furthering our inner and outer personal growth,
    Which is why many choose to commit to the discipline of transformative practices
      As a beneficial means to cultivate a more aware and conscious life.

If we use the circle on the following page to remind us to practice spending time each day:
  Learning (*expanding our awareness of what is true, developing our potential*),
    Aligning (*meditation, living with mindfulness, relaxation, conscious breathing*),
      Creating (*building a better world, creativity, the arts, contributions*),
        And **serving** (*compassionately giving to others and to all of life*),
          Then eventually we may find that the "simple" ways
            To experience **a conscious and balanced life**
              Will get "easier and easier".

The Great Circle of a Conscious and Balanced Life
(Who Would I Be If I Spent Time Every Day ...?)

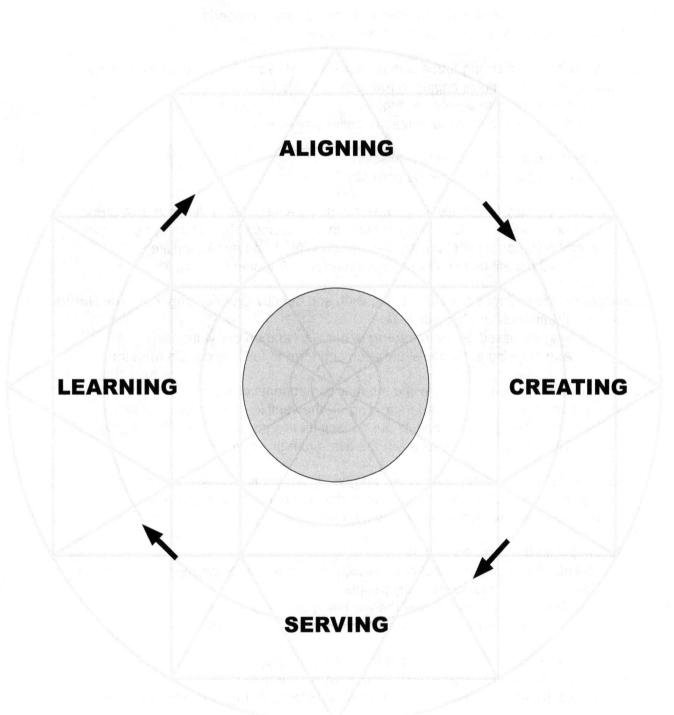

ALIGNING

LEARNING

CREATING

SERVING

AN AWAKENED LIFE

Aligning with my True Nature also aligns me with my purpose, meaning of life, and life mission.

In order for any car to travel down an open road and perform properly
There are certain basic components it must have.

The car must include a strong frame with attached wheels so it can roll over the ground,
Some type of mechanical engine to rotate the wheels forward,
An effective fuel to power the engine,
And a skilled driver to guide the entire process.

If any one of these four components is missing
The car will not be able to operate correctly.

Similarly within our day-to-day life, if we desire to make a valuable shift in our awareness
From an unconscious state of living in fear - to a conscious state of living from *Love*,
In other words - a shift from *an unconscious life* - to *an awakened life*,
It will benefit us to cultivate four important components of our life.

An awakened life emerges from 1) aligning with, and directly experiencing, our **True Nature**,
2) The fulfillment of our life's **purpose**,
3) Living life based on the **meaning** of our life - and on our values,
And 4) giving authentic expression and form to fulfilling our life **mission**.

We can apply the above metaphor using the four components of a car
To describe and expand our understanding of "the vehicle of *an awakened life*",
In which "the <u>driver</u>" represents our conscious alignment with our *True Nature*
That skillfully guides us down the ever-changing road of life.

"The <u>engine</u> of the vehicle" represents our <u>purpose</u> that's continuously revolving within our core
To help us learn what our life is truly about, develop our unlimited potential,
And cultivate our love-centered awareness.

"The <u>fuel</u> to power the vehicle's engine"
Represents the advancement of our values, the broadening of <u>the meaning of our life</u>,
Which currently motivates many people
To compassionately serve the wellbeing of others
And contribute to the beneficial evolution of the Earth.

Finally, "the <u>frame</u> of the vehicle" represents our life's <u>mission</u>,
Or the specific creative expressions, structures, and forms
Which are brought into outer manifestation through our unique gifts and talents.

When all of the aspects of *an awakened life*,
<u>Purpose</u>, <u>meaning</u>, <u>mission</u>, and the realization of our *True Nature*
Are in place and working together smoothly,
"Our vehicle can effortlessly move us along the road of life"
So we may perpetually journey to brand new horizons of awakening
And ever-new emergent possibilities.

Circle of an Awakened Life

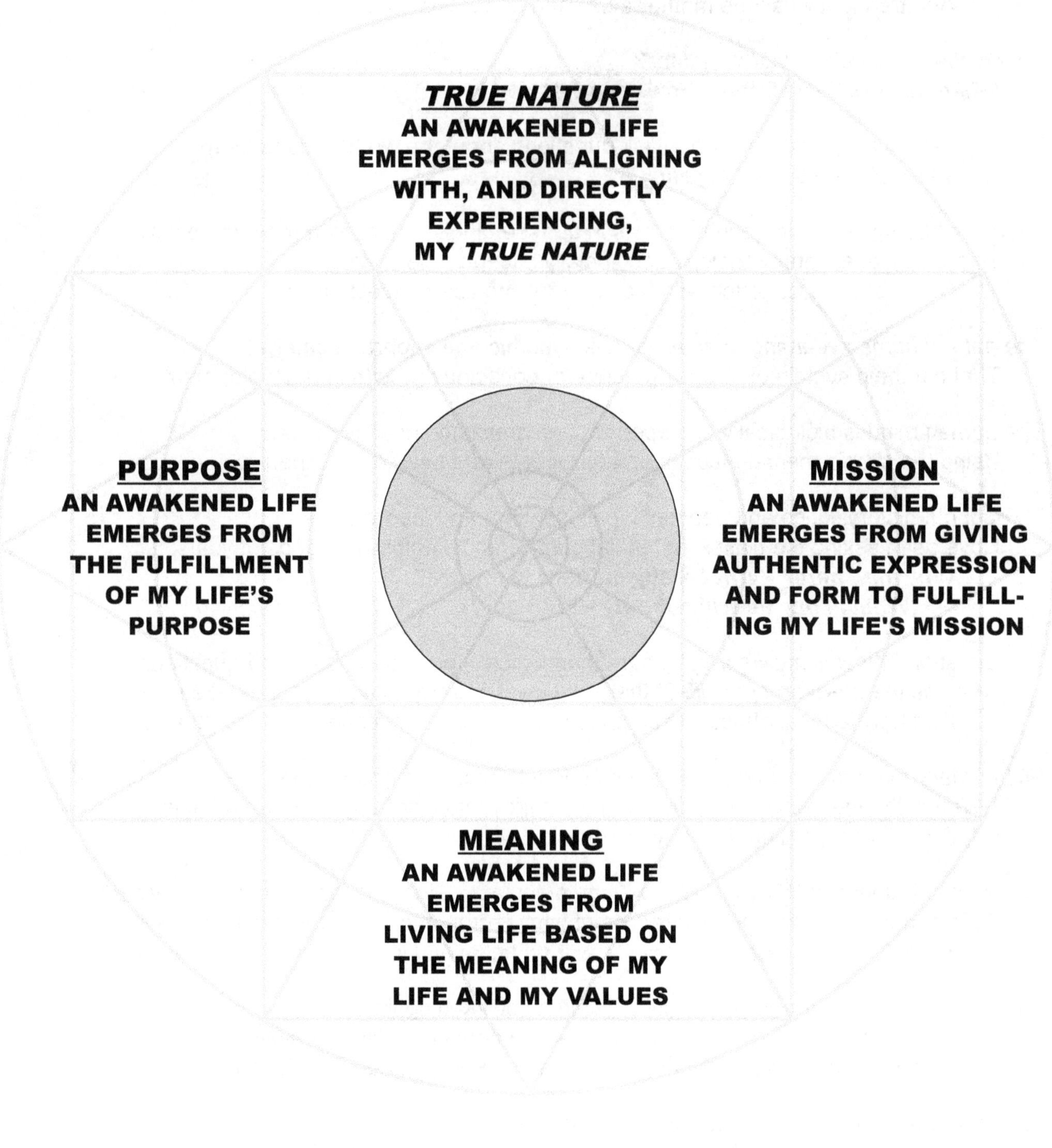

TRUE NATURE
**AN AWAKENED LIFE
EMERGES FROM ALIGNING
WITH, AND DIRECTLY
EXPERIENCING,
MY _TRUE NATURE_**

PURPOSE
**AN AWAKENED LIFE
EMERGES FROM
THE FULFILLMENT
OF MY LIFE'S
PURPOSE**

MISSION
**AN AWAKENED LIFE
EMERGES FROM GIVING
AUTHENTIC EXPRESSION
AND FORM TO FULFILL-
ING MY LIFE'S MISSION**

MEANING
**AN AWAKENED LIFE
EMERGES FROM
LIVING LIFE BASED ON
THE MEANING OF MY
LIFE AND MY VALUES**

THE QUEST FOR INNER FREEDOM

I frequently ask "the Big Questions" as a way to help me learn to live a life of inner freedom.

If you were to observe a healthy four-year old child who is with his or her mother,
  Typically around that age, the child will be very inquisitive about life
    And frequently ask the mother a barrage of curious questions.

Why is the sky blue? - What is that for?
  Where did this come from? - How does that work?

It's very natural for young children to ask questions about the world around them,
  And most of them do this regularly.

Yet as children grow up to become adults in our seemingly regimented modern society
  Of conventional career choices and socially accepted behaviors,
    Some adults lose touch with their natural impulse to question life's mysteries.

The natural human yearning to question is a dynamic and important catalyst
  That can help sustain our ongoing quest for conscious growth and development.

The human mind is biologically equipped with an amazing capacity to learn
  Using the simple mental focus of an appropriate and powerfully expansive question.

Throughout history, kings and peasants, philosophers and laborers,
  Have been asking the classic perennial questions of life for thousands of years:
    Why am I here? - What really matters in my life?
    What is my life truly about? - Who am I?

The question *"What is my life truly about?"* can logically point us to a related question,
  *"What is the **mission** of my life?"* that asks what creative actions we can take in our life
    And how to most effectively contribute our creative gifts and talents to others.

"What really matters in my life?" can point us to a similar type of question,
  *"What is the **meaning** of my life?"* which inquires into what is genuinely valuable
    And what makes our life truly worth living.

The enduring question *"Why am I here?"* can point us to, *"What is the **purpose** of my life?"*
  Referring to expanding our awareness of what is true and living a life of inner freedom,
    As well as the yearning to develop our potential and learn to love unconditionally.

"Who am I?" is a very powerful question within an awakening life
  And is the kind of question each of us, at some time in our life, will likely investigate,
    Which refers to aligning with, and ultimately realizing, our ***True Nature***.

The answers to the first three questions become ever-more clear
  As we sincerely contemplate the unending inquiry of this last existential question.

For when we authentically know who we really are,
  Then all other questions simply melt away.

Circle of the Quest for Inner Freedom
(The Natural Yearning to Live an Awakened Life)

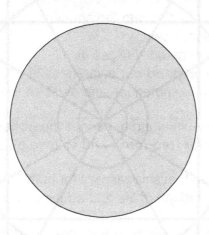

TRUE NATURE
(FORMLESS TRANSCENDENT)
"THE ONE"
MY *TRUE NATURE* IS ABOUT:
+ ALIGNING WITH
   THE SOURCE OF LIFE
+ BEING FULLY PRESENT
+ REALIZING THAT WHO
   I REALLY AM IS ETERNAL
+ EMBRACING PERFECTION

PURPOSE
(INTERIOR YEARNING)
EVOLUTION OF
MY CONSCIOUSNESS
MY PURPOSE IS ABOUT:
+ LEARNING
+ EXPANDING
+ DEVELOPING
+ AWAKENING

MISSION
(EXTERIOR YEARNING)
EVOLUTION OF
MY CREATIVITY
MY MISSION IS ABOUT:
+ CREATING
+ EXPRESSING
+ TRANSFORMING
+ CONTRIBUTING

MEANING
(RELATED TO FORM)
"THE MANY"
THE MEANING OF MY LIFE IS
   ABOUT:
+ SERVING
+ LOVING
+ GIVING
+ OFFERING KINDNESS

PURPOSE OF LIFE

Each day is really about learning to live a life of inner freedom - and to love unconditionally.

A flower innately yearns to grow towards the direction of the Sun,
  A young tree instinctually strives to reach for the sky,
    And an infant naturally longs to stand up tall.

There is a natural impulse in every facet of life which acts as an intrinsic invitation "to expand",
  "To develop", "to (metaphorically) reach upwards toward the stars".

The timeless question, *"What is the purpose of my life?"* is an inquiry of inner discovery,
  And is an investigation of our natural longing to awaken something grander within us.

This question is an inward pursuit "to reach higher into the unlimited sky",
  Stretch farther beyond our self-imposed boundaries,
    Travel to new places where we discover novel possibilities,
      And realize our Oneness with every expression of life.

This *journey of discovery* invites us to dive into the sanctuary of silence,
  The spacious stillness of our inner being
    Where *the Source of Life* constantly urges us
      To **learn** what is true, **expand** our awareness of what really matters,
        Develop our creative potential, and **awaken** to who we truly are.

This innate yearning is constantly whispering to us that **the collective purpose of our life**
  Is **to learn to live a life of inner freedom - and to love all of life unconditionally**.

This awareness is an essential step that's necessary for humanity to take its next leap forward
  In embodying a whole new paradigm of life and a new glorious stage of human evolution.

This perpetual whisper inspires us **to expand our understanding of what is true**
  As well as our awareness of the magnificent evolutionary unfolding of the Universe
    So we may be better stewards
      For the blossoming of a more enlightened global society.

When we align ourselves with this intrinsic impulse,
  It informs us that the common purpose of our life
    Is to awaken our conscious awareness of who we really are,
      For when we know who we truly are - we naturally explore creative ways
        Of manifesting the promise of a more cooperative humanity.

This impulse also evokes in us a natural yearning **to develop more facets of our potential**
  Knowing the possibilities that lay ahead on this human journey of discovery
    Are unlimited and boundless.

If we desire "to continue growing toward the light" and "to reach for the sky",
  It will serve us to take time to ponder and listen deeply within the fields of silence
    As we ask ourselves again and again the perennial question,
      "What is my life truly about?"

Circle of the Purpose of Life
(In Response to the Question "What is My Life Truly About?")

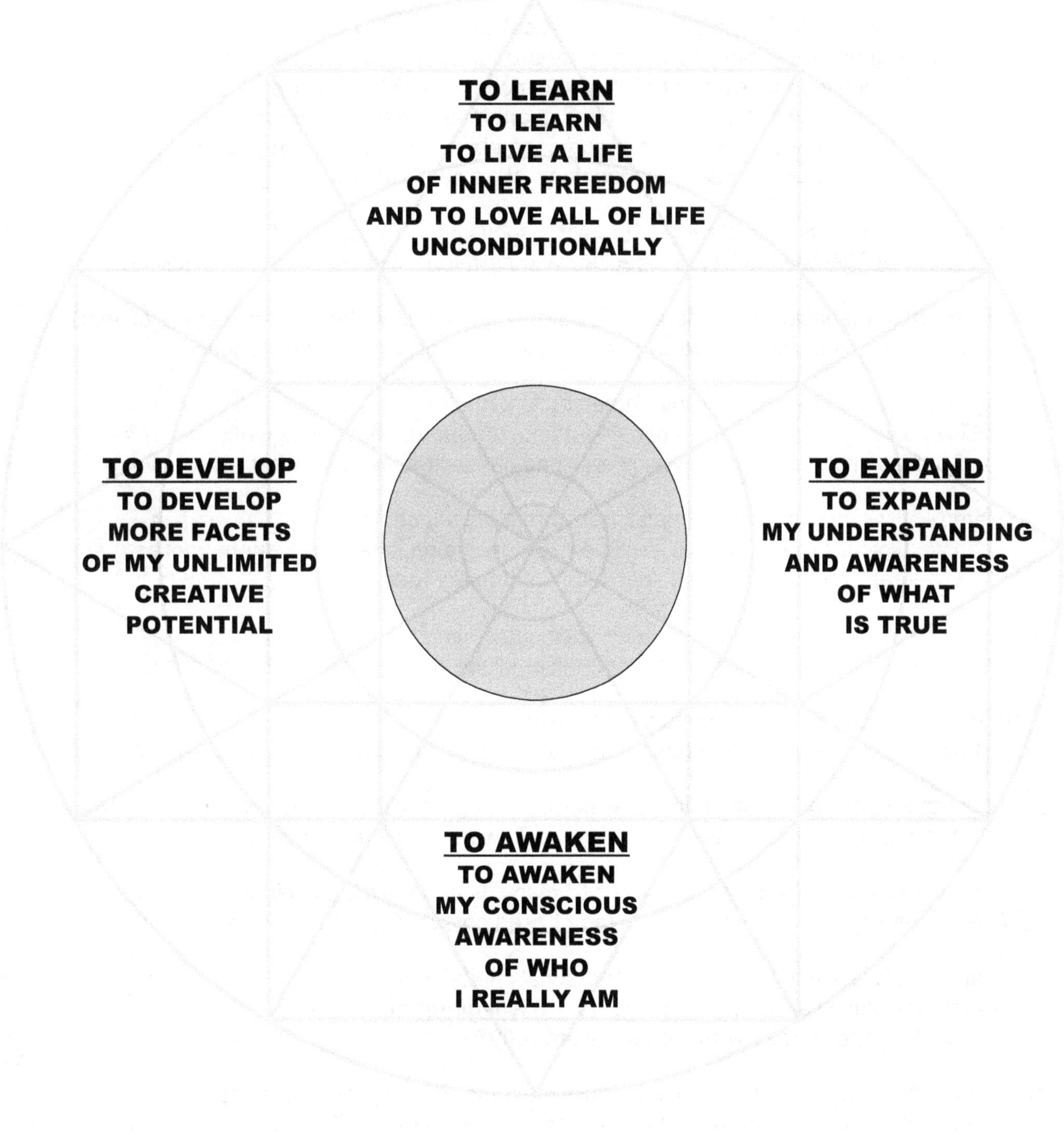

TO LEARN
TO LEARN
TO LIVE A LIFE
OF INNER FREEDOM
AND TO LOVE ALL OF LIFE
UNCONDITIONALLY

TO DEVELOP
TO DEVELOP
MORE FACETS
OF MY UNLIMITED
CREATIVE
POTENTIAL

TO EXPAND
TO EXPAND
MY UNDERSTANDING
AND AWARENESS
OF WHAT
IS TRUE

TO AWAKEN
TO AWAKEN
MY CONSCIOUS
AWARENESS
OF WHO
I REALLY AM

MEANING OF LIFE

I choose the particular meaning I give to everything - based on my current values and beliefs.

In high school science class, students are taught that every photon of light
    Has the paradoxical characteristic of being both a *particle* and a *wave* at the same time.

In the first part of the 1900's, the early mathematical pioneers of quantum physics
    Discovered a unique scientific tenet they referred to as *The Uncertainty Principle*
    Which declared that every photon of light naturally exists as a *wave*
        (Or explicitly, "a wave existing in a quantum realm of infinite probabilities"),
        And the conscious act of someone observing a particular photon
            Is what *collapses* a photon's wave into the form of a *particle*.

In fact, it is only the act of observation ("the act of focusing the attention of the mind")
    That enables the *wave* to have a specific finite form from all of its infinite possibilities.

In relationship to *meaning*, we humans have been doing a similar thing for thousands of years
    By "giving our own distinct *meaning*" to everything we observe and experience.

Nothing in this world has any particular *meaning* to it at all
    Until we place our individual attention on it and, therefore, choose to give it a *meaning*
        That fits into our personal worldview - and has value based on what we believe.

For example, if we've collected a special rock from a distant country during a vacation,
    Then we typically place our own sentimental *meaning* on it based on our memories,
        Whereas someone else just sees it as an ordinary rock.

The home we live in usually has generated special *meaning* to us,
    But to others, it might be just a common assemblage of wood, shingles, and bricks.

Each of us gives an explicit *meaning* to every aspect of our life,
    Yet our current *meaning* can change, over time, as our awareness changes.

Eons ago, the *meaning* for early humans was simply "to survive" in a harsh and hostile world,
    For that instinctual thought was the only primal awareness available to them at the time.

In today's world where people have developed many different levels of spiritual consciousness,
    One's *meaning of life* continues to change based on evolving awareness and values.

There are individuals who have made the personal choice that *the meaning of their lives*
    (What they place value on) is - **"to serve the wellbeing of others"**
        Or **"to experience loving others more fully"**.

If nothing in this world has any *meaning* at all except the *meaning* we choose to give it,
    Then *meaning* could become - **"to give generously to others"** or **"to offer kindness"**.

For when we perceive *the meaning of life* in this way, there appears to be a Universal Law
    Which is always at work (similar to *The Uncertainty Principle* of quantum physics)
        That yearns to awaken freedom in us - based on what we believe really matters.

Circle of the Meaning of Life
(In Response to the Question, "What Really Matters In My Life?")

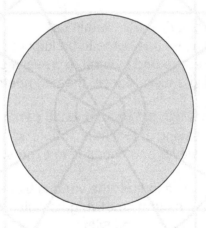

TO SERVE
TO SERVE
THE WELLBEING
OF OTHERS
AS WELL AS ALL OF LIFE

**TO OFFER
KINDNESS**
TO OFFER KINDNESS
TO THOSE
I MEET TODAY

TO LOVE
TO LOVE OTHERS
AND EVERY PART
OF LIFE
UNCONDITIONALLY

TO GIVE
TO GIVE
GENEROUSLY
TO THE PEOPLE
IN MY LIFE

ONE'S MISSION IN LIFE

Today I contribute my creative gifts and talents in ways that uplift and serve the lives of others.

The Italian sculptor, Michelangelo, started each new carving from a large block of marble
    And then slowly chipped away all of the stone which was not the intended design
        Until his exquisite masterpiece was finally revealed.

The painter, Vincent Van Gogh, began a new work of art with a blank canvas
    And then found colors, shapes, lines, and textures
        That portrayed an evocative scene and elicited a host of human emotions.

The musician, Amadeus Mozart, initially had an empty page of staff paper
    That he filled with the novel language of musical notations
        Providing the precise structure for a magnificent melodic composition.

These gifted individuals created unique and imaginative forms of their **mission in life**,
    Which can be thought of as what they each contributed to others as *a creative artist*
        By offering their expressions of beauty to their communities - and to the world.

But we don't need to think of "the creative artist within us"
    As only being associated with what has come to be known
        As the more traditional creative and cultural expressions of art
            Like sculpture, painting, music, dance, theater, poetry, architecture, etc.

"The true creative artist" that lives within the heart of each person abides in every facet of life,
    Such as in the everyday professions of teachers, laborers, economists, car mechanics,
        Bankers, politicians, or however one chooses to express their time and energy.

The day-to-day challenge for all of us is to find "the various blank canvases within our lives"
    That express and contribute the natural creative gifts which constantly flow through us
        In whatever we are personally involved with.

The Impulse of Universal Intelligence has been shaping its countless forms of creativity
    Throughout the entire Cosmos for the last 13.8 billion years of evolution
        And the expression of these forms can be referred to as its *function* or *mission*.

The Infinitely Creative Impulse that flows within us is constantly inviting us **to participate**
    By <u>transforming</u> ourselves so we may more effectively help build a better world.

This *Intelligence* also urges us **to <u>create</u> more diverse and pleasing forms of beauty**
    And to <u>contribute</u> to the unfolding and never-ending blossoming
        Of a more enlightened global society.

It continually encourages us **to <u>express</u>, in the outer world of form,**
    Our creative gifts and talents so we may uplift and serve the lives of others.

Everyone, no matter what career they choose or level of talent they possess,
    Has his or her unique way to express and contribute to the family of humanity
        As an unparalleled *artist of life*.

Circle of One's Mission in Life
(In Response to the Question, "Why am I here?")

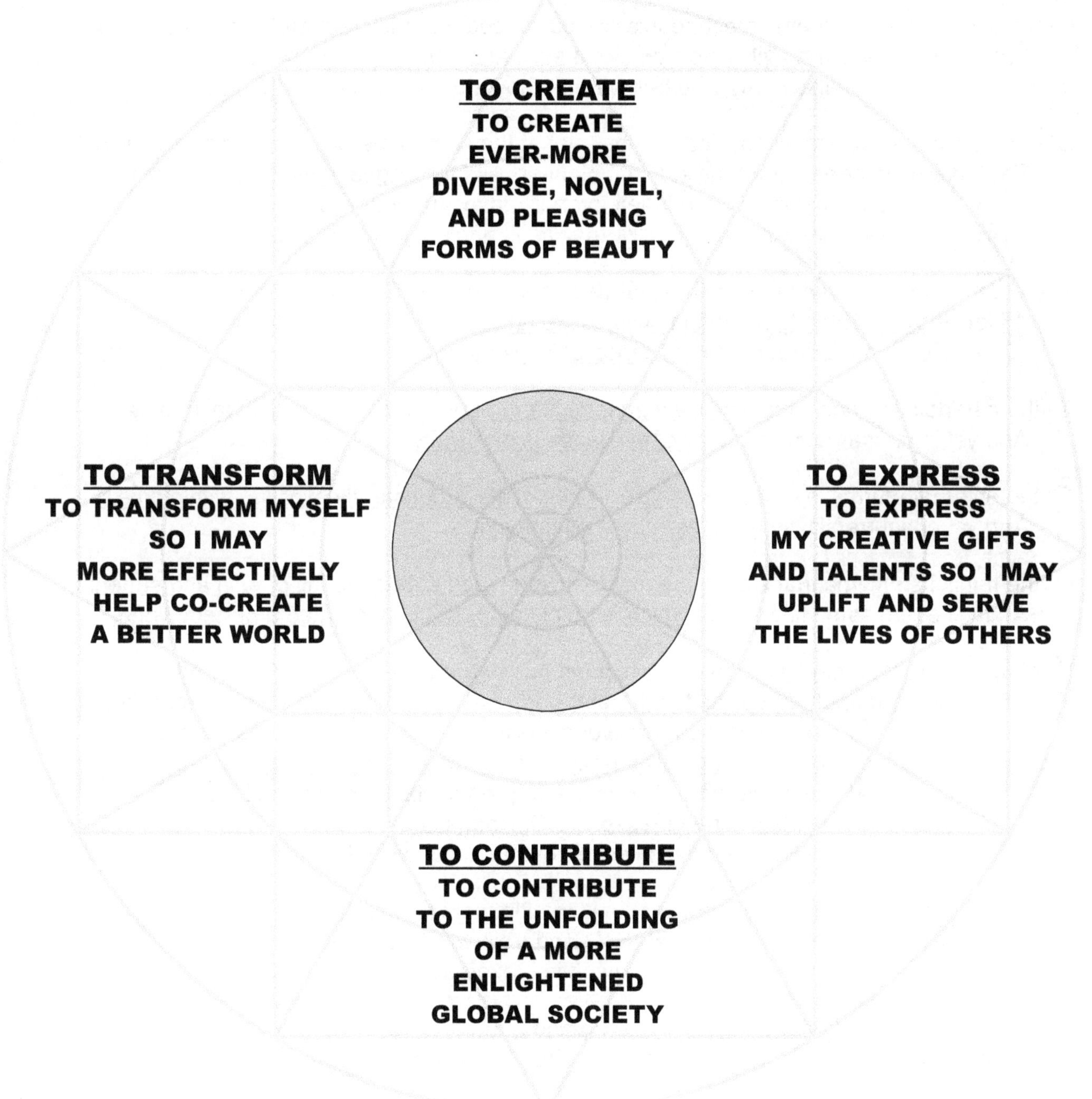

TO CREATE
TO CREATE
EVER-MORE
DIVERSE, NOVEL,
AND PLEASING
FORMS OF BEAUTY

TO TRANSFORM
TO TRANSFORM MYSELF
SO I MAY
MORE EFFECTIVELY
HELP CO-CREATE
A BETTER WORLD

TO EXPRESS
TO EXPRESS
MY CREATIVE GIFTS
AND TALENTS SO I MAY
UPLIFT AND SERVE
THE LIVES OF OTHERS

TO CONTRIBUTE
TO CONTRIBUTE
TO THE UNFOLDING
OF A MORE
ENLIGHTENED
GLOBAL SOCIETY

ONE'S TRUE NATURE

I consciously live with the paradox that my body's life is finite, yet at the same time, I am eternal.

At a physical level of reality we humans are fragile creatures, for when we fall - we get bruised,
When we cut ourselves - we bleed, and when we're out in the sun too long - we burn.

Generally speaking, it seems most people are convinced that they're merely corporal beings
With frail bodies which will simply cease to exist at death,
Yet there are also many who believe that they are so much more than this.

Of course it's true we are all physical beings - yet at the same time, we are also non-physical
For there have been numerous spiritual pioneers like the sages, mystics, and saints,
Who have intimately explored their interior realms (their non-physical realities)
And who have come to realize that life is riddled with *paradox*.

There are various *existential paradoxes* for us to consider, such as the paradox that states:
All forms of life come to an end in physical death,
And yet simultaneously, the essence of life is eternal.

Or the paradox that declares: we all experience life through our distinct individual bodies,
And yet in the same moment, all of existence is one Unity.

Or the one that affirms: every physical expression of life is constantly evolving within time,
And yet concurrently, timeless eternity is all that exists.

Or the religious enigma that states: the material world God created is full of pain and suffering,
And yet at the same time, God, which is unfolding perfection, created a perfect world.

All of us are on *a journey of discovery* to expand our awareness of who we really are,
And in order to open ourselves to a greater understanding of the vast *Mystery of Life*,
We must learn to live with paradox, especially the arcane paradox that states:
We are each a unique individual expression of evolving creation,
And simultaneously at some incomprehensible dimension of life,
We also abide in **Absolute Oneness**,
In other words, we're both humanly mortal and eternal.

What a powerfully transforming realization it is to ultimately discover
That our *True Nature* is our **Eternal Self** - and from a transcendent perspective
Our life is destined to be lived as a sublime expression of **Limitless Love**.

What a profound breakthrough it is to wake up and directly experience
That our *True Nature* is *Infinite Presence* - **the Perfection of What Is**.

Humanity may possibly be on the verge of making a quantum leap into a whole new paradigm,
A novel and emergent expression of magnificent evolutionary expansion,
And this expansion is taking place via the direct realization of one's *True Nature*.

This evolutionary leap in consciousness that we're all awakening to is "a universal gift",
The blessed and mysterious gift of directly experiencing and knowing who we really are.

Circle of *One's True Nature*
(In Response to the Question, "Who Am I?")

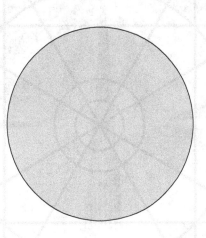

LOVE
I AM
LIMITLESS LOVE
+ + +
I AM
*THE UNBOUNDED ESSENCE
OF ALL THAT IS*

PERFECTION
I AM
INFINITE PRESENCE
+ + +
I AM
*THE PERFECTION
OF WHAT IS*

ETERNITY
I AM
THE ETERNAL SELF
+ + +
I AM
*THE TRANSCENDENT
SELF*

ONENESS
I AM
ABSOLUTE ONENESS
+ + +
I AM
*UNITY
CONSCIOUSNESS*

XVI

THE ART OF TRANSFORMATION AND HEALING

THE GREAT CIRCLE OF DEVELOPMENT AND TRANSFORMATION

As my inner development expands, I open to greater levels of transformation and healing.

When a professional magician performs a magic trick in front of an audience
    Such as transforming a red rose into a white rabbit,
        He or she usually places the rose into a container like a hat or a handkerchief
            Where the magic happens in "a secret space" that no one else can see.

If the trick involves a woman that's to be sawed in half,
    The magician will typically put her in a long wooden box
        Where the mysterious forces of transmutation will take place.

The hat, handkerchief, or wooden box serves the magician as *a transition space*,
    Where "the mystery of magic" transforms, for a moment, the world we believe to be true.

For the performing magician who executes theatrical illusions before an audience,
    There are *three primary levels of perceived reality* which the magician uses:
        1) *The object to be transformed*, 2) *the transition space*, and 3) *"the magic"*.

In relation to everyday life, there are also *three levels of reality* we use to co-create with *Life*
    Which are portrayed in the contemplation circle on the following page:
        1) Our awareness of who and what we believe we are in the present moment,
            2) The growing development of our awareness within our heart and mind
                That is mirrored in our body as our healing and transformation,
                    And 3) our conscious alignment with *the Source of Life*.

As a metaphor to help increase our understanding of **The Great Circle** (the dynamics of life),
    The magician's *object to be transformed* (such as a red rose or a compliant woman)
        Represents our current awareness of our self (displayed in the lower quadrant)
            With a willingness to expand our awareness - and thus be transformed.

The magician's *transition space* (i.e. hat, box) is like "the inner chamber of our heart and mind",
    In other words - it's our choice to love and expand our awareness of what is true
        Which we cultivate over time and express outwardly (left and right quadrants).

As we (with focused intention and heartfelt commitment) surrender this expanded awareness
    To *a Greater Transcendent Power* within us (to *the Infinite Intelligence of the Universe*),
        In other words, as we align our awareness with *the Source of Life* (top quadrant),
            This is where "the magic", or spiritual transmutation, takes place within us.

Our expanded **inner development** is then mirrored by **the Source of Life** in our body
    Utilizing **the transforming energy of *the transition space* (our heart and mind)**,
        And similar to the seasoned magician who mysteriously transforms the object,
            "The magic" of Limitless Love manifests healing and transformation in us
                Based on the level of our inner development and awareness.

So in a very real sense, we are all discovering how to become Spiritual Magicians
    As we purposely surrender every facet of our lives to *the Infinite Presence of Love*,
        Which is where *the true magic of life* really exists.

The Great Circle of Development
and Transformation
(The Transformative Dynamics of Healing)

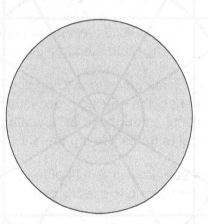

"THE ONE"
THE ONE SOURCE,
INFINITE INTELLIGENCE
+ + +
WITHIN THE REALM OF
ABSOLUTE ONENESS,
I AM ALWAYS ALIGNED
WITH *THE INFINITE*
PRESENCE OF LOVE

INNER
DEVELOPMENT
I CONSTANTLY EXPAND
MY AWARENESS OF WHAT
IS TRUE, LEARN TO LOVE
MORE FULLY,
AWAKEN TO WHO I AM,
AND DEVELOP MY
CREATIVE POTENTIAL

OUTER
TRANSFORMATION
AS MY DEVELOPMENT
EXPANDS, IT IS THEN
MIRRORED WITHIN MY
BODY BY *THE SOURCE*
OF LIFE **IN THE FORM**
OF TRANSFORMATION
OR HEALING

"THE MANY"
I AM A PERFECTLY
UNFOLDING EXPRESSION
OF THE MANY
UNIQUE FORMS OF LIFE
+ + +
IN THE PRESENT MOMENT,
I AM ALREADY HEALED AND
WHOLE

OUTER HEALING MIRRORS INNER DEVELOPMENT

Through a co-creation with the Source of Life my inner development is mirrored as my healing.

Whether it be a puncture wound in an arm, an emotional crisis between two lovers,
    A polluted river where fish are needlessly dying,
        Or an asteroid exploding into an orbiting planet that crosses its path,
            All structures in the Cosmos are, at times, in a natural process of healing.

When any material structure encounters imbalance, or what can also be called <u>outer chaos</u>,
    It always strives to discover creative ways to return to a state of <u>inner balance</u> (<u>order</u>).

Yet imbalance is an integral aspect of reality, for both <u>order</u> and <u>chaos</u> are part of a totality
    And all expressions of life use crisis and chaos as creative drivers to further growth
        Since the Universe intrinsically utilizes these experiences of crisis to "heal",
            In other words - to transform into higher stages of evolution and creativity.

During this natural process of healing (or what can also be referred to as re-balancing)
    Certain new emergent forms of creativity never before expressed, find ways to manifest.

All of creation would not be so rich with exquisite diversity without "this great cosmic dance"
    Of <u>chaos</u> and then <u>order</u> - of <u>imbalance</u> and then <u>healing</u> - of <u>crisis</u> and then <u>renewal</u>.

The fundamental principles that direct and animate the ongoing evolution of the entire Universe
    Are the same principles which affect the healing processes taking place within our life,
        Thus, whether it be a small cut on our hand or "a wound in the body of nations",
            The basic principles that underlie healing are still the same.

Furthermore, we can use the universally known tenets of *the Fields of Light, Love, and Power*
    To help us understand how outer healing is directly related to our inner development.

The arcane words *Light, Love,* and *Power* have been poetically portrayed for centuries
    In numerous spiritual texts and religious scriptures from around the world.

Yet from "a Big Picture perspective", these simple words hold many layers of spiritual meaning
    That can assist us in comprehending the expansive nature of true healing.

The Field of Light is a metaphysical phrase that describes the boundless possibilities
    And unlimited expressions of healing which are potential - and always available to us.

The Field of Love is *the Source of Life, the Infinite Intelligence* of the Universe,
    Which shapes *the Field of Light* into forms of healing based on our inner development.

The Field of Power is the outer <u>effect</u> of healing, the natural result of our inner development
    That awakens a higher stage of awareness (<u>cause</u>) mirroring *healing* within our body,
        And this internal shift of awareness is expressed externally as greater wellbeing.

Our attachments to desires, our emotional resistance, or our loveless beliefs lead to suffering,
    Whereas our expanded awareness which is consciously aligned with *the Source of Life*
        Is naturally expressed in our body - leading to gifts of transformation and healing.

Circle of Outer Healing Mirrors Inner Development
(The Process of Healing In Relation to the Fields of Creation)

QUEST FOR HEALING
MY ATTACHMENTS
TO MY DESIRES, MY
EMOTIONAL RESISTANCE,
OR MY LOVELESS BELIEFS
LEAD ME TO SUFFERING
OR IMBALANCE, WHICH
THEN MOTIVATES ME
TO SEEK *HEALING*

FIELD OF POWER
MY INNER DEVELOPMENT
AWAKENS A HIGHER
STAGE OF AWARENESS IN
ME THAT IS OUTWARDLY
MIRRORED IN MY BODY
AS TRANSFORMATION OR
HEALING AND EXPRESSED
AS GREATER WELLBEING

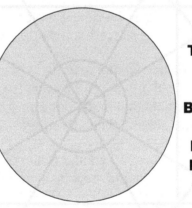

FIELD OF LIGHT
THROUGH MY CONSCIOUS
INNER DEVELOPMENT,
I LEARN THERE ARE
BOUNDLESS POSSIBILITIES
AND UNLIMITED
POTENTIAL FOR *HEALING*
MY BODY OR MIND WHICH
ARE ALWAYS AVAILABLE

FIELD OF LOVE
*THE INFINITE
INTELLIGENCE* OF THE
UNIVERSE *(THE FIELD OF
LOVE)* THEN SHAPES MY
ENERGY BODY *(THE FIELD
OF LIGHT)* INTO A SPECIFIC
EXPRESSION OF HEALING
BASED ON MY AWARENESS

A BALANCED APPROACH TO HEALING
The awakened realization of who I really am is the sublime sanctuary where I am truly healed.

A massive earthquake is simply a release of built-up tension between two tectonic plates
So the Earth's crust can move into a balanced place where it is stable once again.

The still surface of a large lake can be agitated into high waves by the raging power of a storm,
But as the turbulent winds recede, the lake will return to its mirror-like stillness.

It seems that every aspect of creation is in a constant dance of movement and change,
Yet at the same time, is always reaching for a natural state of equilibrium or healing.

To heal is to make whole - to heal is to restore balance - to heal is to establish equilibrium,
And to heal (from a human spiritual perspective) is to awaken to who we really are.

We are multi-dimensional beings that comprise both physical and non-physical aspects,
Including various *dimensions of our self* that need our attention to maintain health,
In other words - we require **a balanced approach to truly healing ourselves**.

Our most obvious area of healing is within the dense material reality that we see, touch, feel,
And observe moving through visible space each day, which we call our physical **body**.

There is also a subtle emotional realm or dimension
That forms a field of energy within and around us that is sometimes called **the heart**,
And is the invisible energy field that holds our emotions and passions
As well as our feelings of connection to others - and the Earth.

Beyond this emotional realm, there's an even subtler realm of energy that exists as **the mind**,
And this field contains all of our concepts, beliefs, intentions, and visions for the future.

And within the mysterious unfolding of our ever-evolving life,
Our *Eternal Self* is the vessel for all expressions of our body, heart, and mind,
And is the formless and timeless essence of who we really are.

During the experiences and exploration of our life, many kinds of imbalance can and do occur,
And a need for healing of our body, heart, or mind may arise in our awareness.

Yet there is an intrinsic impulse in each of us always seeking to make ourselves whole again,
To restore balance, to establish peace of mind, and to embrace our challenges as gifts,
As a natural yearning to reach for greater possibilities of what we can become.

Thus, we can garner our self-responsibility and uncover the many ways (on the following page)
To **care for and maintain balance within our body, nurture our heart,**
Cultivate our mind, and **align with our *Eternal Self*.**

Ultimately, it's a courageous leap in our willingness to grow, a graceful opening of our heart,
An expansion of our spiritual awareness, and a deepening of our compassion and love
That leads to the sacred place of an awakened realization of who we really are,
The sublime sanctuary where we are truly healed.

Circle of a Balanced Approach to Healing

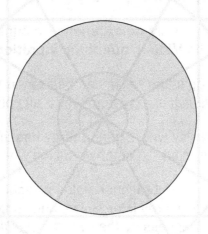

ALIGN WITH
THE ETERNAL SELF
1) ALIGN WITH *THE SOURCE OF LIFE*
2) MEDITATION
3) ABIDE FULLY IN THE PRESENT MOMENT
4) MINDFULNESS

CARE FOR
THE BODY
1) PROPER NUTRITION AND HYDRATION
2) WELLNESS REGIMES
3) ADEQUATE SLEEP
4) CREATE HEALTHY ENVIRONMENTS

CULTIVATE
THE MIND
1) CONTEMPLATE "THE BIG QUESTIONS"
2) FOSTER LIFE-ENHANCING BELIEFS
3) MANAGE STRESS
4) EMBRACE SHADOW

NURTURE
THE HEART
1) SERVE OTHERS
2) PRACTICE GRATITUDE
3) SHARE THE JOY AND LOVE OF COMMUNITY
4) SPEND QUALITY TIME IN NATURE

DIMENSIONS OF REALITY

I'm a multidimensional being living in a multidimensional world - yet at the same time, I am eternal.

When a cut crystal is placed in a window so sunlight can directly shine through the crystal,
    It acts as a prism which refracts the incoming light into a spectrum of rainbow hues
        Sometimes creating a spectacular image of color on an inside wall.

<u>The rays of sunlight</u>, <u>the refracted spectrum of light</u>, and <u>the colorful image projected on a wall</u>
    Are all created with the same energy, but are expressed as completely different forms.

This phenomenon is *one simultaneous act of creation* that's expressing itself in distinct ways
    Depending on where you place the focus of your attention.

We can use this visual metaphor to explore a deeper understanding of how to existentially view
    The various **dimensions of reality** as they influence our everyday lives.

From "the Big Perspective", we are multidimensional beings living in a multidimensional world
    And we each have the ability to experience many diverse dimensions simultaneously.

The various facets or dimensions of reality we experience in our lives
    Can be individually portrayed as *Virtual*, **quantum**, **vibrational**, or **physical realms**.

In the above visual metaphor, <u>the quantum realm</u> can be likened to infinite <u>rays of sunlight</u>
    Which represent *a field of potential energy* from which all possibilities can emerge.

It's the most subtle dimension of reality where pure energy has the potential to come into form
    By the focused intention of our mind - in other words, by where we place our attention.

Energy then flows to the next level, the vibrational realm, a slightly denser dimension of reality,
    And it is here that pure potential energy is organized into individual vibratory patterns
        Or specific fields of consciousness by *the Creative Intelligence* of the Universe.

Continuing this metaphor, <u>vibrational reality</u> can be symbolized by <u>a refracted spectrum of light</u>
    That's produced from a ray of sunlight shining through a prism
        And is expressed in our world as specific *fields of localized energy vibrations*.

<u>The colorful image on the wall</u> represents the <u>physical realm</u>, or that which has come into form,
    Because it's the densest dimension of reality where pure energy is coalesced
        Into, seemingly, "solid" patterns of creation (like trees, mountains, people, etc.).

All of these dimensions of reality, <u>quantum</u>, <u>vibrational</u>, and <u>physical</u>,
    Are different expressions of one universal energy manifesting in various energetic forms
        Which we can learn to attune with, based on the focus of our conscious attention.

Each of these dimensions of reality springs forth out of *The Unified Field*
    From which every form of creation emerges (also referred to as the <u>*Virtual Realm*</u>).

We live in a Universe in which we consist of *pure energy* that seems to emerge "out of nothing"
    And is projected like *a rainbow through a cosmic prism on the infinite screen of our life.*

Circle of the Dimensions of Reality

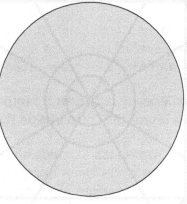

VIRTUAL
REALM
**"A DIMENSION OF LIFE"
THAT'S ALSO REFERRED TO
AS *THE UNIFIED FIELD*
FROM WHICH EVERY FORM
OF CREATION EMERGES
+ *PERFECT ONENESS*
+ *SOURCE OF ALL THAT IS***

PHYSICAL
REALM
**THE DENSEST
DIMENSION OF REALITY
WHERE PURE UNIVERSAL
ENERGY IS COALESCED
INTO "SOLID" MATERIAL
FORMS - SUCH AS
THE PHYSICAL BODY**

QUANTUM
REALM
**THE MOST SUBTLE
DIMENSION OF REALITY
WHERE PURE
UNIVERSAL ENERGY
HAS UNLIMITED
POTENTIAL AND
INFINITE POSSIBILITIES**

VIBRATIONAL
REALM
**A SLIGHTLY DENSER
DIMENSION OF REALITY
WHERE PURE UNIVERSAL
ENERGY IS ORGANIZED
INTO SPECIFIC FIELDS
OF LOCALIZED
VIBRATIONS**

QUANTUM REALM

Through a co-creation with the Source of Life I manifest my intentions into material form.

Imagine that a child is having fun in a colorful toy room
    Where there is a large number of alphabet blocks to play with.

Of course, a full set of toy alphabet blocks provides the child with the creative potential
    To assemble any word or sentence in the English language
        Based on the child's current level of mental development.

Over time as the child grows in greater cognitive awareness,
    He or she is able to create more interesting and useful words.

As a metaphor, **the quantum realm** can be seen as similar to alphabet blocks in a toy room
    Because this realm holds the particles (the unlimited building blocks) of potential energy
        From which all manifested forms in the Universe are shaped into expression.

This realm is **the unbounded ocean of limitless energy that emerges into existence**
    From *The Unified Field* (which is also referred to as *Virtual Reality*).

Just as a child has the potential to form any word using an array of alphabet blocks,
    The quantum realm is also the level of existence
        Where all manifestations and forms of creation exist as infinite potential.

It's **the dimension where universal energy is arranged into infinite forms of expression**
    By using the focus of creative imagination to shape the particles of pure *Light*.

With time, life experience, and as our awareness expands based on our inner development,
    The Infinite Creativity of Life then responds to our expanded level of awareness
        By out-picturing our inner development into the outer world of form.

Physicists have scientifically discovered many unique and bizarre characteristics
    About the strange realm of the quantum world.

One of the most mysterious aspects of **the quantum realm**
    Is that it's **the most subtle dimension of reality** (that we're currently aware of)
        Where universal energy perpetually winks in and out of existence
            From, seemingly, "out of nowhere" (from the void of *The Unified Field*).

The quantum realm is where the world appears to take form - and yet it doesn't,
    Where existence is - and yet it isn't,
        Where the Universe takes shape - and then seems to quickly disappear again.

It's a dimension of mystery, a realm of paradox,
    And an abundant "world of potential and boundless miracles".

You and I, at our current level of development, are like children playing in "a cosmic toy room"
    Where we're learning to assemble "the unlimited building blocks of the quantum realm"
        Into the outer manifestations of whatever we creatively imagine our life can be.

Circle of the Quantum Realm

INFINITE POTENTIAL
QUANTUM REALM –
THE LEVEL
OR DIMENSION
OF REALITY WHERE
ALL MANIFESTATIONS
AND MATERIAL FORMS
OF CREATION EXIST
AS INFINITE POTENTIAL

SUBTLE REALM
QUANTUM REALM –
THE MOST SUBTLE
DIMENSION
OF REALITY WHERE
UNIVERSAL ENERGY
PERPETUALLY
WINKS IN AND OUT
OF EXISTENCE

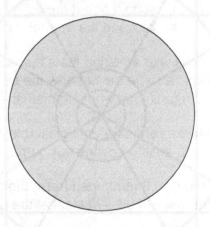

PURE *LIGHT*
QUANTUM REALM –
THE DIMENSION
OF REALITY WHERE
PURE *LIGHT* IS SHAPED
INTO INFINITE FORMS
OF EXPRESSION
WITH THE FOCUS OF MY
CREATIVE IMAGINATION

LIMITLESS ENERGY
QUANTUM REALM –
THE UNBOUNDED OCEAN
OF LIMITLESS ENERGY
THAT CONSTANTLY
EMERGES INTO EXISTENCE
FROM *THE UNIFIED FIELD*
(ALSO REFERRED TO AS
VIRTUAL REALITY)

MIRACLES

Aligning my awareness with the Source of Life opens my heart to receive miracles.

A thousand years ago, there was a common belief "that if you sailed a ship
    Over the distant outline of the ocean horizon, you would fall off the edge of the Earth".

Back then, people believed any ship which did manage to sail past the horizon and then return
    Must have experienced a "miracle" via the divine protection of some supernatural being.

Of course, this "so-called miracle" eventually became commonplace for all ocean vessels
    When it was discovered that the Earth is not flat, but a round spherical globe.

A young man from a nation who lives naturally and sustainably in the remote bush country
    May not know what electricity is - if he has never directly encountered it.

So if this man is taken to a modern country and then experiences electricity for the first time,
    It might appear to him to be some type of unearthly "miracle".

But if the same young man is taught in a school about the science of electricity,
    He finds out what it is and how it works - and the "miracle" is replaced with knowledge.

A magician can mesmerize audiences with amazing feats that appear "miraculous",
    But if you were to learn the magician's secrets of how the tricks were actually done,
        The unknown that seemed miraculous would immediately change to the known.

A "miracle" has been defined as an extraordinary unexplainable event which takes place
    Through an unknown intervention arising beyond our current understanding or beliefs.

"Miracles" seem to be something magical that happen from "the realm of the mysterious",
    And from "a domain that is unfamiliar to us" - at least at the present time.

Yet based on many scientific discoveries from quantum physics, we can **shift our awareness**
    To understanding that a "miracle" is **the acquired ability to bring into material form**
        An intended result from the quantum dimension of infinite possibilities.

There've been many forward-thinking people who revealed that "miracles" are the out-picturing
    Of **a leap of consciousness initiated at the quantum level of reality**.

For millennia, there have been healers, shamans, avatars, and great masters
    Who have inwardly and intuitively discovered a spiritual doorway to this quantum realm
    And have outwardly **created a desired effect that seemed "miraculous"**
        By focusing, with absolute certainty, an intention within their mind.

Nature is diverse and complex, and no matter how much we learn of its wonders in the future
    There will most likely always be some aspects of Nature that appear "miraculous" to us.

But like the healers who have come before us, as we cultivate our awareness, open our hearts,
    Align ourselves with *the Source of Life,* and realize what our life is truly about,
        We will all eventually learn to become "miracle workers".

Circle of Miracles

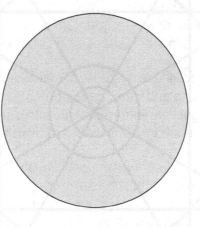

INFINITE POSSIBILITIES
MIRACLE –
MY ABILITY TO MANIFEST
INTO MATERIAL FORM
AN INTENDED RESULT
FROM THE QUANTUM
DIMENSION OF INFINITE
POSSIBILITIES

ABSOLUTE CERTAINTY
MIRACLE –
FOCUSING AN INTENTION
IN MY MIND WITH
ABSOLUTE CERTAINTY
AT THE QUANTUM REALM
AND SURRENDERING IT
TO *A GREATER POWER*

A SHIFT IN AWARENESS
MIRACLE – A SHIFT
IN THE OUTER FORM
OF SOMETHING CREATED
AT THE QUANTUM
DIMENSION AS A RESULT
OF A PROFOUND INNER
SHIFT IN MY AWARENESS

A LEAP OF CONSCIOUSNESS
MIRACLE –
THE OUT-PICTURING
IN THE WORLD OF A LEAP
OF CONSCIOUSNESS IN ME
THAT'S INITIATED
AT THE QUANTUM
REALM

FOUNDATIONS FOR EMERGENT HEALING

I embrace my challenges as "sacred gifts" that Life offers me to learn to love more fully.

In order for Earth to have had the proper biological conditions so life could emerge eons ago,
  It was first necessary for colossal explosions of supernova stars to seed empty space
    With specific primary elements that were essential to shape future life forms.

It was also necessary for countless asteroids that orbited our newly formed central Sun,
  To constantly collide violently into one another for millions of years
    And fashion our rocky planet into a structure which could yield "the womb of life".

It took a few more million years in which massive meteors crashed into the Earth's surface
  Further sculpting the planet's continental contours - and adding to its mineral content.

And then there was a long period of extensive volcanic disruptions and intense surface heat
  Until, over eons of time, our planet slowly cooled from these fires of transmutation
    Which were required to produce the conditions for the first emergent living cells.

Emergent healing is the sudden instantaneous wellbeing that takes place within one's body
  From a profound shift in consciousness, a quantum leap into a new level of wholeness
    In which certain previous forms of disease and imbalance can no longer exist.

Like all that was needed on Earth for life to emerge, for us to attain this shift in consciousness
  A great deal of expansive growth and inner development is usually necessary
    That results from the insights we experience due to our "explosive encounters"
      And the transformative life lessons we learn from these difficult situations.

This shift of awareness arises from "the countless collisions we endure with our inner demons"
  Which must eventually be overcome through surrender, acceptance, and self-love,
    And also arises from "the many crashes" we experience along our life journey
      That give us opportunities to awaken to the knowing of who we really are.

This kind of quantum leap is also generated from being immersed in "the fires of transmutation"
  Where we discover how to let go of our fear, attachments, and self-imposed suffering.

In time, these challenging life experiences can become "the sacred gifts that help us learn"
  To be <u>self-loving</u>, to be fearlessly <u>authentic</u>, to <u>appreciate</u> everything and everyone,
    And to be aware of our Unity, our <u>Oneness</u> with all people and all of life.

These four aspects of our development (**self-love, authenticity, appreciation,** and **Oneness**)
  Form the foundation for a profound expansion in consciousness
    Where we suddenly leap, or emerge, into a higher stage of spiritual awareness.

Our "explosions, collisions, crashes, and fires" (in other words, the disturbing events of our life)
  Are all essential building blocks that help shape our future radiant temple of wholeness.

For without these difficult life experiences, or "sacred gifts", that help us expand our awareness
  And cultivate our intention to love all of life unconditionally,
    The foundations for emergent healing would not be able to bestow their *miracles*.

Circle of the Foundations for Emergent Healing
(Ways to Cultivate My Intention to Love Unconditionally)

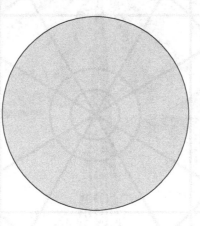

SELF-LOVE
I AM GRATEFUL FOR
WHAT I'M LEARNING
FROM EVERY EXPERIENCE
OF MY LIFE, I SURRENDER
MY ATTACHMENTS TO
MY DESIRES, AND I ACCEPT
MY LIFE IS UNFOLDING
PERFECTLY JUST AS IT IS

APPRECIATION
I APPRECIATE THE
UNIQUE CREATIVE GIFTS
AND TALENTS IN EVERY
PERSON, THE BLESSED
LIFE I EXPERIENCE EACH
DAY, AND ALL THAT I'M
DISCOVERING ABOUT
WHAT REALLY MATTERS

AUTHENTICITY
I INTEND EVERY DAY
TO BE THE MOST REAL,
GENUINE, AND HONEST
EXPRESSION OF ME
I CAN BE COURAGEOUSLY
EXPRESSING
MY UNIQUENESS
AND VULNERABILITIES

ONENESS
I EMBRACE MY ONENESS
WITH ALL OF LIFE
- AND CULTIVATE THE
CONSCIOUS AWARENESS
THAT MY *TRUE NATURE*
IS THE SAME ESSENTIAL
NATURE AS IN EVERY
FACET OF CREATION

XVII

CONCLUSION - SACRED DESTINY

BALANCE

I feel balanced when I'm fully present, and thus able to respond with love to the events of life.

The entire Universe is an infinite sea of radiant energy in constant motion and change,
   An unbounded ocean of pure universal energy shifting through endless evolving forms.

Life forms are always changing from a state of *balance* to one of *imbalance*, then back again,
   As part of a natural unfolding progression of continuous growth and expansion
      On a never-ending journey of exploring life's unlimited possibilities.

There is both a force reaching for *balance* or *order*, as well as a force reaching for *disorder*,
   And together, these two dynamic forces perpetually move the Universe forward.

Within the many spheres of science, **balance is sometimes referred to as *equilibrium***,
   And as a key universal principle, every material form is constantly striving for it.

To illustrate this idea using a physical example, if you take a glass of pure water
   And pour crystals of salt into the water in small amounts,
      The salt crystals will dissolve into the liquid and harmonize in a balanced way
         Because the water ions will bond with the salt ions creating *equilibrium*.

But if you then pour more and more salt into the glass,
   There eventually won't be enough water ions to bond with, or absorb, all of the salt,
      And *imbalance* will occur as salt crystals form at the bottom of the glass.

We humans are always longing to attain balance simply because being in balance feels good
   And our natural inborn *feeling mechanism (our emotional body)*
      Is *Life's* way of inwardly guiding each of us toward greater growth and expansion
         By reaching for our next experience of balancing what feels imbalanced.

By consciously aligning the choices we make
   With the awareness of what naturally feels good within the aliveness of our body,
      We're more able to be present and responsive
         To the changing circumstances of our life.

And as we align our awareness with *the Source of Life*,
   Our ability to tune into our feelings then becomes a mechanism of inner guidance
      That can help us maintain a healthy equilibrium
         As we courageously follow the guidance we receive from within.

Balance can also be thought of as **being fully present** and embracing the perfection of our life
   While we "absorb" all of the events we deal with each day - with ease and grace.

It is **the harmonizing experience** that's possible for us to achieve, no matter what's going on,
   When we're **able to flow** with any situation that arises.

From the perspective of how we are integrally connected to the changing rhythms of life,
   Balance and *imbalance* are "two dancers moving together in perfect harmony"
      As they perpetually turn round and round the upward-spiraling Circle of Life.

Circle of Balance
(In Relation to My Life Experience)

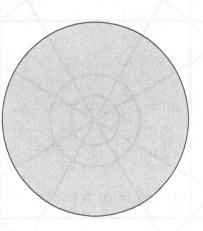

EQUILIBRIUM
BALANCE –
THE SENSE
OF EQUILIBRIUM
I FEEL AND EMBODY
WHEN I MAINTAIN
AN ALIGNMENT WITH
THE SOURCE OF LIFE

HARMONY
BALANCE –
WHAT I FEEL
WHEN I'M
IN HARMONY WITH
ALL OF THE DYNAMIC
AND DISTINCT FACETS
OF MY LIFE

FLOW
BALANCE –
WHAT I FEEL
WHEN I'M ABLE
TO EFFORTLESSLY
FLOW WITH
ANY SITUATION
THAT ARISES

PRESENCE
BALANCE –
MY EXPERIENCE
OF BEING
FULLY PRESENT
AND ABLE TO EMBRACE
THE UNFOLDING
PERFECTION OF MY LIFE

This series of Contemplative Practices continues in

The Autumn Volume: September 22 – December 20

The Winter Volume: December 21 – March 18

The Spring Volume: March 19 – June 19

The Great Circle Mantra

My life is unfolding perfectly
Just the way it is
Because all that truly exists
Is *Perfect Love*
Yet I am here
To help the world become more perfect
By living my life
Perfectly guided by *Love*

Introduction To The Poem - *The Diver*

It was a scorching June of 2008. I placed all of my camping gear into a canoe and headed down river into the wilderness. The morning winds were still with river water that reflected like a silvery mirror. A few echoes of birds sliced through the silence.

The idea for this poem came while I was in deep contemplation as the dawning sun was just rising over the silhouetted trees. There were jagged rock cliffs on the other bank of the river. I imagined that a man was standing on a rock precipice with a yearning to courageously dive into the cool waters below.

Then one of my Contemplation Circles came to mind regarding the foundational theme: Pillars of Awakening. These Pillars are qualities for cultivating inner freedom, a life of self-mastery. The four qualities depicted as the Pillars of Awakening are:

1) **Gratitude** - I am grateful for what I'm learning from every experience of my life.

2) **Surrender** - I let go of my attachments and surrender everything in my life to *a Greater Power*.

3) **Acceptance** - I accept that my life in unfolding perfectly just as it is.

4) **Oneness** - I am aware of my Oneness with all of life.

I imagined that the four unique stages of his dive from the rock ledge were portraying these four awakening qualities.

For many years, I have started my morning meditation by consciously connecting with these four pillars. Now as I bring them into my awareness each day, I sometimes visualize "the diver" as well.

— *Oman Ken*

This poem is an excerpt from Oman Ken's poetry book entitled
"Infinite Awakenings – Philosophical Story Poems Envisioning A More Glorious World".

The Diver

His bronze sculpted body stood suspended
　For what seemed an endless eternity
　　Both feet anchored
　　　At the edge of a high rock precipice
　　　　Overlooking the rippling waters of the sea below
　　　　His eyes gazing out in all directions

He patiently watched the slow turning of seasons
　The bitter cold biting at his skin
　　The soft blanket of air cradling him
　　　Storms, cyclones, and haunting whirlwinds
　　　　And the glories of a perfect twilight

Finally he discovers his moment of absolute stillness
　The sanctified place where he revels in whatever arises before him
　　Giving thanks for how it shaped him
　　　How it formed the curves of his body and mind
　　　　Grateful for the wondrous gifts of every breath
　　　　　For the energy of aliveness pulsing through him

And now ready to proceed
　Taking a final step to the rim of the rocky cliff
　　Looking down at the churning water below
　　　The sight of a swirling emerald ocean
　　　　Awakens an impulse of realization

His body prepares itself
　With a relaxed sigh of commitment
　　Adrenaline surging through the fibers of every muscle
　　　Bending knees in focused anticipation
　　　　Like a tiger perched to lunge on its prey

Then with an explosive vault
　He catapults himself forward
　　Leaping out into the unknown
　　　Letting go of familiar worlds
　　　　And slipping into a field of surrender
　　　　　Where only the courageous are invited

The air is unruffled and silky
        That guides his effortless freefall
                Invisible wings take over his downward flight
                        There is nothing to do
                                But embrace the wonder
                                        The fullness of it all
                                                Accepting the inevitable trajectory
                                                        Into the arms of what is - and what will be

His sculpted body pierces a portal through the water's crust
        Plunges deep within the ocean depths
                Disappears into the blue vastness
                        The droplets which caress his body
                                Were born from the one ocean
                                        That crash gentle waves
                                                Upon every distant shore

He is immersed within the womb
        Of this ubiquitous world
                Where timeless sea creatures
                        Chant their ancient songs
                                Heard by the divers who daringly seek
                                        To be reborn by their hallowed music
                                                To embody their sublime pageantry
                                                        And to dance in their revelations of freedom

For a never-ending instant
        The music engulfs him
                Consumes him - transforms him
                        He effortlessly merges
                                With the symphonic matrix of the oceanic
                                        The canticle of the deep
                                                To become the singer
                                                        The singing - and the song

Ultimately the primal urgency for air
        To fill his lungs with breath
                Magnetizes him toward the surface
                        To the next edge of infinity
                                Where he yearns to offer his virtuosity
                                        To an ever blossoming world

He emerges from the blue water
    Placing his feet upon a fragile Earth
        Knowing that to dive into freedom
            Is to rediscover
                The immeasurable treasures of the gods

For now everything has suddenly changed
    His eager eyes again gaze out in all directions
        Yet he simply notices
            That even though the totality of the Universe
            Has mysteriously awakened
                There is still another precipice to explore
            On the next horizon

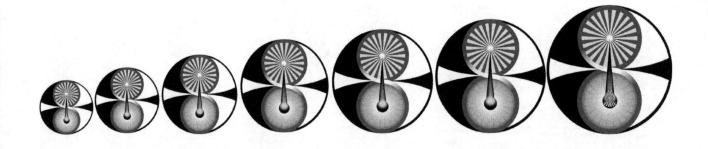

✳ JOURNEY OF *THE GREAT CIRCLE* – GLOSSARY OF TERMS ✳

Being defines the invisible and formless realm of *the Transcendent*. It is the sublime realm of existence in which all that exists is *Transcendent Oneness* - all that exists is *Absolute Perfection* - all that exists is *Unbounded Eternity* - all that exists is *Limitless Love*.

Becoming defines the natural process within any form of life that is developing its potential - which leads to manifesting more diverse creative expressions of itself or its environment. In relation to human beings, *Becoming* is one's *journey of awakening*. It is the *journey of discovery* or *spiritual journey* regarding one's inner development, the expansion of one's awareness, or one's spiritual awakening - which leads to greater contributions of one's creative gifts and talents employed in the service of others. *Becoming* can also be referred to as "one's creative actions and expressions to help make the world a better place".

Biosphere is *the Universal Consciousness* that gives shape to all biological life like microbes, plants, animals, which have evolved physical sensations and basic emotions.

Cause and Effect – The originating cause of everything within the phenomenal Universe is consciousness. The resulting effect from the creative intelligence of consciousness is the manifestations within the world of form (creation).

Consciousness is the invisible *Force of Natural Intelligence* which creates the visible world - the non-physical *Transcendent Power* which creates the physical Universe - an intangible internal *Awareness* which creates a tangible external reality. It is the invisible field of natural intelligence and information of any material or phenomenal structure that determines and gives creative shape to its visible form or pattern. Consciousness is the transcendent interiority of any structure of life which is the animating creative power that brings exterior form to its temporal body.

There is always some facet of consciousness (or natural intelligence) in every form of material expression within the Universe, such as the unique consciousness in every human being, animal, plant, micro-organism, rock, planet, star, galaxy, and beyond.

Consciousness is also the level or ability of a manifested form or structure within the Universe to be aware of, and respond to, experiences in its environment. A plant has a limited ability to respond to its environment. Whereas an animal has a greater, more developed ability. As far as is generally accepted, human beings have the greatest ability to be aware of, and respond to, experiences in their environment, and thus it is said that humans have the most evolved consciousness of all creatures on Earth.

Creation defines the phenomenal embodiment of the material realm. It is all expressions of the Universe - such as galaxies, stars, planets, microorganisms, plants, animals, and humans. Creation is also a word that represents the world of Nature.

In this book, the words Nature, Sun, Moon, Earth, Solar System, Universe, Cosmos are capitalized to represent that at a particular realm of consciousness, they are each a living entity of creation which is to be held in reverence, respect, honor, and is to be seen as sacred.

Emergent Healing is the spontaneous transformation that instantaneously happens within our body, heart, or mind when we experience a radical and profound shift in consciousness. *Emergent healing* is an extraordinary change and sudden balance that occurs in our being when we experience an internal "quantum leap" to a higher stage of awareness.

At these higher stages of awareness where we embody a greater level of wholeness, various forms of disease and imbalance, which we may have encountered previously, can no longer exist within the elevated frequency of *Limitless Love*.

Enlightenment is the sublime embodiment of inner freedom - which is living at a stage of spiritual consciousness where one abides in inner peace no matter what occurs. *Enlightenment* (from the perspective of this book) is not only about one's personal *awakening* or awareness of Oneness with God *(the Transcendent)*, but that any sustained individual alignment with *Ultimate Reality* must also be embodied and grounded within one's physical body and then shared collectively through the personal actions of serving the wellbeing of others.

In some contemporary spiritual groups, the concept of *enlightenment* is now perceived as an ongoing experience of loving others and loving self unconditionally while serving the good within all of life.

Evolution is the creative and natural development within all of life. It is the response within every phenomenon to *the Natural Intelligence* of the Universe which directs each facet of existence to further develop, expand its possibilities, create diversity, and express more of its potential.

The Evolutionary Impulse is *the Natural Intelligence* within the Universe that animates every material form along a path of perpetual creative unfoldment. It is the transcendent organizing principle within all of Creation. It can be thought of as *the Infinite Creativity* within all of existence that intelligently shapes and organizes higher expressions of manifested form such as galaxies, stars, oceans, myriad life forms, and every human being.

The Evolutionary Impulse is (from a religious perspective) the same as *the Universal Force of God* that guides development and manifestation within all forms of the natural world. It is the *Force* that "attracts together" sub-atomic particles, the planets in their solar orbits, all interdependent ecosystems, as well as two lovers who experience romantic passion.

Evolutionary Perspective – see Evolutionary Spirituality

Evolutionary Spirituality is a phrase that describes a "Big Picture Perspective" way of thinking about how our lives develop and transform. Evolutionary spirituality provides us with the gifts of a much larger perspective of reality inspiring us to further develop our higher potential, to motivate us to transform our fear-based self-oriented nature, to create the seeds of greater compassion for all of life, and to take responsible conscious actions toward building a more sustainable future.

Evolutionary spirituality merges both *the Transcendent Power of Consciousness* and the myriad forms of creation. It unifies God with evolution. It is the awareness which embraces a Oneness of an *Infinite and Eternal Intelligence* with an ever-unfolding Universe.

Existence is defined as the totality of the physical and the non-physical, the visible and the invisible, the Immanent and *the Transcendent*. It is the wholeness and merging of consciousness and creation, God and the Universe, Spirit and form, *"The One"* and *"The Many"*, *Being* and *Becoming*.

Fractals are natural objects or mathematical patterns that repeat themselves at smaller scales in which a reduced-size copy of the initial pattern is formed in succeeding generations, typically producing new emergent variations within each later generation.

There is also a group of *fractal patterns* that repeat themselves identically as they get smaller, yet the vast majority of *fractals* repeat their patterns with slight variations each time generating new and novel formations at different levels of magnification.

For example, trees grow in *fractal patterns* both above and below the ground, as well as the veins and arteries within the human body. Other *fractal patterns* that occur in the natural world are not as obvious - such as the way amorphous clouds slowly accumulate and form in the sky, how the ragged rock edges of mountain ranges are structured, the manner in which the coastlines of countries take shape, and how the patterns of galaxies and solar systems are created.

God – see *the Transcendent*

The Great Circle is "a spiritual map of an awakening life" which illustrates that our inner development determines and gives creative shape to how our external reality is expressed in our life. In other words, it portrays the universal dynamics of our inward expansion of consciousness mirrored as our outward creative expression.

There are many examples of traditional iconic images that represent *The Great Circle* - such as the Yin Yang symbol, the Star of David, the medicine wheel, and the sacred cross.

The primary function of **The Great Circle** as a transformative tool is to simply portray a useful collection of words and phrases for the purpose of deeply comprehending the nature of existence. With this awareness we can develop a greater understanding of what our life is truly about and what really matters - and thus, cultivate an unconditional love for each expression of life.

Holiness and Magnificence is another way of describing our *True Eternal Nature*, our *Transcendent Self*, who we really are. In religious language, it is our sacred divinity.

Infinite Awakenings represents the perpetual evolution and constant development that occurs in every phenomenal structure in the Universe - including galaxies, stars, planets, animals, plants, micro-organisms, and humans. "Awakening" describes a natural process of "developing to a higher level of awareness" or "expanding to a more elevated stage of consciousness" or "evolving to a new species". "Infinite" points to the awareness that *Life's* "awakenings" continue on and on without end.

Infinite Intelligence – see *The Transcendent*

The Infinite Presence of Love – see *The Transcendent*

Inner Freedom is when one consciously realizes the perfection that's always unfolding within - and within all of life. Living with this awareness allows the natural states of peace, happiness, joy and harmony to effortlessly arise. It is a life of one who has devotedly learned to love others and all of life unconditionally - and who has gained the joyful awareness of serving the wellbeing of others. In these writings, one who attains this level of mastery is referred to as a **Master of Freedom**.

Therefore, when we are aligned with *the Source of Life* - and gratefully celebrate every experience we have while fully loving and accepting ourselves, as well as every part of life - we are free.

Journey of Awakening is the natural evolutionary journey of ongoing inner development that every person in the world is constantly embarked on (whether he or she is consciously aware of it or not). Over time, this *journey of discovery* becomes conscious and intentional through a process of expanding one's awareness, transforming one's beliefs, discovering how to master a life of inner freedom, and contributing one's creative gifts and talents to the wellbeing of others. This is also referred to as the *spiritual journey* or the *journey of self-mastery*.

Life (when italicized and spelled with a capital) is a word that represents *the Transcendent, the Source of All That Is, the Infinite Intelligence* of the Universe. It is a short way of referring to *the Source of Life*. When "life" is not italicized and capitalized, it represents our human existence in the physical world.

Limitless Love – see *The Transcendent*

"The Many" can be defined in a number of ways, such as the myriad forms of life, the countless expressions of natural creativity on the Earth and throughout the Universe, all that is created, the endless manifestations of creation, etc. In relation to human beings, *"The Many"* is the totality of all humans that exist on the planet. Every person is a unique creative expression of *"The Many"*.

Master of Freedom is a visionary archetype that represents our *Fully Awakened Self,* one's *True Eternal Nature* completely experienced and lived within one's physical body. It is the embodied realization of a person who lives a life of inner freedom, loves all of life unconditionally, and serves the good of all with their creative gifts and talents. It is every person's sacred destiny to embody the *Awakened Self* and fully experience their life as a **Master of Freedom.**

Morphogenetic Field is a phrase used in developmental biology and consciousness studies that proposes there is a tangible field of energy that's generated by all things, both physical structures and even mental constructs, which serves to organize the structure's characteristics and patterns.

When we consciously align ourselves to *the morphogenetic field of a specific visionary archetype*, we begin a process of personally resonating to the archetype - and bringing into our awareness the expansive qualities and visionary characteristics which the archetype symbolizes.

Noosphere is *the Universal Consciousness* that gives shape to both the individual and collective mind, which resides within all intelligent life forms.

"The One" – see *The Transcendent*

Oneness is Ultimate Reality in which every form of creation is a unique expression of one *Unity*. It can be described as Infinite Reality in which each expression of life is an integral part of *one unfolding never-ending spiral of Consciousness*. Oneness can be thought of as Quantum Reality in which all of the manifest world of form is made of the same *universal energy (Light)* in constant motion. It can also be described as Transcendent Reality in which the Universe and everything in it is comprised of *one Universal Love*, and many people simply call this *Love* - "God".

Paradox is the perception that two discrete realities which contradict each other both exist at the same time. It is the notion that two expressions of reality which are complete polar opposites can both take place at once.

In the writings of **Journey of *The Great Circle***, embracing the existential paradoxes of life is a key to the cultivation of spiritual awakening. Embracing certain paradoxes enables us to merge consciousness with creation - God with the Universe - *Heaven* with Earth.

Physiosphere is *the Universal Consciousness* that gives shape to all material structures in the Universe - such as atoms, galaxies, stars, mountains, etc.

The Source of Life (The Source of All That Is) – see *The Transcendent*

Spiritual Journey – see *Journey of Awakening*

The Transcendent is the *Supreme Ubiquitous Intelligence* that is beyond form. It represents the invisible and formless *Natural Intelligence* throughout the Universe. *The Transcendent* is the sublime organizing principle which fashions everything in the manifested world of the material realm.

For millennia, this *Natural Intelligence* has been referred to in many ways throughout the world (The Thousand Names of the Divine) - such as *the Source of Life, Universal Consciousness, Pure Awareness, God, Allah, Tao, the Creator, the Great Spirit, the Great I Am, the Infinite Presence of Love, the Unbounded Ocean of Being, "The One", Infinite Intelligence, Limitless Love,* and so many more exquisite names for this sublime *Transcendent Power*. In many religious traditions this *Natural Intelligence* is simply referred to as "God".

(Note: Words that represent *"The Transcendent"* within **Journey of *The Great Circle*** are capitalized and italicized)

The Transcendent Impulse is defined as a constant spiritual yearning that we become aware of in our lifetime. It is the natural impulse to expand our awareness of what our life is truly about, to develop our potential, and to awaken to who we really are (an ascending impulse).

At the same time, it is the constant spiritual yearning of our expanding inner development to manifest ever-new expressions of creativity in our life (a descending impulse). This intrinsic and constant yearning (which is both the longing for spiritual awakening and for spiritual embodiment) that perpetually exists within us and within all forms of life - is called *the Transcendent Impulse*.

True Eternal Nature is the invisible transcendent consciousness of who we really are. It is the part of us that is eternal, unbounded, and limitless. Our *True Nature* is the aspect of who we are that guides and directs our life when we have learned to be aware of it.

There are numerous names for our *True Eternal Nature* - such as *the Higher Self, the Transcendent Self, the Authentic Self, the Essential Self, the Divine Self.* In many religious traditions, it is commonly referred to as the *"Soul".* Within **Journey of The Great Circle** it is also called our "holiness and magnificence".

The Unbounded Ocean of Being – see *The Transcendent*

The Unified Field is a term, which comes from quantum physics, that's defined as a limitless field of all possibilities that is formless and unbounded from which everything in the entire known Universe has emerged. Many religious traditions speak of this *Field* simply as "God" - or "The Kingdom of God" - or the Divine.

Unisphere is *Universal Consciousness* - which can also be referred to as *"The One", the Oneness within all of Consciousness, the Source of All That Is, Infinite Intelligence, The Unified Field, God.*

Universal Consciousness – see *The Transcendent*

Visionary Archetypes are poetic images of our greater potential or possibility. They represent qualities and virtues on ever-higher levels of human consciousness. Visionary archetypes are symbolic templates that point us to higher stages of inner development and to the qualities and realms of creative expression we strive to achieve. They can be thought of as pictorial representations of superior moral qualities which can empower and motivate us to express something greater in ourselves, a promise of a more positive future for our life.

✳ THE STORY OF AWAKENING WITHIN THE FIRST NARRATIVES ✳

IN THE CONCEPTUAL DESIGN of **Journey of The Great Circle**, there is a poetic interweaving of themes within the first four contemplative narratives of each volume. Together these four narratives reveal "a hidden archetypal story" about every person's *spiritual journey of discovery*.

The first four narratives of the Summer Volume are:
    1) Gifts of Summer
    2) Qualities Within the Seasons of Life
    3) The Great Story of Awakening
    4) *Journey of Awakening*

The Transcendent Gifts of the Four Seasons

The first narrative of every volume depicts the transcendent gifts of each season, such as "Gifts of Summer" in this volume. Each season has four qualities listed that describe important interior aspects of our unfolding lives. Every quality has a particular placement either in the north, east, south, or west orientation.

Qualities Within the Seasons of Life

The second narrative within each of the four volumes is called "Qualities Within the Seasons of Life". This narrative lists all the transcendent qualities from the season on the previous page as well as all four qualities from each of the other seasons from the remaining volumes. Therefore, each of the four seasons displays four essential qualities (totaling sixteen individual qualities) that relate to our human developmental journey.

The Great Story of Awakening

The third narrative of each volume is called "The Great Story of Awakening". This narrative explains how the universal archetypal story of our spiritual awakening can be derived from organizing the four transcendent qualities from each of the four seasons into four specific chapters of a "story" that we are calling "The Great Story". These four chapters are the key components of the universal story of an awakening life (The Great Story) - and are listed as:

    1) *The Great Circle*
    2) Pillars of Awakening
    3) Master of Freedom
    4) Spheres of Contribution

"The Great Story of Awakening" can be thought of as "the spiritual portrayal of an awakening life" - and is the personal story of our conscious inner development and expansion of our awareness. It is our individual *journey of awakening*, our *journey of self-mastery*, in which we learn to awaken to a higher stage of spiritual consciousness.

The First Chapter: *The Great Circle*

The first chapter of "The Great Story of Awakening" is called **The Great Circle**. This chapter is formulated by gathering the first or top quality of each season from the previous narrative entitled "Qualities Within the Seasons of Life". The chapter of **The Great Circle** includes the following four qualities:

1) From **Winter:**   Align With *"The One"*   - (renewal and alignment)
2) From **Spring:**   Outward Expression   - (creativity and contribution)
3) From **Summer:**   Serve *"The Many"*   - (service to others and cultivating self-care)
4) From **Autumn:**   Inward Expansion   - (development and expanding awareness)

As we explore the daily narratives throughout this book, we will be introduced to the various dynamics at play in the world and in our lives. The first chapter called **The Great Circle** speaks to the natural invitation from *The Transcendent Impulse of Life* to learn what our life is truly about, discover what really matters, and cultivate an awareness of how to live a life of inner freedom.

The Second Chapter: Pillars of Awakening

In the first chapter, **The Great Circle** invites us to explore the Big Questions of *Life* and what our life is truly about. The personal inner development from this pursuit provides us with insights about the next segment of our unfolding story of discovery.

The second chapter, **Pillars of Awakening**, is created by gathering the second set of transcendent qualities from the narrative "Qualities Within the Seasons of Life". This includes the four following qualities:

1) **Winter:**   Oneness
2) **Spring:**   Acceptance
3) **Summer:**   Surrender
4) **Autumn:**   Gratitude

These four qualities are actually different ways to describe self-love and unconditional love - and are the personal attributes we develop using daily transformative practice to consciously transform our suffering into a life of inner freedom.

As an *artist of life*, we practice these spiritual attributes as a way to develop our highest expression of ourselves, as a means to cultivate our creative potential, and as a vehicle to reach for the next horizon of possibility of what we can become. Through our daily practice, we learn to maintain an ongoing alignment with *the Essence of Creation, the Source of Life, the Love of God*. And we reconnect with a natural transcendent yearning within us to feel this alignment in every moment of our life.

The Third Chapter: Master of Freedom

As we develop spiritual maturity and learn to maintain an alignment with *Life*, with *the Source of All That Is* we enter into the third chapter of our *awakening journey*, **Master of Freedom**.

Master of Freedom is the visionary archetypal image of an individual who is a fully integrated awakened being - and who experiences inner freedom, consciously maintains an alignment with *the Source of All That Is,* and uses his or her unique gifts and talents to serve the good of all. The chapter **Master of Freedom** is formulated by gathering the third set of transcendent qualities from the narrative "Qualities Within the Seasons of Life". This includes the qualities:

1) **Winter:**   Awakened Presence
2) **Spring:**   Endless Creativity
3) **Summer:** Unconditional Love
4) **Autumn:** Limitless Development

Through dedicated daily transformative practice these four qualities empower us to integrate our inner development into our everyday life as an embodied and anchored experience. These are the qualities of consciously cultivating the mastery of living a life of inner freedom - in other words, living an awakened life. Once this level of spiritual awareness has been realized, it becomes obvious that the most important way to use our creative energy is to offer our unique mission to the world through our personal contributions. Furthermore, we recognize how natural it is to follow the inner guidance of our heart as we share our novel contributions to help create a more glorious world.

The Fourth Chapter: Spheres of Contribution

The fourth chapter of "The Great Story of Awakening" is called **Spheres of Contribution**. As we explore this chapter, we discover ever-greater ways of living in this world and offering our creative gifts and talents. The chapter **Spheres of Contribution** gathers the fourth set of transcendent qualities from the narrative "Qualities Within the Seasons of Life". These include:

1) **Winter:**   Contributions to Oneself
2) **Spring:**   Contributions to Family
3) **Summer:** Contributions to Community
4) **Autumn:** Contributions to the World

When we learn to maintain an experience of living our life with peace of mind and inner freedom, the next obvious and intrinsic awareness is for us to serve the wellbeing of others - and to contribute our unique creative gifts and talents.

When these four chapters, *The Great Circle*, **Pillars of Awakening**, **Master of Freedom**, and **Spheres of Contribution** are placed together sequentially, they form the universal great story of our spiritual awakening, or what has been referred to in this book as **"The Great Story of Awakening"**.

Quadrant Directions	Gifts of Summer		Qualities Within the Seasons of Life	The Great Story of Awakening
NORTH Winter	Serve *"The Many"*		* Align With *"The One"* + Oneness – Awakened Presence x Contributions to Oneself	***The Great Circle*** * Align With *"The One"* * Outward Expression * **Serve *"The Many"*** * Inward Expansion
EAST Spring	Surrender		* Outward Expression + Acceptance – Endless Creativity x Contributions to Family	**Pillars of Awakening** + Oneness + Acceptance + **Surrender** + Gratitude
SOUTH Summer	Unconditional Love		* **Serve *"The Many"*** + **Surrender** – **Unconditional Love** x **Contributions to Community**	**Master of Freedom** – Awakened Presence – Endless Creativity – **Unconditional Love** – Limitless Development
WEST Autumn	Contributions to Community		* Inward Expansion + Gratitude – Limitless Development x Contributions to the World	**Spheres of Contribution** x Contributions to Oneself x Contributions to Family x **Contributions to Community** x Contributions to the World

Journey of Awakening

The fourth contemplative narrative found within each volume is entitled *"Journey of Awakening"*. It has been written as another pragmatic version and additional way of understanding the preceding narrative **"The Great Story of Awakening"**.

"Journey of Awakening", with its four stages that describe our *spiritual journey*, form the foundation for our conscious exploration and inner development of self throughout the four volumes of **Journey of *The Great Circle*.** The four stages are:

1) Development   = *The Great Circle*
2) Transformation = Pillars of Awakening
3) Mastery   = Master of Freedom
4) Contribution = Spheres of Contribution

✳ THE DANCE, POETRY, AND SONG OF THE FRONT COVER ART ✳

THE FRONT COVER ART of **Journey of _The Great Circle_** is a visual representation of the relationship between three facets of reality: the transcendent aspect of life, one's _Eternal Nature_, and one's physical embodiment. In other words - it is a symbolic representation of the integration of _Spirit_, _Soul_, and body.

We are so much more than we appear to be. Our physical bodies are just a small part of the magnificent totality of who we really are. The realm of our physical body is like an iceberg that appears above the surface of the water. Yet ninety percent of the mass of an iceberg remains invisible underneath the ocean's waters. Similarly a vast part of who we really are remains invisible to our senses, yet it is present in, and determines, every aspect of our life.

Our physical body is obviously visible in the world of form, yet our _True Eternal Nature_ and _the Infinite Intelligence within All That Is_, which created everything in the Cosmos, is invisible to our five senses.

The artwork of the front cover symbolically represents this awareness, and gives us a visual metaphor to use to deepen our understanding of it.

The black and white meditator represents our physical body that is embarked on a _journey of discovery_ to learn to love all of life unconditionally.

The gold branches and roots of the Tree of Life represent our _True Eternal Nature_, our _Higher Self_, our _Soul_, which is eternal and unbounded - and is the consciousness that is mirrored in our physical body.

The circle around the Tree of Life, as well as the Universe of infinite stars, represent _the Transcendent_, _the Infinite Intelligence_ of the Universe, _the Source of All That Is_.

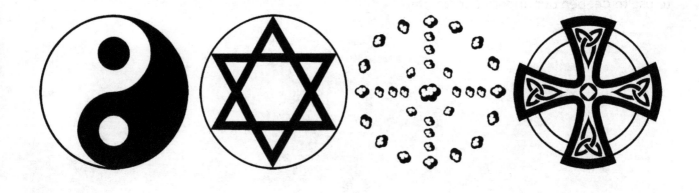

✳ RESOURCES ✳

Braden, Gregg. *The Isaiah Effect + The Divine Matrix*

Brown, Michael. *The Presence Process*

Capra, Fritjof. *The Tao of Physics*

Chopra, Deepak. *The Path of Love + The Seven Spiritual Laws of Success + How To Know God*

Cohen, Andrew. *Evolutionary Enlightenment + What Is Enlightenment Magazine*

Davies, Paul. *The Mind of God*

Dispenza, Joe. *Becoming Supernatural + Breaking the Habit of Being Yourself*

Dowd, Michael. *Thank God For Evolution*

Green, Brian. *The Fabric of the Cosmos*

Hawkins, David. *Power Vs. Force + Discovery of the Presence of God + The Eye of the I*

Houston, Jean. *The Possible Human + Life Force + A Mythic Life*

Hubbard, Barbara Marx. *Conscious Evolution*

Lipton, Bruce and Steve Bhaerman. *Spontaneous Evolution: Our Positive Future and a Way To Get There From Here*

Mandelbrot, Benoit. *The Fractal Geometry of Nature*

McTaggert, Lynne. *The Field*

Millman, Dan. *Way of the Peaceful Warrior*

Moore, Robert and Douglas Gillette. *King, Warrior, Magician, Lover*

Morter, Sue. *The Energy Codes*

Murphy, Michael. *The Future of the Body*

Patten, Terry. *A New Republic of the Heart*

Ra, Kaia. *The Sophia Code*

Reich, Robert. *The Common Good*

Swimme, Brian. *Canticle to the Cosmos*

Swimme, Brian and Thomas Berry. *The Universe Story*

Teilhard de Chardin. *The Human Phenomenon*

Tolle, Eckhart. *The Power of Now + A New Earth*

Trott, Susan. *The Holy Man*

Wilbur, Ken. *The Marriage of Sense and Soul + Sex, Ecology, Spirituality - The Spirit of Evolution*

Williamson, Marianne. *A Return To Love + Enchanted Love + The Healing of America*

Yogananda, Paramahansa. *Autobiography of a Yogi*

Your mission ~ to dance with the *Light*
Your purpose ~ to polish the perfection
Your meaning of it all ~ to give for the good of all.

It's just what diamonds
Who spend their life *Being*
In the course of *Becoming*
Do

✳ ACKNOWLEDGEMENTS ✳

I THANK THE FOLLOWING PEOPLE for helping me bring this creative project into form.

First, I thank my dear friend, Bob Sizelove, with whom I've shared many adventurous camping trips for over a decade. During one of these camping trips at a place we call "paradise", I received my first Contemplative Circle which became the springboard for **Journey of *The Great Circle*.** For years, Bob and I have discussed the primary themes of this book around a blazing campfire under a star-strung sky. Bob's deep devotion to God and his commitment to ongoing self-development and service has been an inspiring aspect for me in writing this book.

Next, I thank my friend, Jo Norris, for her constant support of my writings. Jo is a progressive and creative catalyst for change and has touched so many people with her loving presence and wisdom. She has touched and inspired me profoundly. Jo has been a supportive angel at many steps during the evolution of this book.

I thank my Beloved partner, Yana DiAngelis, for her unconditional love and perpetual support of seeing the holiness and magnificence within me. Her unwavering recognition of who I really am has been a powerful testament of the unconditional love and compassion that is possible for our glorious world. Her love gave me inner strength during the completion of this project.

I thank my Soul Friend and Anum Cara, Enocha Ranjita Ryan, for years of listening to me read each morning the daily contemplative narrative. She has been such a fervent and constant support of my creativity. Her steady love and the inspiring way she lives her life was so empowering to me in bringing these writings into manifestation.

Furthermore, I thank my dear friend, Maria Cavendish, for her loving support and encouragement all the many years as I spent time contemplating at the creek to bring through this body of work.

I thank my long time friend, Shambhu, who is a masterful guitar recording artist and creative wonder. Shambhu's consistent support and encouragement of all my creative endeavors has been a blessed gift in my life.

And I thank the following editing angels: Maureen Levy for her Amazonian feats, Chaka Ken-Varley, Robert Varley, Kathleen Havercamp, Rhianne Teija Newluhnd, and those who have given me discerning feedback and assistance in various ways toward the polishing of this work: Shanti Norman, Karl Anthony, Mia Margaret, Charley Thweatt, and Iala Jaggs for showing me a magical place at the creek where I spent over 10 years downloading the inspiration for this book.

As a final note, I thank the following inspiring teachers of philosophical and spiritual viewpoints that have pointed me to embracing larger perspectives of what I believe my life is truly about and what really matters: Marianne Williamson, Jean Houston, Barbara Marx Hubbard, Deepak Chopra, Joe Dispenza, Dr. Sue Morter, Gregg Braden, Alan Cohen, Andrew Harvey, Ken Wilber, Michael Dowd, Brian Swimme, Andrew Cohen, Kaia Ra, and Paramahansa Yogananda.

✳ ABOUT THE AUTHOR ✳

Oman Ken has devoted his life to being a multi-instrumentalist and singer. He lives in a home filled with exotic instruments from around the world, and professionally has focused his musical presentations on the harp, guitar, piano, Native American and ethnic flutes, as well as the gift of his voice. He has performed hundreds of concerts and celebrations across the United States while creating 15 professional recordings of his original vocal and instrumental music.

Oman has also composed three Ritual Theater musicals which he directed and produced in Hawaii, entitled "Genesis: A Ritual of Transformation", "Starwheel: Journey of the Sacred Circle", and "The Mask and the Sword". Furthermore, he has produced myriad multi-media Solstice and Equinox Celebrations with a troupe of 25 people in Houston, Texas and Cincinnati, Ohio.

Oman has presented his transformational workshops: "The Ceremonial Art of Celebration", "Dance Movement as Spiritual Practice", and "The Power Within the Archetypes of the King, Warrior, Magician, and Lover", in various spiritual conferences and retreats around the United States.

After a challenging physical condition made it unfeasible to continue his musical travels, Oman deepened his spiritual quest for inner freedom by spending an abundance of time in Nature contemplating what life is truly about - and what really matters.

The result of his personal investigations was a host of poetic contemplative narratives that became the foundation for this book **Journey of _The Great Circle_**.

Oman now lives in the majestic Red Rocks of Sedona, Arizona.   JourneyOfTheGreatCircle.com

JOURNEY OF *THE GREAT CIRCLE*
DAILY AFFIRMATION STATEMENTS FOR SUMMER

(Copy - then cut along the dotted lines to carry an affirmation with you each day)

I - THE DANCE OF THE INFINITE SEASONS

JUNE 20 or 21   GIFTS OF SUMMER
Today I consciously deepen my understanding of the meaning of my life.

JUNE 20 or 21   QUALITIES WITHIN THE SEASONS OF LIFE
My life is interconnected with the lives of all people through a vast Field of Universal Energy.

JUNE 22   THE GREAT STORY OF AWAKENING
Every day has meaningful opportunities to learn to serve the wellbeing of others.

JUNE 23   *JOURNEY OF AWAKENING*
My life is a perpetual journey of discovery - a quest to live an awakened life of inner freedom.

JUNE 24   CULTIVATING THE MASTERY OF *BEING* AND *BECOMING*
Each day I cultivate a life of inner freedom using the gifts of daily transformative practice.

JUNE 25   INNER FREEDOM
I accept what is, embrace that my life is unfolding perfectly, and love myself just as I am.

JUNE 26   THE INTEGRAL STAGE OF CONSCIOUSNESS
In the quiet of my heart, I integrate the many aspects of my life into an expression of harmony.

JUNE 27   ALIGNING WITH *THE TRUE SELF*
Today I align my awareness with who I really am, my True Self, the Essence in me that is eternal.

II - <u>THE POETRY OF *THE GREAT CIRCLE*</u>

JUNE 28   *THE GREAT CIRCLE*
From the perspective of living in the present moment, my life is unfolding perfectly just as it is.

JUNE 29   *THE GREAT CIRCLE* OF AWAKENING AND CONTRIBUTION
Greater awareness of what is true leads to greater contributions of my creative gifts to others.

JUNE 30   *THE GREAT CIRCLE* OF THE MEDICINE WHEEL
Today I embrace the existential paradox that I live in an ephemeral body - yet I am also eternal.

JULY 1   ALTERNATIVE WAYS TO DESCRIBE *THE GREAT CIRCLE*
Today I develop a greater awareness of what my life is truly about - and what really matters.

JULY 2   *BEING* AND *BECOMING*
My life is unfolding perfectly, at the same time, I'm here to help the world become more perfect.

JULY 3   GOD
I realize there is no place where the Omniscient Intelligence of Limitless Love is not.

JULY 4   GOD AS "THE BELOVED"
I radiate my love to the people in my life - and honor the beauty and goodness within them.

III - <u>HEART AWARENESS PRACTICES</u>

JULY 5   FOUNDATIONAL TRANSFORMATIVE PRACTICES
Through my commitment to daily transformative practice, I cultivate a life of inner freedom.

JULY 6   SPHERES OF APPRECIATION
My appreciation grows each day for the many gifts and blessings I constantly receive.

JULY 7   SERVICE

Being in service to the wellbeing of others is a natural, joyous, and fulfilling part of my life.

IV - THE SONG OF EMBODIED LOVE

JULY 8   THE NATURAL STATES THAT EMERGE FROM *BEING*

I take time throughout the day to feel the ever-present peace and harmony that's within me.

JULY 9   THE NATURAL STATE OF JOY

Joy is the natural state that arises in me when I'm fully present to each experience of my life.

JULY 10   PILLARS OF AWAKENING

I let go of my attachments and surrender everything in my life to a Greater Power.

JULY 11   SURRENDER

I surrender to the vast Intelligence of the Universe that knows how to accomplish everything.

JULY 12   TRUST

Today I let go of my need to control others and, instead, I trust in the perfect flow of life.

JULY 13   EMBRACING THE UNKNOWN

Today I embrace the unknown by trusting unwaveringly in the unfolding perfection of life.

JULY 14   BLACK HOLE

I choose forgiveness in every situation and pray for the power of grace to carry it into my heart.

JULY 15   FORGIVENESS

Within the present moment everything in my life - right now - is unfolding perfectly just as it is.

V - HEART AWARENESS PRACTICES

JULY 16   PRAYERS FOR THE "DEMONS"

People who seem to bring me difficulty are really here to help teach me to love unconditionally.

JULY 17   WELLBEING OF THE HEART

I courageously follow the guidance of my heart so I may live my life with ease and grace.

JULY 18   SHADOW WORK

Today I mindfully witness my thoughts and feelings without judgment or attachment.

VI - ARCHETYPES OF LIFE MASTERY

JULY 19   RELIGIOUS ARCHETYPES

I feel a natural yearning in me that is directing me to creatively envision who I desire to become.

JULY 20   *THE GREAT CIRCLE* OF THE ARCHETYPES

I use my creative imagination to envision myself experiencing the next level of my potential.

JULY 21   ARCHETYPES OF LIFE MASTERY

Today I use transformative practices to help me cultivate peace of mind and inner freedom.

JULY 22   MYSTICAL LOVER

One way I share my love for life is by doing what I can to contribute to the wellbeing of others.

JULY 23   KINDNESS

Today I intend to be the most loving, caring, and kind person I can be in every situation.

JULY 24   AUTHENTICITY

I live an honest, authentic, and vulnerable life while feeling each of my emotions as they arise.

JULY 25   HUMILITY
I offer my creative gifts and talents to bless others from the sacred altar of a humble heart.

JULY 26   FLEXIBILITY
I surrender any attachments to my desires - and let go of my need to control the flow of life.

VII - <u>HEART AWARENESS PRACTICES</u>

JULY 27   PASSION FOR LIFE
Today I am willing to live a more vibrant and radiant life with passion, aliveness, and curiosity.

JULY 28   HEART AWARENESS
Today I expand my awareness of the diverse emotions that constantly pass through me.

JULY 29   CULTIVATING THE MIRACULOUS
I celebrate that the Universe is naturally "wired" to create miracles for me - and for everyone.

VIII - <u>ARCHETYPES OF HIGHER KNOWLEDGE</u>

JULY 30   THE GIFTS OF PAIN
The pain that I feel is also a gift in disguise which is in my life to teach me to love more fully.

JULY 31   EXTRAORDINARY MOMENTS OF AWARENESS
I recognize that every moment of this day has the possibility to be extraordinary.

AUGUST 1   EXPERIENCES OF EPIPHANY
My search for the true, the good, and the beautiful is also about discovering who I really am.

AUGUST 2   ARCHETYPES OF HIGHER KNOWLEDGE
There is a natural yearning in me that constantly invites me to become who I truly desire to be.

AUGUST 3   AWAKENED ARTIST
Today I consciously live my life as a creative expression of beauty with everything I do.

AUGUST 4   THE NATURAL IMPULSE OF CREATIVITY
The Natural Creative Impulse that I feel in me is constantly inviting me to fully love all of life.

AUGUST 5   BEAUTY
I keep my heart open so I can experience more of the natural beauty that's all around me.

IX - HEART AWARENESS PRACTICES

AUGUST 6   AWAKENING THE INNER ARTIST
Focusing my energy on what I'm passionate about helps me to cultivate my creative potential.

AUGUST 7   CULTIVATING AN OPEN HEART
Today I keep my heart open so I may feel the Universal River of Life flow through me.

AUGUST 8   AFFIRMATIONS FOR PRIMARY EMOTIONAL NEEDS
I feel safe, loved, empowered, and connected with the beauty and goodness within all of life.

X - THE EVOLUTIONARY PERSPECTIVE

AUGUST 9   GIFTS FROM AN EVOLUTIONARY PERSPECTIVE
Embracing a "Big Picture perspective" helps me to cultivate compassionate service to others.

AUGUST 10   EVOLUTION OF COMPASSION
The Natural Intelligence within me is constantly inviting me to cultivate greater compassion.

AUGUST 11   THE FRACTAL NATURE OF EMERGENT EVOLUTION
I am a small but integral part of the Universe that's learning to love all of life unconditionally.

AUGUST 12   EVOLUTION OF CONSCIOUS CREATIVITY
I maintain an alignment with Life so that my daily choices help contribute to a better world.

AUGUST 13   EVOLUTION OF GOOD AND EVIL
Everything I perceive and experience in the world is a perfect expression of Limitless Love.

AUGUST 14   EVOLUTION OF MORALITY
I choose to live my life with integrity so my actions contribute to the wellbeing of others.

AUGUST 15   EVOLUTION OF JUDGMENT
I constantly listen to my inner guidance so each day, I make the most life-affirming choices.

AUGUST 16   CULTIVATING HEART WISDOM
I frequently take time to be quiet, so I may listen to the guiding wisdom within me.

XI - ARCHETYPES OF SPIRITUAL AWAKENING

AUGUST 17   ARCHETYPES OF SPIRITUAL AWAKENING
I am on a journey of awakening in which I'm learning the gift of serving the wellbeing of others.

AUGUST 18   COMPASSIONATE HEART
Today I shine "the light of spiritual awareness" into the sanctuary of my heart.

AUGUST 19   THE INTRINSIC NATURE TO CARE
I am aligned with Limitless Love, - and thus, being caring towards others is my intrinsic nature.

AUGUST 20   COMPASSION
I stay aligned with Life, keep my heart open, and celebrate compassion flourishing within me.

AUGUST 21   EMPATHY
I keep my heart open so I may better empathize with the feelings and experiences of others.

AUGUST 22   GENEROSITY
Today I deepen my awareness of how I can compassionately give, and be of service, to others.

AUGUST 23   VARIOUS FORMS OF ARCHETYPES OF SPIRITUAL AWAKENING
Mastery of inner freedom is natural, for it is every person's destiny - and thus, it is my destiny.

XII - HEART AWARENESS PRACTICES

AUGUST 24   NURTURING THE FEMININE NATURE
As a means to cultivate my wellbeing, I nurture the vital part of me that is my feminine nature.

AUGUST 25   NURTURING THE MASCULINE NATURE
As a means to cultivate my wellbeing, I nurture the vital part of me that is my masculine nature.

AUGUST 26   PARADOX SURRENDER PRAYER
Today I cultivate the intuitive faculty in me that helps me embrace life's existential paradoxes.

XIII - ARCHETYPES OF CONSCIOUS CONTRIBUTION

AUGUST 27   SPHERES OF CONTRIBUTION
I give to my community by cultivating integrous relationships, equality, and cooperation.

AUGUST 28   CONTRIBUTION TO COMMUNITY
I give of my time, talents, and creativity to help others live a more peaceful and fulfilling life.

AUGUST 29   ARCHETYPES OF CONSCIOUS CONTRIBUTION
Today I consciously align my awareness with all that is good and beautiful in this world.

AUGUST 30   VISIONARY STORYTELLER
I consciously create, and fully live, the most benevolent and loving story of life I can imagine.

AUGUST 31   CELEBRATION
Every moment that I experience has the possibility of becoming a unique celebration of life.

SEPTEMBER 1   INSPIRATION
I maintain an alignment with the Source of Life and thus, I naturally align my heart to inspiration.

SEPTEMBER 2   HOPE
Today I accept my life just as it is - yet at the same time, I imagine myself creating a better future.

SEPTEMBER 3   "THE UNIVERSE STORY"
Embracing an evolutionary perspective of life empowers me to help co-create a better world.

XIV - HEART AWARENESS PRACTICES

SEPTEMBER 4   CONSCIOUS SPIRITUAL PARTNERSHIP
Today I honor and celebrate the holiness and magnificence within every person in my life.

SEPTEMBER 5   INTIMACY
Today I am committed to be honest, authentic, and vulnerable with the people I love.

SEPTEMBER 6   SACRED SEXUALITY
Today I consciously choose to be present, keep my heart open, and fully relax in each moment.

XV - NAVIGATING THE JOURNEY OF THE GREAT CIRCLE

SEPTEMBER 7   THE GREAT CIRCLE OF A CONSCIOUS AND BALANCED LIFE
Today I align with the Source of Life, learn what is true, create more beauty, and serve others.

SEPTEMBER 8   AN AWAKENED LIFE
Aligning with my True Nature also aligns me with my purpose, meaning of life, and life mission.

SEPTEMBER 9   THE QUEST FOR INNER FREEDOM
I frequently ask "the Big Questions" as a way to help me learn to live a life of inner freedom.

SEPTEMBER 10   PURPOSE OF LIFE
Each day is really about learning to live a life of inner freedom - and to love unconditionally.

SEPTEMBER 11   MEANING OF LIFE
I choose the particular meaning I give to everything - based on my current values and beliefs.

SEPTEMBER 12   ONE'S MISSION IN LIFE
Today I contribute my creative gifts and talents in ways that uplift and serve the lives of others.

SEPTEMBER 13   ONE'S TRUE NATURE
I consciously live with the paradox that my body's life is finite, yet at the same time, I am eternal.

XVI - THE ART OF TRANSFORMATION AND HEALING

SEPTEMBER 14   *THE GREAT CIRCLE* OF DEVELOPMENT AND
                      TRANSFORMATION
As my inner development expands, I open to greater levels of transformation and healing.

SEPTEMBER 15   OUTER HEALING MIRRORS INNER DEVELOPMENT
Through a co-creation with the Source of Life my inner development is mirrored as my healing.

SEPTEMBER 16   A BALANCED APPROACH TO HEALING
The awakened realization of who I really am is the sublime sanctuary where I am truly healed.

CPSIA information can be obtained
at www.ICGtesting.com
Printed in the USA
LVHW051923310721
694026LV00008B/239